Hotels
Country Guesthouses
in Italy
for less than €100

CONTENTS

REGIONAL MAPS

Symbols used in the guide

	**Hotel or Bed & Breakfast**
	**Country Guesthouse**
40-50 €	Price per person in low and high season
62-70 €	Price for two people in low and high season
	The little extra that makes the hotel or country guesthouse different
8	Hotel on the regional map
18	Country guesthouse on the regional map
	Breakfast included in the price of the room
	Credit cards not accepted

How to use this guide

This new edition of **Michelin's Hotels and Guesthouses in Italy for less than €100** features a selection of 340 establishments at reasonable prices throughout Italy. Having travelled the length and breadth of the Bel Paese, our incognito inspectors were left free to make their own choices. A few lines at the top of each description, indicated by our familiar "We most liked" aim to highlight the little extra that we particularly liked and want to share with you, whether it be "The beautiful pool in the shade of olive trees", "Your hosts' friendly welcome" or simply a few words to set the scene.

Finding your way round the guide

The guide is divided into the 19 administrative regions of Italy, organised in alphabetical order, with the exception of the "Abruzzo & Molise" chapter, which brings these two regions together. The establishments are listed by place, again in alphabetical order, within each region. The name of each place is followed by the two letters which correspond to the regional capital, for example, RM for Rome. The number at the top of the establishment's description corresponds to its location on the map at the beginning of each chapter.

Maps

A map at the beginning of the guide shows the different regions of Italy. At the beginning of each chapter is a photo and text illustrating the countryside or important tourist sites, together with a regional map showing our selection of establishments (hotels are marked in blue and rural guesthouses in green). The maps and directions in this guide use the metric system for reasons of practicality; as a reminder 1km = 0.6miles.

Hotels

Our selection of hotels has been chosen for their location, atmosphere and hospitality. Some offer dining facilities and half board accommodation.

We definitely recommend booking ahead; you should also call if you think you may arrive late in the evening.

Rural Guesthouses (Agriturismi)

Rural guesthouses were originally conceived as an opportunity to combine accommodation and the chance to taste the products made on the farm (among them olive oil, wine, honey, vegetables and meat). Often converted mills, country houses or farmsteads, they are also the private homes of the people who will welcome you and endeavour to make your stay as pleasant as possible. They are ideal for those looking for quiet, restful accommodation in the countryside. Because of the ever-increasing popularity of this type of establishment, it is important to book well in advance, particularly during the summer or for long weekends, and to reconfirm your booking if you expect to arrive late.

Meals

In the text relating to each establishment, we indicate whether meals are served.

Rates

Prices are per single or double room in low or high season. For example:

€40-50: the price of a single room is €40 out of season rising to €50 in high season.

€60-80: the price of a double room is €60 out of season rising to €80 in high season.

Note that all establishments offer several rooms for under €100. However, certain establishments do also offer rooms or suites at higher rates. Please ensure, therefore, that you check the room rate at the time of reservation.

Breakfast

Breakfast is sometimes included in the price of the room. Whenever this is not the case, we have indicated the price of breakfast per person.

Credit cards

Where credit cards are not accepted, the symbol indicates this.

Reservations

A credit card number or deposit is often required to confirm the reservation of a room.

Telephoning

To telephone Italy, dial 00 + 39 + the telephone number, including the first 0.

Facilities, directions and things to do

For each establishment, we give:

- the facilities on offer: swimming pool, tennis courts, sauna...
- directions from the nearest town
- suggestions for things to do and see in the local area.

Indexes

All the establishments in the guide are listed in alphabetical order in several indexes:

Activity breaks index, by region and place: these establishments offer at least one sporting activity (gym, riding, tennis, golf, etc.).

Local produce index, by region and place: this index lists all the establishments which offer tasting sessions and sell local produce.

Hotels index, by region and place.

Country Guesthouses index, by region and place.

Exploring Italy with Michelin

To find out more about the area of Italy you intend to visit, you might also want to delve into the Michelin Green Guide Italy for further historical and cultural information. Michelin map 735 Italia is a practical map on a scale of 1:1 000 000 which shows the whole Italian road network. Michelin maps 561-566 give detailed information on the area you wish to tour. Internet users can access personalised route plans, Michelin maps and town plans through the website at www.ViaMichelin.com

Your viewpoint

We have endeavoured to make this guide practical and readable and trust that it will accompany you on family holidays and romantic weekends. We have included a questionnaire at the back of the guide: all your comments and suggestions for new addresses are most welcome.

Jesi
Macerata
Civitanova Marche
Fabriano
Fermo
385
S. Benedetto
d. Tronto
Ascoli Piceno
E 55
219
2
5
7
8
Teramo
66
A 24
A 14
S 16
4
Pescara
Gr. Sasso d'Italia
2914
96
Chieti
E 80
L'Aquila
131
ABRUZZO
Vasto
Termoli
A 25
Maiella
2795
A 24-E 80
Avezzano
Sulmona
177
S 16
3
211
Tivoli
148
A 14
6
Fiuggi
S 6
A1
MOLISE
1
Frosinone
Sora
S. Severo
Velletri
E 45
Isernia
Montecassino
S 85
S 17
Campobasso
137
Cassino
S 17
Latina
210
117
Terracina
Formia
S 6
111
S 213
A1
Gaeta
Ariano Irpino
E 45
Benevento
S 7qu
Volturno
Caserta
NAPOLI
50
Vesuvio
Avellino
37
1277
Pozzuoli
Pompei

ABRUZZO & MOLISE

Prior to being absorbed by the Kingdom of Naples in the 12C, Abruzzo and Molise were fought over by a succession of kings, emperors and dynasties. This wild and rugged region of empty plains, rocky massifs and forests was prized not for its riches, but as a strategic gateway to neighbouring areas.

Today, it has three national parks within its boundaries, making it one of Italy's most unspoilt regions and a haven for flora and fauna.

Beach lovers will be pleased to know that the coastline has in recent years greatly improved its facilities; the seaside resorts of Abruzzo and Molise are an increasingly popular family holiday destination, not least because of the excellent value for money which they represent.

The region's cities and towns are rich in artistic heritage, and make for a pleasant alternative to the packed streets of Italy's most famous tourist centres. In bygone times, poets celebrated the local countryside and its fecundity; today that same natural abundance is evident from the ubiquitous lamb dishes, always appetising whatever the recipe and to be found in every restaurant.

8 establishments

1

SELVAGGI

Sig.ra Lucarino
Strada provinciale Montesangrina km 1
86061 Agnone (IS)
Tel. 0865 77785 – Fax 0865 77177
staffoli@staffoli.it – www.staffoli.it

37/52€

Closed 10 Oct-23 Nov • 15 double rm • Half board €47 • Menu €16-30 • Parking, small dogs welcome • Riding, tasting and sale of cured meats and cheeses

The harmonious setting in the surrounding landscape.

A country track leads to this fortified farmhouse dating from 1720, tucked away among woods and fields which provide the ideal backdrop for riding, walking and fishing. The genuine and sincere hospitality here manifests itself in the friendly service and the rustic simplicity of the interior; in the vaulted dining room guests can savour locally-produced cheese, and cured and cooked meats. The perfect spot for a holiday of complete relaxation, or for those fond of walking and riding.

Access
From Isernia: SS 17 for 3.5km towards Vasto, then left onto SS 650 for 9.5km to Pescolanciano, 7km on the SS 651, then right onto SS 86 for 21km

Sights nearby: Church of Sant'Emidio, Fonderia Pontificia Marinelli, International Bell Museum

2

LA PERGOLA

Fam. Zibelli-Ischi

Via Emilia, 19
64011 Alba Adriatica (TE)
Tel. 0861 711068 – Fax 0861 711068
info@hotelpergola.it – www.hotelpergola.it

40-50/70-100€

Closed 11 Jan-28 Feb and 1 Oct-19 Dec • 1 single rm, 9 double rm • No restaurant • No dogs • Bicycles available, beach with facilities

The cheery atmosphere created by the management.

A little slice of Switzerland on the Adriatic Riviera, this seemingly paradoxical establishment is an utter delight. The management are of Swiss descent, and an alpine theme is very much to the fore, most notably in the decorative scheme employed in the bedrooms. Breakfast hours are flexible, and there is a pleasant seafront restaurant.

Access
From Teramo: SS 80 for 19km, then A 14 for 16km to Alba Adriatica exit, continue for 2km

Sights nearby: Tortoreto: historic centre; Colonella: scenery

3

LE GOLE

Sigg. Aldo e Achille Paris
Via Sardellino
67041 Aielli (AQ)
Tel. 0863 711009 – Fax 0863 711101
info@hotellegole.it – www.hotellegole.it

50/76-100€

Open all year • 40 double rm • Half board €51-70 • Menu €15-30 • Parking, garden

The imposing beams supporting the roof.

Carefully used, the simplest building materials such as brick, stone and wood, can create a work of art. After several years' work, the result here is striking, giving the feel of a Tuscan fortified farmhouse. Inside, a courtyard with well gives onto the rooms, all of which are decorated in period style with plenty of dark wood and exposed beams in evidence. Despite the ambience of days gone by, levels of comfort and technology are up to the minute.

Access
From L'Aquila: A 24-A 25 for 44km to Celano-Aielli exit, continue for 3km to Celano

Sights nearby: Grotte di Stiffe, gole di Celano

4

LE MAGNOLIE

Sig. Tortella
Contrada Fiorano, 83
65014 Loreto Aprutino (PE)
Tel. 085 8289804 – Fax 085 8289534
lemagnolie@tin.it – www.lemagnolie.com

45-60/ 50-65€

Closed 1-28 Feb • 12 double rm • Half board €50-60 • Menu €23 • Parking, garden, swimming pool, no pets • Organised trips, cheese and wine tasting, sale of oil

The hearty agricultural feel of the place.

A truly rural location. This 17C farmhouse, which has been completely restored, is set in 26 hectares of olive groves, orchards and market gardens. There is a minimum two night stay, but this is no imposition; the rooms have antique furniture coupled with comfortable modern beds, and guests who enjoy outdoor cooking can use the barbecue facilities near the pool. Those in quest of the rustic idyll can gather fruit and vegetables from the surrounding farmland, and eggs from the hens which roam freely in the courtyard.

Access
From Pescara: SS 16 bis to Cappelle sul Tavo, then left for 12.2km to Loreto Aprutino, and follow west for 5km

Sights nearby: Moscufo: church of Santa Maria del Lago

5

CASALE DELLE ARTI

Sig. Di Domenico
Strada Selva Alta
64023 Mosciano Sant'Angelo (TE)
Tel. 085 8072043 – Fax 085 8072776
casalearti@tin.it – www.casaledellearti.it

47-50/ 75-80€

Open all year • 1 single rm, 13 double rm • No restaurant • Parking, no dogs

The contrast between the verdant countryside and the hues of the house.

As the name implies, the emphasis here is on art; in the garden is a fountain incorporating an unusual modern sculpture, while inside the well restored building there is a fine collection of contemporary works, some by better known artists than others. The rooms have a simple elegance, with period furnishings and wrought iron beds. The restaurant is a hive of activity; popular with the locals, it also hosts functions and receptions. Located in a panoramic spot and well placed for both the sea and the Gran Sasso mountain range.

Access
From Teramo: SS 80 for 17km, then left for 3km

Sights nearby: Historic centre of Montone and convento dei Santi Fratelli; Giulianova: archaeological museum

6

VILLA LA RUOTA

Sig.ra Gentile

Colle Massarello, 3
67032 Pescasseroli (AQ)
Tel. 0863 910516 – Fax 081 2471303
bnb@villalaruota.it – www.villalaruota.it

60/80-90€

Open all year • 6 double rm • No restaurant • Parking, garden, no dogs

The bathrooms with fine ceramics and co-ordinated accessories.

Situated out of town, this delightful B&B retains the charm of a private house. In the public areas the ambience of hospitality is elegantly conveyed by features such as the open fireplace and small bar area. Although not large, the rooms are enhanced by many personal touches. At any time of the year, this is an ideal spot from which to explore the natural beauties of the Abruzzo region, much of which is protected parkland.

Access
From Pescara: SS 5 for 23km to join A 25 for 65km to Pescina exit, then onto the SS 83 for 37km

Sights nearby: Abruzzo National Park

7

TONINO-DA ROSANNA

Sig.ra Maggetti
Via Volturno, 11
64026 Roseto degli Abruzzi (TE)
Tel. 085 8990274 – Fax 085 8990274

45-60€

Closed 20-30 Sep and 1-30 Nov • 7 double rm • Breakfast €4; half board €40-55 • Menu €30-50 • No dogs

The mosaics and wall paintings; not just a restaurant, but a homage to the sea.

This establishment's distinctive atmosphere is instantly apparent, its 19C furnishings and pictures making for a nautical theme. The focal point is the restaurant, which is equally adept at creating ambience and fine food. One room is almost completely covered in mosaics depicting fishermen at work, chronicling the family history of the owner, Signora Rosanna.

Access
From Pescara: A 14 for 33km to Roseto exit; left onto SS 150 for 5km

Sights nearby: Atri: historic centre, grotte (caves), Calanchi National Park

DON AMBROSIO

Sigg. Rossi

Contrada Piomba, 49
64029 Silvi Marina (TE)
Tel. 085 9351060 – Fax 085 9355140
info@donambrosio.it – www.donambrosio.it

80-95€

Closed 5-20 Nov • 10 double rm • Menu €23-43 • Garden, parking, no dogs in the restaurant • Bicycles available, tasting and sale of local produce

The history and local heritage of the place.

Named after the grandfather of the current owners; his wooden bed is still in use in one of the rooms, a symbolic link between bygone times and life today. Much older still is the main house, which remains little altered since its original construction in the 15C. The accommodation is pleasant and welcoming, as is the restaurant with its brick vaulting and rustic furnishings. The cuisine here is worthy of note, based as it is on typical hinterland dishes which are little known and overshadowed by coastal cooking.

Access
From Pescara: SS 16 for 12km

Sights nearby: Atri: cathedral; Pescara: birthplace of Gabriele D'Annunzio and Museum of Folklore

Promon del Gargano
300
1055
Manfredonia
Lucera
Foggia
Barletta
Trani
Molfetta
Bari
Cerignola
Canosa
Andria
Bitonto
Irpino
243
Melfi
1
Altamura
Gioia d. Colle
Matera
4
Potenza
7
5
212
BASILICATA
Scanzano
2
6
M. Pollino
2248
Sapri
3
Castrovillari
Sibari
Rossano
Golfo

BASILICATA

Bordering both the Tyrrhenian and Ionian seas, Basilicata manages to unite disparate shorelines, traditions and communities, but it is its hinterland rather than its coasts which defines the region's character. Matera, the second city after Potenza, is renowned for its rock dwellings, where for centuries its inhabitants have found shelter deep in the ground.

The local economy remains primarily agrarian, which means that Basilicata's landscape remains beautiful and unspoilt.

These days Basilicata is renowned for its proud and united people but is popular with tourists looking to get off the beaten track in unspoilt surroundings. Its countryside is virtually untarnished by industrialisation and is rich in natural beauty sought out by the film and advertising businesses.

Visitors heading home would be well advised to return with the odd bottle of Aglianico del Vulture in addition to their holiday snaps.

7 establishments

1

LA LOCANDA DEL PALAZZO

Sig. e Sig.ra Botte

Piazza Caracciolo, 7
85022 Barile (PZ)

Tel. 0972 771051 – Fax 0972 771051

info@locandadelpalazzo.com – www.locandadelpalazzo.com

72/ 98€

Closed 15-30 July • 2 single rm, 9 double rm • Breakfast €6 • Menu €40-60 • Gardens, small dogs welcome • Riding, organised trips, bicycle hire, tasting and sale of wine

The tasteful use of colour and materials, here elevated to an art form.

Once overlooked, the borderlands between Puglia and Basilicata are now very popular, and deservedly so on account of the colourful local landscape and people. Formerly used for wine making, this well presented establishment has an elegant lobby and spacious, luxuriously restored accommodation with splendid bathrooms. The restaurant offers sophisticated cuisine to satisfy even the most exacting of palates.

Access

From Potenza: SS 93 for 10km, then 30km on the SS 658, left for 1.2km, then right for 3km on the SS 93

Sights nearby: Melfi: cathedral; Monticchio lakes

2

COSTA CASALE

Sig.ra Cucinotta
Contrada Vito
85032 Chiaromonte (PZ)
Tel. 0973 642346 – Fax 0973 642346

52€

Open all year • 5 double rm • Half board €42 • Menu €25 • Parking, garden, no dogs • Riding, organised trips, cured meats and cheeses for sale

The presence of hares and fallow deer in the vicinity of the farmhouse.

Previously the farmstead of the De Salvo family, this establishment nestles among the olive groves and orchards of the Lucania countryside. Little has changed over the years; the natural lushness of the place has been further enhanced by the establishment of the Pollino National Park, while the old farmstead has become an agriturismo (after careful restoration) and the De Salvo family, who continue to farm the surrounding land, extend a warm welcome to visitors to the area. The restaurant offers dishes cooked with home reared ingredients.

Access
From Potenza: Eboli-Potenza road for 8km to Tito exit, then onto the A 3 for 53km to Lauria Nord exit, onto the SS 653 for 34km, then left for 7km

Sights nearby: Palazzo Vescovile and its churches; Pollino National Park

3

LA TANA

Sig. Salerno

Contrada Castrocucco
85040 Maratea (PZ)
Tel. 0973 871770 – Fax 0973 871720
latana@tiscali.it

45-65/56-104€

Closed 23 Dec-27 Jan • 4 single rm, 10 double rm • Half board €40-85 • Menu €18-36 • Parking, swimming pool, no dogs • Organised trips, bicycle hire

The location, one of the most beautiful spots along the Basilicata coastline.

Situated on the coast to the south of Maratea, this hotel is set against a backdrop of rocky outcrops, little beaches and crystal clear waters. Those who prefer freshwater can lounge under a sun umbrella by the large swimming pool, but the sea here is hard to resist. This is a well organised, efficiently run establishment, where the service and facilities seem to improve year on year. The welcoming rooms are tastefully furnished, and most have air conditioning.

Access

From Salerno: 9km to Pontecagnano junction, then A 3 for 103km to Lagonegro Nord exit, left onto SS 585 for 22km, then right for 1km to Castrocucco

Sights nearby: Scenery of the Golfo di Policastro

SASSI HOTEL

Sassi Hotel Srl

Via San Giovanni Vecchio 89
75100 Matera (MT)
Tel. 0835 331009 – Fax 0835 333733
hotelsassi@virgilio.it – www.hotelsassi.it

60-70/ 90-95€

Open all year • 5 single rm, 21 double rm • No restaurant

The primeval experience of sleeping in a rock dwelling.

This hotel defies standard terms of definition; a curious labyrinth of a structure incorporating 18C buildings and rock dwellings laid out over six storeys, with accommodation accessed by an external staircase. The rooms carved from the rock face are without doubt the most appealing, albeit the simplest. In addition, there are fine views over the Unesco World Heritage site of the town of Matera and its cathedral.

Sights nearby: The sassi (rock dwellings), cathedral

5

BOUGANVILLE

Sig. Figliuolo

Strada Provinciale 83
85055 Picerno (PZ)
Tel. 0971 991084 – Fax 0971 990921
info@hotelbouganville.it – www.hotelbouganville.it

62/85€

Open all year • 10 single rm, 24 double rm • Half board €60 • Menu €22-35 • Parking, garden, no dogs

The accommodation's high standards of comfort.

In a convenient roadside location, this modern hotel is run with business travellers in mind but tourists would be unwise to dismiss it out of hand. Outside there is ample parking and a welcoming garden, while beyond the lobby the interior has a bar, breakfast room and restaurant (which also hosts receptions). Upstairs, the modern and functional rooms occupying the first and second floors are very spacious.

Access

From Potenza: SS 407 for 13.7km to Picerno exit, then onto SP 83 for 3km

Sights nearby: Churches of San Nicola and the Annunziata, medieval tower

6

PICCHIO NERO

Sig.ra Genovese

Via Mulino, 1
85030 Terranova di Pollino (PZ)
Tel. 0973 93170 – Fax 0973 93170
picchionero@picchionero.com – www.picchionero.com

50/67€

Closed Nov • 25 double rm • Half board €57 • Menu €22-32 • Parking, garden, no dogs • Organised trips, tasting and sale of jam, cakes and cured meats

The splendid position in the Pollino National Park.

Few places in Italy have managed to remain as unspoilt as the Pollino National Park, established a little over ten years ago to protect the fauna, flora and landscape of this area. Occupying two buildings situated within the park boundaries, this hotel is the ideal base from which to discover the beauties of the surrounding mountain scenery. After a hard day's exploring, guests can return to savour some delicious local cuisine, the area's other great natural resource.

Access

From Taranto: SS 106 for 70km, right onto the SS 653 for 26km, then left onto the SS 481 for 15km, right onto the SS 92 for 14km

Sights nearby: Pollino National Park

7

LA FORESTERIA DI SAN LEO

Sig. Guarini
Contrada San Leo, 11
85018 Trivigno (PZ)
Tel. 0971 981157 – Fax 0971 442695

40-55/62-80€

Closed 1 Nov-31 Mar • 6 double rm • Half board €45-60 • Menu €25-40 • Parking, garden, no dogs • Riding, bicycle hire, fishing, honey and cheese for sale

The serenity of the hermitage setting up in the hills.

The well presented rooms are colourfully decorated in contrast to the plain stonework in the public areas, giving visitors a feel for the long history of this secluded place, previously a Benedictine monastery dedicated to Saint Leo. In addition to its interesting heritage, the hotel also has its own stables, giving guests a chance to explore the meadows and woods which stretch out over the surrounding hills towards the high mountains beyond.

Access
From Potenza: SS 407 for 18km to Anzi exit, continue for 9km to San Leo

Sights nearby: Matera: Sassi, cathedral

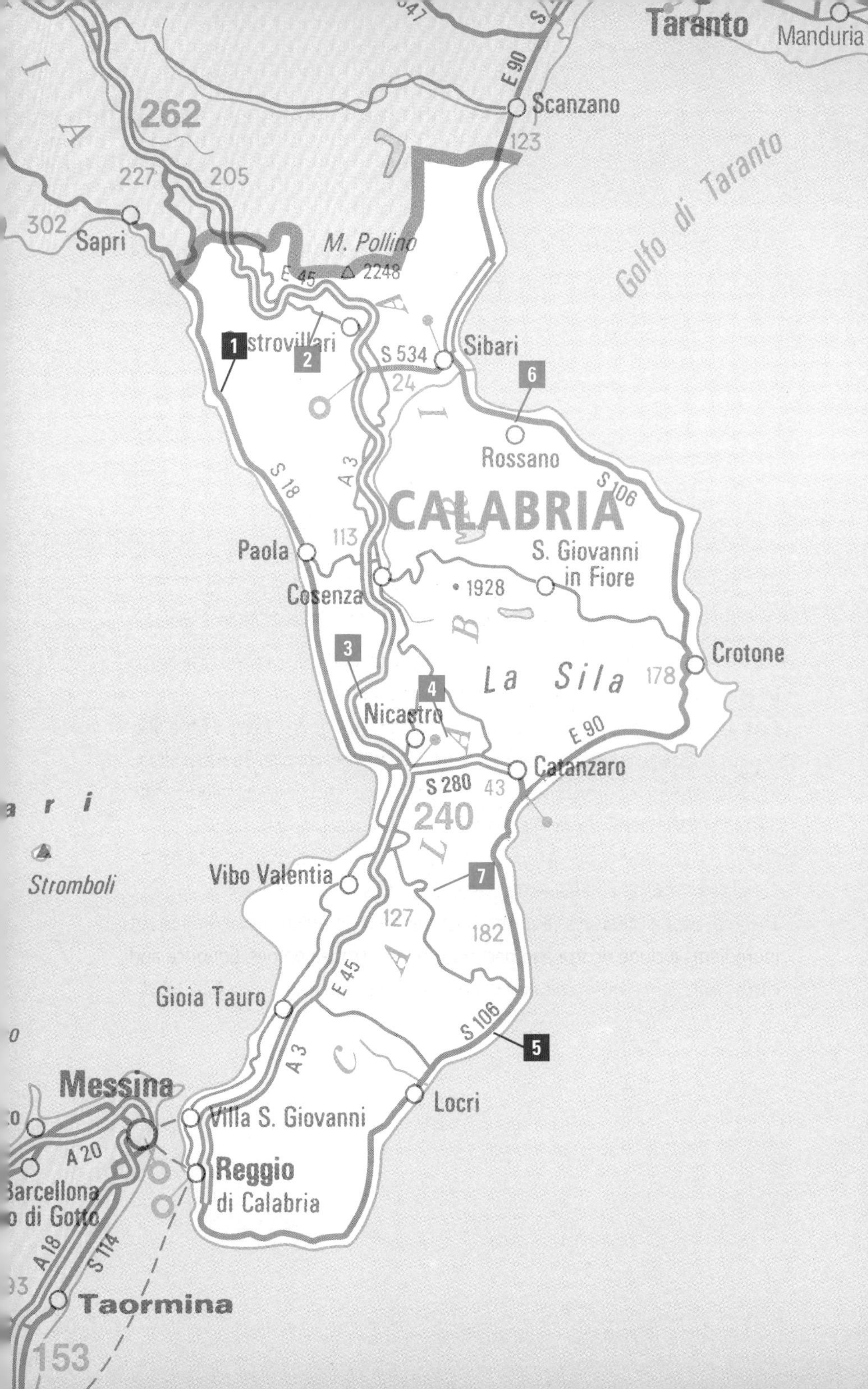

Taranto
Manduria
E 90
Scanzano
123
262
Golfo di Taranto
227
205
302
Sapri
M. Pollino
2248
E 45
1
2
Castrovillari
S 534
Sibari
24
6
Rossano
S 18
A 3
S 106
CALABRIA
113
Paola
S. Giovanni
in Fiore
Cosenza
1928
3
Crotone
4
La Sila
178
Nicastro
E 90
Catanzaro
S 280
43
240
Stromboli
Vibo Valentia
7
127
182
E 45
Gioia Tauro
S 106
5
A 3
Messina
Locri
Villa S. Giovanni
A 20
Reggio
di Calabria
Barcellona
A 18
S 114
Taormina
153

CALABRIA

Forming the toe of the Italian peninsula, this harsh and wild region is the home of the red pepper, and has some areas of unimaginable beauty.

Each season has its own appeal here: in winter the snowy slopes of the Sila, Pollino and Aspromonte draw skiers and visitors from all over southern Italy; in autumn and spring the woods and plains are a fragrant blaze of colour, while in summer the long coastline attracts sun worshippers in their droves.

Against this backdrop, certain places stand out: Maratea, Tropea, Stilo, Pentadattilo, Scilla and Palmi, to name but a few.

The red pepper features large in Calabrian cuisine, while other important ingredients include ricotta and pecorino cheese, Tropea onions, liquorice and citrus fruits. Wine buffs will be familiar with the region's famous Cirò label.

7 establishments

1

DUCALE VILLA RUGGERI

Sig.ra Ruggeri
Via Vittorio Veneto, 254
87020 Cirella (CS)
Tel. 0985 86051 – Fax 0985 86401
info@ducalehotel.net – www.ducalehotel.net

45-55/65-85€

Open all year • 22 double rm • Half board €44-86 • Menu €20 • Parking, private beach, bowls, no dogs in the restaurant • Organised trips, archery and fishing

The well-kept lawned gardens.

The rocks, pebbled beaches, turquoise waters and islets of the Calabrian coast form the backdrop of the Villa Ducale, built by descendants of the Gonzaga family in the 18C and subsequently owned by the Ruggeri, who today continue to run the establishment. The ambience is genteel and refined, and there are delightful well planted gardens. Inside, the furnishings vary in origin; some are unusual antiques, while others are more everyday. The spacious restaurant offers Calabrian and other Italian dishes. Meals are also served in the gardens.

Access
From Cosenza: SS 19 for 4km, then left onto SS 18 for 28km to Paola, right onto SS 18 for 43km, then left for 6km

Sights nearby: Pollino National Park; Diamante: murals

LA LOCANDA DEL PARCO

Sig.ra Tamburi

Contrada Mazzicanino, 12
87016 Morano Calabro (CS)
Tel. 0981 31304 – Fax 0981 31304
info@lalocandadelparco.it – www.lalocandadelparco.it

30-35/70€

Open all year • 12 double rm • Half board €45-50 • Menu €20-25 • Parking, garden, swimming pool, no dogs in the restaurant • Riding, tasting and sale of jam, cured meat and oil

The rocky setting of the extraordinary spa pool.

Conveniently close to the motorway but set in open country, this hotel is dominated by Mount Pollino and its national park. Inside, guests will find a welcoming lounge area with a family ambience, while the dining room is more rustic in feel with communal tables. The rooms take their names from musical notes and have many personal touches including period style furnishings. A second building close to the pool has two further rooms. Horses may also be hired from the stables.

Access

From Cosenza: A 3 for 74km to Morano Calabro exit, continue for 0.3km

Sights nearby: Pollino National Park

3

VOTA

Fam. Mauri

Contrada Vota, 3
88047 Nocera Terinese (CZ)
Tel. 0968 91517 – Fax 0968 91517
infomail@agrivota.it – www.agrivota.it

52-60€

Open all year • 8 double rm • Breakfast €3; half board €46-55 • Menu €13-23 • Parking, garden, swimming pool, bowls, no dogs • Bicycle hire, walks, tasting and sale of cured meat, cheese, olives and oil

The panoramic view towards the sea.

Situated high up in a panoramic spot halfway between Nocera and Falerna, this agriturismo is a truly original holiday destination offering something for everyone. From the poolside terrace, beach lovers can see the beach, 5km away and easily reached by car. Those in quest of unspoilt countryside can explore the 35 hectares of olive groves and citrus orchards. However guests choose to spend their days, come evening they will welcome the traditional Calabrian cuisine incorporating genuine local products.

Access

From Catanzaro: SS 280 for 28km, then onto the A 3 towards Napoli to Falerna exit, continue for 4km, then turn right, follow road for 8.5km to Vota

Sights nearby: Golfo di Sant'Eufemia; Nicastro: castle, cathedral

4

LE CAROLEE

Sig.ra Gaetano
Contrada Gabella, 1
88040 Pianopoli (CZ)
Tel. 0968 35076 – Fax 0968 35076
lecarolee@lecarolee.it – www.lecarolee.it

50-60/80-100€

Open all year • 7 double rm • Half board €65-75 • Menu €30-35 • Parking, garden, swimming pool, small dogs welcome • Bicycle hire, tasting and sale of cured meat and oil

The rugged Calabrian scenery, impervious to the passage of time.

The Calabrian hinterland is one of Italy's wildest landscapes; over the centuries it has been the domain of those seeking isolation, be they saints or brigands. Such a history explains why this 19C residence was originally fortified. The building encloses a small inner courtyard, while a swimming pool is set in its garden. On the whole, this hotel represents Calabria updating itself by drawing upon its past and presenting it with modern enhancements.

Access
From Catanzaro: SS 280 for 20km to Pianopoli exit, onto the SS 18 for 5km, then right for 4km

Sights nearby: Nicastro: castle, cathedral

5

FEDERICA

Sig. Baggetta

Via Nazionale, 152
89040 Riace (RC)
Tel. 0964 771302 – Fax 0964 771305
hotelfederica@bagetur.it – www.bagetur.it

45-60/ 75-90€

Open all year • 16 double rm • Half board €55-78 • Menu €23-33 • Garden, no dogs in the restaurant

We most liked

The contrasting colours of sea and sand close to the hotel.

This attractive new building stands close to the beach on the Gelsomini riviera. Modernity prevails inside and out, the rooms are comfortable and many offer fine views of the azure waters of the Ionian sea, so intense in colour that guests might imagine themselves in the tropics. It is a delight to walk barefoot beneath the garden's palm trees, moving from the cool lawn to the warm sand of the beach, with an unbroken view of sea and sky as far as the eye can see. Also worthy of note is the restaurant, which is renowned for its grilled meat and fish dishes.

Access

From Catanzaro: SS 19 for 7km to Catanzaro Lido exit, then right onto the SS 106 for 57km to Riace Marina

Sights nearby: Gerace: cathedral; Locri: Locri Epizefiri archaeological site

6

TRAPESIMI

Sig. Pace
Contrada Amica
87068 Rossano Stazione (CS)
Tel. 0983 64392 – Fax 0983 290848
info@agriturismotrapesimi.it – www.agriturismotrapesimi.it

37/74€

Open all year • 7 double rm • Half board €52 • Menu €16-18 • Parking, no dogs in the restaurant • Organised trips, bicycles available, cured meat and oil tasting

Views of the sea to the front, flanked by the olive groves of the Sila.

Situated several hundred metres down a narrow track, this isolated building is of recent construction but is in the style of the farmhouse which preceded it on this site. From the terrace there are views over the timeless landscape of the plain with its ancient olive groves, and the gulf of Sibari, a crossroads of society since the days when the Greeks founded colonies here. This agriturismo also hosts conventions on various subject from ecological issues to history; the ideal place for combining a relaxing holiday with a little culture.

Access
From Cosenza: A 3 to Roggiana Gravina exit, onto SS 19 to Tarsia, right for 8km, then right onto SS 106 to Amica

Sights nearby: Sibari: Parco Archeologico della Sibaritide, Museo Archeologico

7

I BASILIANI

Sig.ra Martelli
Strada Statale 182 - Contrada San Basile
88060 Torre di Ruggiero (CZ)
Tel. 0967 938000 – Fax 0967 938000
info@ibasiliani.com – www.ibasiliani.com

40-50/70-80€

Closed 7 Jan-16 Apr, 1 Nov-27 Dec • 1 single rm, 8 double rm • Half board €60-65 • Menu €20-30 • Parking, garden, swimming pool, no dogs in the restaurant • Cookery courses, fishing, tasting and sale of jam, cheese and liqueurs

The remains of the monastery, redolent of timeless contemplation.

Once dedicated to prayer, this place became a farmhouse before its latest transformation into a country guesthouse. The path through the woods remains, winding towards the village of Torre di Ruggiero; travelling along it on foot or on horseback it is easy to imagine how pilgrims would have come this way, crossing the land which divides the Ionian and Tyrrenhian seas, perhaps heading for the Cattolica church in Stilo, a thousand year old masterpiece of Byzantine art.

Access

From Catanzaro: SS 19 for 7km, onto the SS 106 for 19km to Soverato, then onto the SS 182 for 25km

Sights nearby: Church of S. Domenica, ruins of the convent of S. Agostino

Vasto
Tremiti
Termoli
La Maiella
2795
Sulmona
Promontorio del Gargano
1055
S. Severo
Manfredonia
Isernia
Lucera
Campobasso
Foggia
Cassino
Cerignola
Canosa
Ariano Irpino
Benevento
Caserta
Volturno
NAPOLI
Vesuvio
1277
Avellino
Pompei
Pozzuoli
Salerno
Castellammare
Sorrento
Amalfi
Melfi
Potenza
CAMPANIA
Capri
Costa Amalfitana
Paestum
Cagliari
Palermo
Sapri
Paola

CAMPANIA

Those in quest of an authentic flavour to their travels will not be disappointed by Campania, its rich cuisine – pastries made with ricotta cheese and candied fruit, seafood dishes, homemade pasta with a rich Neapolitan sauce, not to mention its trademark pizzas with buffalo mozzarella topping – reflecting the warmth of the local people.

Visitors more interested in sightseeing cannot fail to be impressed by Vesuvius, Capri and Ischia; the Sorrento peninsula reaching out into the Tyrrhenian sea, its steep scrubby slopes interspersed with the rocky outcrops of the Lattari hills. Inland, the wild Appenine landscape is softened by farmland plains irrigated by the Volturno, Calore and Sele rivers. Those still not convinced by Campania's charms should be swayed by its history, both Ancient, as represented by Pompeii and Herculaneum, and more recent, namely the golden age of the Kingdom of Naples. Its sumptuous court occupied some of Italy's most impressive palaces, most notably at Caserta, symbol of the Bourbon apogee and Naples at its height.

20 establishments

1

IL CEPPO

Fam. Laureana

Via Madonna del Carmine, 31
84043 Agropoli (SA)
Tel. 0974 843044 – Fax 0974 843234
info@hotelristoranteilceppo.com – www.hotelristoranteilceppo.com

45-65/ 72-82€

Open all year • 1 single rm, 12 double rm • Menu €16-26 • Parking, no dogs • Tasting and sale of oil, wine and cakes

The palm fronds shading the first floor windows.

Palm trees and bougainvillaea surround this little hotel, a two-storey establishment opened in 1994. There are around 15 rooms, mostly suites, which are simply furnished and functional. This is a good location for those seeking to explore the area's archaeological heritage or enjoy the beaches a short drive away, and is also used by business travellers during the week. Opposite the hotel is the restaurant, run by the same family for nearly 30 years.

Access

From Salerno: A 3 for 21km to Battipaglia exit; onto SS 18 for 27km and then SS 267 for 5km

Sights nearby: Castle and walls; Paestum: archaeological site and museum

2

LA COLOMBAIA

Sig. Botti

Via Pian delle Pere
84043 Agropoli (SA)
Tel. 0974 821800 – Fax 0974 829781
colombaia@tin.it – www.lacolombaiahotel.it

70-100€

Closed 1 Jan-28 Feb • 10 double rm • Half board €55-70 • Menu €16-18 • Parking, garden, swimming pool, no dogs

The pool situated among olive trees.

An imaginative development project has transformed an imposing country residence into a little fairytale castle; the results are extraordinary and undoubtedly very original. The distant sea is framed by the hills, and the surrounding grounds planted with olive groves create an air of calm and relaxation for the hotel's privileged clients. Inside, there is an air of gentility, both in the public areas and in the well-equipped rooms. The terrace is another attractive feature, with seating, umbrellas and a fine pool.

Access

From Salerno: A 3 to Battipaglia exit; onto SS 18 for 27km and then SS 267 for 5km, on reaching Agropoli head south for 2km

Sights nearby: Scenery of the Cilento coastline

3

CIVITA

Civita Srl

Via Manfredi, 124
83042 Atripalda (AV)
Tel. 0825 610471 – Fax 0825 622513
info@hotelcivita.it – www.hotelcivita.it

68/ 90€

Open all year • 4 single rm, 24 double rm • Half board €60.50-65 • Menu €16-40 • Parking, no dogs

The comfort, cleanliness, spaciousness and service.

The archaeological remains of Civita and Abellinum attract many visitors to this area. After spending the day admiring these sites, tourists can be sure of a well-deserved rest at this spacious and well-run establishment of recent construction, a family concern with attractive white and blue decor. The rustic style accommodation has good carpeting and curtains; the well-presented bathrooms are a decent size and impeccably clean. The restaurant serves Mediterranean cuisine, with four options per course and a set menu at lunch.

Access
From Avellino: 4km to the east

Sights nearby: Mercoliano: Loreto abbey and National library; Montevergine: Santuario

VILLA OTERI

Sig. Faga

Via Lungolago, 174
80070 Bacoli (NA)
Tel. 081 5234985 – Fax 081 5233944
reception@villoteri.it – www.villaoteri.it

65-85/75-100€

Open all year • 9 double rm • Half board €55-75 • Menu €25-40 • Parking, small dogs welcome • Organised trips, bicycles available

The breakfast of freshly squeezed orange juice, cappuccino and croissants...and the view.

Delightful setting, breathtaking views, conveniently located for exploring the delights of Campagna far from the madding crowd. Villa Oteri meets all these criteria, a patrician residence in a splendid location, now transformed into a hotel which is a happy union of the convenient and the stylish. The well-equipped rooms are kitted out in up to the minute style but retain a period feel, while the service is first class. The restaurant serves a wide variety of dishes, though the emphasis is on fish.

Access

From Naples: follow the by-pass (tangenziale) for 18km to Pozzuoli, then right for 6.5km

Sights nearby: Cento Camerelle, Terme di Baia; Pozzuoli: Tempio di Serapide, amphitheatre, volcanic crater (solfatara)

5

CASERTA ANTICA

Sig. Giaquinto
Via Tiglio, 45
81020 Caserta (CE)
Tel. 0823 371158 – Fax 0823 371158
info@hotelcaserta-antica.it – www.hotelcaserta-antica.it

45-55/70-75€

Open all year • 2 single rm, 24 double rm • No restaurant • Parking, swimming pool, small dogs welcome • Riding, tasting and sale of cheese and cured meat

The large pool, situated in a peaceful sunny spot.

Close to the medieval quarter of old Caserta, in a quiet residential area, this newly built hotel is ideally equipped to satisfy the requirements of the thousands of tourists who each year visit the city and surrounding area. The limited public areas consist of a small lobby and breakfast room, while the average-sized rooms have balconies; those on the top floor are more interestingly furnished. Outside, in addition to the underground parking (note the very steep ramp), there are gardens and, best of all, a large and pleasant pool. In addition to all this, the rates are very competitive.

Access
From Caserta: SS 87 for 2km, then right for 7km

Sights nearby: Historic centre; Caserta: Reggia

LA PETROSA

Sig. Soffritti
Via Fabbrica, 25
84052 Ceraso (SA)
Tel. 0974 61370 – Fax 0974 61370
staff@lapetrosa.it – www.lapetrosa.it

35-55/ 50-90€

Closed 1 Nov-28 Feb • 5 single rm, 5 double rm • Half board €80-100 • Menu €22-25 • Parking, garden, swimming pool • Organised trips, local produce tasting and crochet work for sale

The rooms in the castle and the marvellous surrounding countryside.

Also known as Vigna della Corte, La Petrosa is part of the district of Ceraso in the Palistro valley (within the Cilento national park) around 10km from the sea and also close to Monte Sacro (1700m). The surrounding landscape is a lush mix of olive groves, orchards and fields. Visitors may opt for camping, apartments or rooms. This last category occupies the finest building, the old main house (a castle-like edifice) and a farmhouse near the pool.

Access
From Salerno: 9km to Pontecagnano junction, then onto the A 3 for 10km to Battipaglia exit, 68km on the SS 18 to Ceraso, right for 7.5km to Petrosa

Sights nearby: Velia: archaeological zone, Promontorio di Palinuro and Grotta Azzurra

7

VILLA DE PERTIS

Sig. De Pertis

Via Ponti, 30
81010 Dragoni (CE)
Tel. 0823 866619 – Fax 0823 866619
info@villadepertis.it – www.villadepertis.it

59/70€

Open all year • 7 double rm • Half board €48 • Menu €21-28 • Garden, no dogs in the restaurant • Bicycle hire

The staircase with stone steps and unusual arches.

Dagomi is a small village around 30km from Caserta on the Volturno coast, a peaceful setting for the Villa De Pertis, a country residence of 17C origin. Dynamism and originality are the key words to describe this establishment, which has an organic quality in its structure. An informal hospitality pervades the place, which owes more to the atmosphere of a private house than to that of a commercial hotel. In addition to the restaurant, lounge with open fireplace and garden with fine views, guests can enjoy the pool table and table tennis. There are also bicycles with which to explore the surrounding countryside.

Access

From Caserta: SS 87 for 16km to Caiazzo, then left onto the SS 158 for 14km

Sights nearby: Alife: Roman walls; Piedimonte Matese: Santuario della SS Annunziata

8

BARONE ANTONIO NEGRI

Sig.ra Negri
Via Teggiano, 8
84084 Fisciano (SA)
Tel. 089 958561 – Fax 089 891180
info@agrinegri.it – www.agrinegri.it

40-65/60-110€

Open all year • 6 double rm • Half board €50-75 • Menu €25 • Parking, garden, swimming pool, bowls, small dogs welcome • Tasting and sale of hazelnut products

The cakeshop, where guests can savour fresh hazelnut biscuits.

In a panoramic and peaceful position among the hills that separate the Salerno coastline from Avellino, this historic establishment, the grandest of the estates in the Fisciano district, is run in dedicated fashion by the last of the line of the Negri family. Hospitality and comfort go hand in hand with history and tradition here, making this relaxing place the ideal spot from which to explore the Sorrento peninsula and Naples.

Access
From Salerno: A 3 for 2.5km, then 7km on the E 84 to Penta-Baronissi exit, 2km on the SP 91

Sights nearby: Salerno: cathedral and archaeological museum; Vietri sul mare: scenery and ceramics

9

IL VITIGNO

Sig.ra Turrisi
Via Bocca, 31
80075 Ischia (NA)
Tel. 081 998307 – Fax 081 998307
info@ilvitigno.com – www.ilvitigno.com

70/ 80€

Closed Dec, Jan, Feb • 1 single rm, 17 double rm • Menu €15 • Parking, swimming pool, garden, no dogs

The attractive wrought iron tables and chairs.

Panoramically situated among olive groves and vineyards in a hilly part of the island, this verdant oasis has stunning views over the sea. There are around ten rooms, all of which are attractively furnished in simple, tasteful style. Although the sea is close by, those wishing to stay put can enjoy the small but charming swimming pool. The residents-only restaurant offers Ischian and Campanian specialities using locally grown produce.

Access
By ferry from Naples or Pozzuoli, then SS 270 for 10km

Sights nearby: View of Mount Epomeo; Ischia: Castello Aragonese

10

SANT'ALFONSO

Sig.ra Cuomo
Via Sant'Alfonso, 6
84010 Furore (SA)
Tel. 089 830515 – Fax 089 830515
info@agriturismosantalfonso.it – www.agriturismosantalfonso.it

60-90€

Closed Nov • 10 double rm • Half board €50-65 • Menu €19-29 • Garden, small dogs welcome • Organised trips, tasting and sale of jam, liqueurs and wine

The terrace, offering fine views of the sea.

A steep climb up 500m of stone steps leads to this haven of peace and quite tucked away in the terraced hillside between the coastline and the Monti Lattari. The building's origins are lost in the mists of time, but it is thought to date from the 16C and was definitely in use as a convent in the 19C. Today it is the ideal place for a relaxing break in peaceful surroundings; named after aromatic herbs, the rooms are simply furnished, in keeping with the architectural style of the house. The house wine is made on the premises and fresh water is drawn from a working well.

Access
From Salerno: SS 163 for 24km to Conca del Marini, then right for 6km

Sights nearby: Vallone di Furore, Grotta di Smeraldo

11

PALAZZO PENNASILICO

Sig. Luigi Pennasilico

Via Le Piazze, 27
84090 SIETI (SA)
Tel. 089 881822 – Fax 089 881822
info@palazzopennasilico.it – www.palazzopennasilico.it

90/ 100€

Closed Jan, Feb • 2 double rm • Breakfast €10 • No restaurant • Parking, garden, no dogs

The terrace overlooking the village of Sieti.

The property of the Pennasilico family since the 16C, this delightful palazzo is located in Sieti, a small textile village deep in the Monti Picentini Park. The palazzo has only recently opened its doors to guests, who will delight in the magnificent frescoes and decor of the drawing rooms, corridors and private chapel. The bedrooms, also furnished in a very individual style, are grouped into two categories; the Alcova suite is particularly stunning. Also worthy of note is the courtyard where the bread oven, oil press and stables were once situated. Friendly, hospitable owners.

Access

From Salerno: A 3 towards Reggio di Calabria for 3km, then 18km along SS 88

Sights nearby: Salerno: cathedral; Vietri sul Mare: views and ceramics

12

PICCOLO PARADISO

Sig. Antonino Cacace

Piazza Madonna della Lobra, 5
80061 Massa Lubrense (NA)
Tel. 081 8789240 – Fax 081 8089534
info@piccolo-paradiso.com – www.piccolo-paradiso.com

56-74/95-111€

Closed 16/11-14/03 • 4 single rm, 50 double rm • Half board €70.50-79 • Menu €25-40 • Swimming pool, no dogs in the restaurant

The Vietri-style ceramics.

Far from the noise and sophistication of the famous hot-spots of the Bay of Naples and the Amalfi Coast, Massa Lubrense is a typical fishing village built from tufa stone. The Piccolo Paradiso is a more modern construction, regularly renovated by the enterprising Cacace family who have managed the hotel for years. The bedrooms here are light and the bathrooms furnished with colourful ceramics. One of the highlights of the hotel is the attractive swimming pool located on the spacious, panoramic terrace. The restaurant, which serves a selection of fresh Mediterranean dishes, is situated in a large dining room.

Access

From Naples: A 3 towards Salerno for 24km, then SS 145 for 31km

Sights nearby: Amalfi coast; Capri: Blue Grotto and view from Monte Solaro

13

MESOGHEO

Sig. Carola

Contrada Valle Corrado, 4
82030 Melizzano (BN)
Tel. 0824 944356 – Fax 0824 944130
info@mesogheo.com – www.mesogheo.com

65/100€

Open all year • 10 double rm • Half board €80 • Menu €30 • Parking, garden, swimming pool, no dogs in the restaurant • Archaeological trips, horse riding

The open fireplaces in every room, perfect for cooler evenings.

A little dedication is required to find this establishment, tucked away as it is up a poorly signposted track, but the visitor will find the extra effort worthwhile. The main building is a typical local farmhouse, with the restaurant on the ground floor and the owner's apartment upstairs. Guests will find their accommodation in one of two smaller buildings closer to the pool; there are around ten rooms, with many personal touches in evidence and a pleasant feel. All in all, a great place to stay.

Access

From Benevento: SS 88 for 8km, left onto the SS 372 for 15km, then left for 12km

Sights nearby: Benevento: Arco di Traiano, Roman theatre, church of Santa Sofia, Egyptian obelisk

14

B&B L'ALLOGGIO DEI VASSALLI

Sig. Antonelli
Via Donnalbina, 56
80134 Napoli (NA)
Tel. 081 5515118 – Fax 081 4202752
info@bandbnapoli.it – www.bandbnapoli.it

55-65/93-99€

Open all year • 4 double rm • No restaurant • Small dogs welcome

Dvd player and free drinks in every room.

Centrally located close to the city's artistic and cultural highlights, this gem of a place stands out among the many hotels which have sprung up in recent years to cater for the ever increasing number of tourists. Occupying an 18C palazzo, the well presented rooms have a historic charm which, along with frescoed ceilings, preserve the original atmosphere of the place.

Sights nearby: Convento di S. Chiara, churches of S. Anna dei Lombardi and S. Domenico Maggiore, Cappella Sansevero

15

B&B MORELLI 49

Sigg. Musella

Via Domenico Morelli, 49
80121 Napoli (NA)
Tel. 081 2452291 – Fax 081 288435
bedmorelli49@libero.it – www.bbmorelli49.it

55-65/ 85-95€

Open all year • 4 single rm, 4 double rm • No restaurant

The warm Neapolitan ambience and the central location.

Lying between piazza del Plebiscito and the seafront, the narrow streets of the scenic Chiaia district are only a short walk from some of the city's greatest historic monuments. The accommodation here is composed of four simple but well presented rooms on the first floor of a period building, their dark wood furnishings contrasting with colourful bathrooms. A lively Neapolitan family atmosphere pervades the place without detracting from the courteous nature of the service.

Sights nearby: Palazzo Reale, Piazza del Plebiscito, Castel Nuovo, Galleria Umberto I

CAPPELLA VECCHIA

Sigg. Raia
Via Santa Maria a Cappella Vecchia, 11
80121 Napoli (NA)
Tel. 0812405117 – Fax 081 2405117
info@cappellavecchia11.it - www.cappellavecchia11.it

50-65/80-100€

Open all year • 1 single rm, 4 double rm • No restaurant • Small dogs welcome • Organised trips, bicycle hire

The light and comfortable interior.

The first floor accommodation of this B&B is modern in feel but equipped to a high standard and all rooms have private bathrooms. This period building is only 500m from the Palazzo Reale and the Santa Lucia district with its splendid views over the gulf of Naples, making it the ideal base from which to explore the artistic and historical riches of the city.

Sights nearby: Palazzo Reale, Piazza del Plebiscito, Castel Nuovo, Galleria Umberto I

17

PRINCIPE NAPOLIT'AMO

Sigg. Napolitano

Via Toledo, 148
80132 Napoli (NA)
Tel. 081 5523626 – Fax 081 5523626
info@napolitamo.it – www.napolitamo.it

50-80/ 70-95€

Open all year • 13 double rm • No restaurant

Looking down onto the city from an open window.

Occupying the first floor of a 17C palazzo on one of the city centre's finest streets, this is the ideal place from which to discover the real Naples. Although the external façade looks a little austere, inside is a courtyard which encapsulates the city's charms, with delicious aromas emanating from the kitchens as the visitor climbs the stairs to the entrance. The spacious rooms have high ceilings and all overlook either the street or the courtyard.

Sights nearby: Palazzo Reale, Castel Nuovo, Galleria Umberto I, convento di Santa Chiara, church of Sant'Anna dei Lombardi

18

LE OLIVE DI NEDDA

Sig.ra De Majo
Via Crucelle Superiore, 14
81010 Ruviano (CE)
Tel. 0823 863052 – Fax 0823 863052
info@olinedda.it – www.olinedda.it

45-50/ 90-100€

Open all year • 7 double rm • Half board €70-75 • Menu €32 • Parking, garden, no dogs • Horse riding, bicycle hire, fishing, tasting and sale of cured meat, oil, liqueur and wine

Enjoying the evening breeze from the pergola.

The Telesina valley derives its name from Telesia, an ancient Samnite and subsequently Roman settlement, the ruins of which still exist. This rustic establishment sits in a plain, with views of olive groves along the valley which extends between hills. Nearby flow the waters of the river Volturno, and all around the farmhouse are fields, woods and a garden with pergola offering a cool retreat from the heat of the day. Out of season, guests can enjoy views over the landscape from the comfort of the fireside.

Access
From Caserta: SS 87 for 25km, then right for 0.5km to Alvignanello

Sights nearby: Caserta: Reggia; Caserta Vecchia: historic centre

19

CASA SOFIA

Sig. Katz

Via Sant'Angelo, 29/B
80070 Ischia (NA)
Tel. 081 999310 – Fax 081 904928
info@hotelcasasofia.com – www.hotelcasasofia.com

50/ 100€

Closed 11 Nov-14 Mar • 2 single rm, 9 double rm • No restaurant • No dogs

The stunning views and the many personal touches.

It is difficult to decide which view is best here; there are so many from which to choose. The hotel is tastefully furnished, with each piece seeming to have been selected individually, thus giving every room a unique feel. With books and magazines the lounge area is very welcoming, while the restaurant serves diners on a fine terrace in summer, or indoors (yet equally panoramic) in poor weather.

Access
By ferry from Naples or Pozzuoli, then 12km on the SS 270, left for 3km to Sant'Angelo

Sights nearby: View of Mount Epomeo; Ischia: Castello Aragonese

20

LA GINESTRA

Sig.ra Anna Belforte
Moiano - Località Santa Maria del Castello
80060 Moiano (NA)
Tel. 081 8023211 – Fax 081 8023211
info@laginestra.org – www.laginestra.org

70-80€

Open all year • 1 single rm, 6 double rm • Half board €45-50 • Menu €16-20 • Parking, garden, no dogs in the restaurant • Bicycle hire, organised trips, tasing and sale of organic produce

The elegance of this patrician villa between the scrubby hinterland and the sea.

It is no accident that the original builders decided on this spot for their patrician villa; 600m above the gulf of Salerno and flanked by the scrub covered slopes of Monte Faito, this is a stunning location which time has left untouched. The restored property has well equipped accommodation, a terrace where meals are served in summer, and a games area. Nuts, honey, oil and fruit are on sale in the large lounge area converted from the old stables. The proprietors will arrange guided tours of the area on request.

Access
From Naples: A 3 to Castellammare di Stabia, then 12.5km to Vico Equense, then left for 8km to Santa Maria del Castello

Sights nearby: Monta Faito, view of the gulf of Naples

EMILIA-ROMAGNA

In order to understand this region, it is worth following the course of the Po, the great river which emerges from the hills of Piedmont before making its way across the plain and forming the boundary with Lombardy. Dykes separate it from the surrounding flat farmland which extends to the Apennine foothills. Parallel to its course runs the via Emilia, forming a cultural route which takes in the marble of Parma's Romanesque baptistery, the terracotta of Bologna's university, the gold of Ravenna's mosaics, and the ducal splendours of Ferrara, bearing witness to the historical legacy of Romans, Byzantines, the medieval communes and the warring states of the Renaissance period. The landscape is on a human scale, with town and country remaining distinct, and a network of roads which invite travel by bicycle or on foot. The region's cultural richness is matched by its gastronomy; the birthplace of Verdi boasts cuisine which is a veritable symphony of flavours, accompanied by wines such as Sangiovese and Lambrusco.

30 establishments

Bergamo
Iseo
Riviera
Brescia
Sirmione
Gallarate
Monza
Treviglio
Novara
MILANO
Vigevano
Lodi
Pavia
Cremona
Mantova
Piacenza
Salsomaggiore
Terme
Parma
Reggio
Emillia
E M I L I A
GENOVA
Cisa
1039
Cerreto
1261
1388
Rapallo
Sestri
Levante
La Spezia
Carrara
Massa
Abetone
Montecatini-Terme
Forte dei Marmi
Viareggio
Lucca
Empoli
Pisa
Livorno
Volterra
Cecina
Golfo di Genova
Ligure
Bastia
Palermo
Ile-Rousse
Olbia, Cagliari
Porto Torres
Tunis
Barcelona, Palma
A 4
A 7
A 1
A 12
A 15
A 21
E 35
E 80
P 1
19
4
2
9
28
29
1
27
8
10
12
25
11
18
20

Treviso
Vicenza
Grado
Trie
Piran
Mestre
VENEZIA
Padova
109
Lido di V.
Golfo
di Venezia
Monselice
Chioggia
Poreč
Adige
Rovigo
Po
Ferrara
Comacchio
Reno
Ravenna
EMILIA - ROMAGNA
Imola
Faenza
Forlì
Cervia
Cesena
Rimini
Riccione
Raticosa
968
Cattolica
San Marino
Pesaro
Fano
Bagno
di Romagna
Pontassieve
FIRENZE
Urbino
Senigallia
Jesi
Sansepolcro
Arno
Arezzo
Città di Castello
Gubbio
Macerata
Fabriano
Siena
Cortona
Perugia
Montepulciano

1

GARDEN VIGANÒ

Sig. Vincenzi e Sig.ra Specuglia

Via Garibaldi, 17
42020 Albinea (RE)
Tel. 0522 347292 – Fax 0522 347293
info@hotelgardenvigano.it – www.hotelgardenvigano.it

55/77€

Open all year • 5 single rm, 17 double rm • Breakfast €10 • No restaurant • Parking, park, no dogs

The delightful dining room where breakfast is served.

The winding roads heading up from the plain lead to this haven of tranquillity located within the Fola park. The ancient cypress preceding the entrance heralds the visitor's arrival. Of 18C origin, the building is typical of the local area, an elegant construction in austere brickwork. There are just under 20 rooms of various sizes, all furnished in rustic style and spotlessly clean.

Access
From Reggio Emilia: south for 7km on the SP 25

Sights nearby: Reggio Emilia: Parmeggiani Gallery, churches of la Ghiara and San Prospero

2

VILLA BELLARIA

Sig.ra Cazzaniga Calderoni

Cortina di Alseno - Località Fellegara
29010 Alseno (PC)
Tel. 0523 947537
info@villabellariabb.it – www.villabellariabb.it

35-39/ 55-59€

Open all year • 3 double rm • No restaurant • Parking, garden, no dogs • Organised trips, jam and cake tasting

Breakfast on the veranda overlooking the garden.

The ancient agricultural settlement of Alseno lies between the Via Emilia and the outlying foothills of the mountains. Not far away, this little villa sits in a quiet and panoramic spot surrounded by a well kept garden, at its best when its trees take on the colours of autumn. Inside, there is a family atmosphere, akin to a B&B, which pervades both the accommodation and the public areas, where the sofas' azure hues blend well with the pictures and walls, and the fireplace blazes.

Access

From Piacenza: SS 9 towards Parma for 28km to Alseno, right for 4km, then left for 2km to Fellegara

Sights nearby: Castell'Arquato: historic centre; Fidenza: cathedral

3

VAL CAMPOTTO

Sig. Poppi

Strada Margotti, 2
44010 Campotto (FE)
Tel. 0532 800516 – Fax 0532 319413
agriturismo@valcampotto.it – www.valcampotto.it

48/68€

Open all year • 9 double rm • Half board €52 • Menu €14-24 • Parking, no dogs • Bicycle hire, organised trips, jams, honey and liqueurs for sale

The wood-beamed ceilings in the rooms.

The farming spirit which for generations has created the rich and fertile conditions so evident in the surrounding area has inspired Patrizia and Stefano to throw open the doors of their home to guests; nine rooms are available, decorated in an elegant rustic style, while the restaurant serves dishes prepared from locally-grown produce, and home made pasta. Bicycles may be hired by those wishing to explore the countryside.

Access

From Ferrara; SS 16 for 35km, then left along Via VIII Settembre for 4km before reaching Via Margotti

Sights nearby: Ferrara: Cathedral, Castello Estense, Palazzo Schifanio, Palazzo dei Diamanti, Casa Romei

4

LE COLOMBAIE

Sig.ra Merli
Via Bersano, 29
29010 Besenzone (PC)
Tel. 0523 830007 – Fax 0523 830735
lecolombaie@colombaie.it – www.colombaie.it

45/90€

Closed 20 Nov-28 Feb • 6 double rm • No restaurant • Parking, garden • Bicycles available

The childlike pleasures of cycling through the countryside.

Imagine an unspoilt village at the heart of the Po plain, in the area between Piacenza and Parma known as Verdi country. From here a dirt track leads through open country to this hotel. Beyond its rose garden, the recently restored building appears, its colourful interior tastefully furnished with contemporary design objects which blend well with the rustic Lombard backdrop. Once a humble stable block with hay barn, it is difficult to believe that such a transformation has taken place here.

Access
From Piacenza: SS 10 for 5km, then onto the SS 587 for 13km to Cortemaggiore, then left for 8.5km to Bersano

Sights nearby: Sant'Agata: Villa Verdi; Busseto: Villa Pallavicino

5

A CASA DI DOLLY

Sig.ra Calebotta

Via Della Libertà, 9 (ingresso da via Mura di Porta d'Azeglio)
40123 Bologna (BO)
Tel. 051 331937 – Fax 051 331937
info@acasadidolly.it – www.acasadidolly.it

50-75/80-100€

Closed Aug • 3 double rm • No restaurant • No dogs

The family's video library.

The location of this bed and breakfast, just a few metres from the main avenue in Bologna and ten minutes' walk from Piazza Maggiore, makes it an ideal base for exploring the city. Situated on the second floor of a modern condominium, it has a large sitting room, part of which is used as the breakfast room, where the family's video collection is available for guests to enjoy. The guestrooms are spacious and embellished with occasional piece of ethnic furniture; two of the rooms share a bathroom. Friendly, welcoming owners who are particularly fond of cats.

Sights nearby: Basilica of San Petronio, Piazza Maggiore, leaning towers, churches of San Francesco and San Domenico

GALILEO

Sig. Cicognani

Piazza Galileo, 3
40123 Bologna (BO)
Tel. 051 237452 – Fax 051 237452
galieleobeb@libero.it – www.galileobedandbreakfast.com

40-60/ 60-80€

Open all year • 1 single rm, 3 double rm • No restaurant • No dogs

Having the centre of Bologna on the doorstep.

This B&B has four simple rooms, furnished in unremarkable style but all spotlessly clean, as are the two bathrooms. What distinguishes it from the competition, however, is its location. Within five minutes, guests can walk to the very heart of Bologna, Piazza Maggiore, dominated by the church of San Petronio, the town hall and the palazzo Re Enzo, named after the son of Emperor Fredrick II, imprisoned here after the battle of Fossalta.

Sights nearby: Basilica of San Petronio, Piazza Maggiore, leaning towers, churches of San Francesco and San Domenico

7

VILLA AZZURRA

Lord Snc

Viale Felsina, 49
40139 Bologna (BO)
Tel. 051 535460 – Fax 051 531346

80/100€

Closed 10-20 Aug • 5 single rm, 10 double rm • No breakfast • No restaurant • Parking, garden

The tranquil atmosphere and spaciousness of the rooms.

From the exterior, this appears to be a private residence and the same impression prevails inside. Situated away from the centre in a quiet leafy area, the hotel has its own garden (with children's play equipment) but the main attraction is its spacious accommodation. The well equipped rooms are furnished in a modern functional style, having been refurbished recently. No breakfast, but excellent value for money by the standards of the city.

Sights nearby: Basilica di San Petronio, Piazza Maggiore, leaning towers, churches of San Francesco and San Domenico

8

CA' BIANCA

Sig. Turini e Sig.ra Urso
Loc. Ostia Parmense, 84
43043 Borgo Val di Taro (PR)
Tel. 0525 98003 – Fax 0525 98213
m.turini@libero.it – www.agriturismo-cabianca.it

55/90€

Closed 1 Nov-30 Apr • 1 single rm, 6 double rm • Half board €70 • Menu €19-28 • Parking, garden • Horse riding, bicycle hire, tasting and sale of jams, mostarde and liqueurs

The monumental wooden fireplace in the "club house".

The woods, mountain streams and cultivated fields of the Val di Taro completely surround this large white house, a farm and agriturismo run by Graziella and Mauro and their family. The perfect base for a holiday at any time of year, the property stands at an altitude of 400m. Activities on offer include mushroom picking, mountain biking, fishing and, in particular, horse riding. The house has seven spacious, comfortable rooms, a games and billiard room, plus an attractive, rustic dining room offering the perfect backdrop for the home-made cuisine served here.

Access
From Parma: SS 9 towards Piacenza for 10km, then A 15 for 36km and SS 523 for 19km

Sights nearby: Compiano: castle and medieval village

9

I DUE FOSCARI

Sigg. Bergonzi e Morsia
Piazza Carlo Rossi, 15
43011 Busseto (PR)
Tel. 0524 930031 – Fax 0524 91625

62/87€

Open all year • 20 double rm • Breakfast €8; half board €77.50 • Menu €25-45 • Parking, garden, no dogs

The uniquely majestic dining room.

The ideal place to stay for those looking for something a little different. From the exterior, this unusual establishment looks like a castle, an imposing edifice with stone gateways. On entering the lobby, the overall style becomes clearer: gothic without being dark, making for a curious theatrical effect. Spacious rooms, antique furniture and carefully-sourced fixtures all make this a place well worth a visit.

Access
From Parma: SS 9 for 22km, then right onto the SS 588 for 12km

Sights nearby: Villa Pallavicino; Roncole: birthplace of Verdi; Sant'Agata: Villa Verdi

10

LE SCUDERIE

Le Scuderie Scrl
Via Regigno, 77
42033 Carpineti (RE)
Tel. 0522 618397 – Fax 0522 718066
www.carpineti.com

30/52€

Open all year • 8 double rm • Half board €40 • Menu €18-28 • Parking, garden • Tasting and sale of local produce

The relaxing atmosphere in which to bask after exploring the surrounding area on horseback.

'Paradise lost among the Reggiano Alps' announces the brochure; perhaps an exaggeration but only a slight one. Occupying a fine stone built country house, this establishment is surrounded by unspoilt woodland and fields. There are some fine local landmarks, most notably the castle where in 1077 Matilda of Canossa sheltered Pope Gregory VII during his flight from the wrath of Emperor Henry IV. The restaurant offers classic Emilian cuisine. Those yet to be convinced of the merits of the place may be interested to know that there is also the opportunity to discover the area on horseback.

Access
From Reggio Emilia: SS 63 for 29km, then left for 4.5km to Carpineti, then right for 1.5km to Via Regigno

Sights nearby: Reggio Emilia: Galleria Parmeggiani, churches of la Ghiara and San Prospero

11

LA FENICE

F.lli Girandoni

Via Santa Lucia, 29
40040 Castel d'Aiano (BO)
Tel. 051 919272 – Fax 051 919024
lafenice@lafeniceagritur.it – www.lafeniceagritur.it

60/ 80€

Closed 7 Jan-7 Feb • 15 double rm • Half board €60-64 • Menu €23-37 • Parking, garden, swimming pool, no dogs • Horse riding, tasting of cured meat and woodland fruit

The stone and woodwork, the open fireplaces and the hidden passageways.

The Giarandoni brothers were pioneers of the agriturismo sector, having opened their doors to guests in the late 1980s. Their experience built up over the years means that this establishment is today one of the best run in the area. It is charmingly situated in a small village of wood and stone construction, surrounded by delightful countryside. The many open fireplaces and hidden passageways linking the different parts of the building give it great character, also evident in the restaurant which specialises in traditional Emilian cuisine.

Access

From Bologna: SS 64 for 29km, then right for 10km to Rocca di Rofeno

Sights nearby: Bologna: basilica of San Petronzio, Piazza Maggiore, leaning towers, churches of San Francesco and San Domenico

12

VILLA GAIDELLO

Sig.ra Bini

Via Gaidello, 18/22
41013 Castelfranco Emilia (MO)
Tel. 059 926806 – Fax 059 926620
gaidello@tin.it – www.gaidello.com

65/93€

Closed Christmas, Easter and Aug • 2 single rm, 2 double rm • Menu €35-45 • Parking, garden, no dogs • Bicycle hire, tasting of jams and onions pickled in balsamic vinegar

Life on the plains... at its most authentic.

The open landscape is typical of the local area. Tomato fields surround the historic range of buildings, their interiors providing a welcoming atmosphere for visitors. Accommodation is available in the main house and a second building a little distance away, both of which are well proportioned with period fixtures, wood beamed ceilings and a rustic ambience. The restaurant, serving traditional Emilian cuisine and excellent home made pasta, occupies another building.

Access
From Modena: SS 9 towards Bologna for 13km

Sights nearby: Modena: Cathedral, Galleria Estense, Palazzo Ducale

13

IL LOGHETTO

Sig.ra Mazza
Via Zenzalino Sud, 3/4
40055 Castenaso (BO)
Tel. 051 6052218 – Fax 051 6052254

55/ 95€

Closed Jan, Aug • 3 single rm, 7 double rm • Menu €20-35 • Parking • Bicycle hire, fishing, organised trips, jams, fruit and liqueurs for sale

A game of billiards after dinner in the lounge area.

The entrance to this hotel is easily missed, being tucked away in a narrow and busy street. After overcoming this initial hurdle, the visitor can begin to enjoy the charming particularities of this large establishment. The recent extensive renovation has greatly enhanced levels of comfort without detracting from the typically rustic structure. A friendly and helpful family management team, well-proportioned rooms and great attention to detail all serve to make this an attractive place to stay.

Access
From Bologna: SS 253 for 10km to Budrio junction

Sights nearby: Bologna: basilica of San Petronio, Piazza Maggiore, leaning towers, churches of San Francesco and San Domenico

B&B CORTE DEI GIOGHI

Sig.ra Tagliavini
Via Pellegrina, 8
44100 Ferrara (FE)
Tel. 0532 745049 – Fax 0532 745050
info@cortedeigioghi.com – www.cortedeigioghi.com

55-60/75-85€

Open all year • 3 double rm • No restaurant • Parking • Bicycles available

The magnificent wooden beds which give such character to the rooms.

At the entrance to the city, close to the cathedral in the old San Giorgio district, this hotel is reminiscent of a picturesque country residence, with imposing brick walls, dark wooden shutters and an attractive portico which provides welcome shade in the hot summer months. The charming rooms are well proportioned, with beamed ceilings and period furnishings. Breakfast is served in a welcoming, rustic-style dining room, or outside in summer. Ample parking available to guests.

Access
From Ferrara: SS 16 for 2km, then left into Via Pellegrina

Sights nearby: Cathedral, Castello estense, Palazzo Schifanio, Palazzo dei Diamanti, Casa Romei

15

ALLA CEDRARA

Sig. Marzetti

Via Aranova, 104 località Porotto
44044 Porotto (FE)
Tel. 0532 593033 – Fax 0532 772293
agriturismo@allacedrara.it – www.allacedrara.it

35-45/ 62-72€

Open all year • 1 single rm, 3 double rm • No restaurant • Parking, garden, no dogs • Bicycle hire, organised trips, tasting of typical regional cakes

The large open fireplace in the lounge area.

This establishment is approached down a long dirt track, with visitors leaving a trail of dust and the stresses of urban life behind them. Situated only 10km from Ferrara, yet already in the heart of the countryside, this hay barn conversion is surrounded by gardens and parkland with a wide variety of recently planted trees. Bicycles may be borrowed (no charge) to explore the area, and the comfortable rooms guarantee a restful stay.

Access
From Ferrara: SS 496 for 5km

Sights nearby: Cathedral, Castello Estense, Palazzo Schifanio, Palazzo dei Diamanti, Casa Romei

16

LOCANDA CORTE ARCANGELI

Fam. Arcangeli

Via Pontegradella, 503
44030 Ferrara (FE)

Tel. 0532 705052 – Fax 0532 752606

info@cortearcangeli.it – www.cortearcangeli.it

50-70/ 73-85€

Open all year • 6 double rm • Half board €55-65 • Menu €27-58 • Parking, no dogs • Bicycles available, tasting of jams, cured meats and mostarde

Excursions on the bicycles available to guests.

The Arcangeli family, the owners of this charming farmhouse in the countryside outside Ferrara, have prudently reinvented themselves; these days they provide welcoming hospitality to visitors, offering a cheerful, restful ambience in which to stay. The charming surroundings boast brick vaulted and wood beamed ceilings, and rustic furnishings typical of country residences. The excellent breakfasts are robust, varied and generous.

Access

From Ferrara: 2km to the north-east

Sights nearby: Cathedral, Castello Estense, Palazzo Schifanio, Palazzo dei Diamanti, Casa Romei

17

LOCANDA IL BAGATTINO

Sig.ra Maurillo

Via Porta Reno, 24
44100 Ferrara (FE)
Tel. 0532 241887 – Fax 0532 217546
info@ilbagattino.it – www.ilbagattino.it

55-65/85-95€

Open all year • 6 double rm • No restaurant • Bicycle hire

The combination of elegance and convenient location.

Named after a long redundant denomination of coinage, this fine building is a short walk from the cathedral and the castle. A warm welcome awaits from the professional management, who have created an ambience of understated refinement. The six rooms offer every imaginable comfort; the top floor accommodation is particularly charming. To sum up, this tranquil spot is the ideal base from which to discover the beauties of the city of the dukes of Este.

Sights nearby: Cathedral, Castello Estense, Palazzo Schifanio, Palazzo dei Diamanti, Casa Romei

18

CA' DI FOS

Sig.ra Zaccanti

Via Rondichioso, 731
40041 Gaggio Montano (BO)
Tel. 0534 37029 – Fax 0534 38521
cadifos@computermax.it – www.agriturismo-cadifos.com

40/80€

Closed Jan, Feb • 8 double rm • Half board €50-60 • Menu €25-30 • Parking, garden, swimming pool, small dogs welcome • Bicycles available, archery, tasting and sale of jams and honey

The trout leaping in the lake.

Although it would be an exaggeration to say that this place touches the sky, it certainly does provide breathtaking views over the hills around Bologna. Surrounded by fields and woods, it also benefits from a lovely setting. The owners opened their doors in 1987 offering simple accommodation, while the characterful dining room offers delicious local cuisine. Visitors can purchase numerous specialities including fresh trout from the small lake, not far beyond the swimming pool.

Access

From Bologna: SS 64 for 54km to Silla, then right for 7km

Sights nearby: Church of Santi Michele e Nazario, Rupe landscape, Parco Regionale del Corno alle Scale

19

CROARA VECCHIA

Sig. Milano
Località Croara Vecchia
29010 Gazzola (PC)
Tel. 333 2193845 – Fax 0523 957628
gmilanopc@tin.it – www.croaravecchia.it

75/90€

Closed Nov, Dec, Jan, Feb • 1 single rm, 4 double rm • No restaurant • Parking, garden, swimming pool • Horse riding, bicycles available

The covered riding school, available in all weathers.

It is difficult to imagine how the friars who lived here in the 16C would have felt about this place becoming a rural guesthouse, and plenty of changes have taken place since then. Situated on the banks of the Trebbia and surrounded by gardens, the hotel also has an equestrian centre for horse lovers. The accommodation is furnished with tastefully simple pieces, as is the pleasant breakfast room. The perfect spot for a weekend away from it all.

Access
From Piacenza: southwest on the SP 28 for 14km to Rivalta Trebbia

Sights nearby: Piacenza: Palazzo del Comune, cathedral

20

MONTEGRANDE

Sig. Bartolomei e Sig.ra Zani

Via Marconi, 27
40049 Vidiciatico (BO)
Tel. 0534 53210 – Fax 0534 54024
info@montegrande.it – www.montegrande.it

56-60€

Closed 25 Apr-15 May, 15 Oct-30 Nov • 14 double rm • Breakfast €7; half board €45-50 • Menu €20-30 • Bowls, no dogs • Organised trips, bicycles available

The comfortable armchairs in the lounge.

Situated on Vidiciatico's main street, this small establishment has been steadily improved by its proprietors to create a splendid place to stay for summer holidays or winter breaks on the Apennine slopes. The rooms are of average size: some benefit from terrace access, while others are decorated with brightly coloured wallpaper. The owner-run restaurant serves regional specialities and seasonal dishes including truffles and mushrooms.

Access

From Bologna: SS 64 for 50km, then right onto the SS 324 for 16km, then left for 0.7km to Vidiciatico

Sights nearby: Gaggio Montano: church of Santi Michele e Nazario, Rupe landscape; Parco Regionale del Corno alle Scale

21

IL CUCCO

Sig. Emili e Sig.ra Tosatti

Via Nazionale, 83
40051 Altedo (BO)
Tel. 051 6601124 – Fax 051 6601124
ilcucco.bo@libero.it – www.ilcucco.it

52/ 72-105€

Closed Aug • 3 single rm, 8 double rm • Half board €72.50 • Menu €16-30 • Parking, garden, no dogs in the restaurant • Bicycle hire, vegetables for sale

The home-made specialities, available for tasting and purchase.

Heading north from Bologna, this country guesthouse is to be found on the outskirts of Altedo near Malalbergo; visitors must leave the main road and follow a dirt track for several hundred metres prior to reaching their destination, a classic farmhouse surrounded by gardens, vegetable plots and chicken runs. Behind the brick façade is spacious and characterful accommodation with exposed beams, and well equipped bathrooms. The owners prepare the excellent cuisine themselves; the local speciality bread (tigella) is not to be missed.

Access
From Bologna: SS 64 for 22km

Sights nearby: Bologna: basilica of San Petronio, Piazza Maggiore, leaning towers, churches of San Francesco and San Domenico

22

LA CARTIERA DEI BENANDANTI

Sig.ra Cevenini
Via Idice, 13
40063 Monghidoro (BO)
Tel. 051 6551498 – Fax 051 6551498
lacartiera@tin.it – www.lacartiera.it

45-50/70-80€

Closed 15 Jan-20 Mar • 1 single rm, 4 double rm • Half board €50-55 • Menu €15-25 • Parking, garden • Bicycle hire, archery, tasting and sale of jam, fresh cheeses and vegetables

A day's mountain biking followed by a hearty meal.

This old mill has been completely rebuilt in stone and its charming appearance belies the newness of its construction. Its light interior has an elegant ambience and high standards of comfort. The cuisine relies heavily on home grown products and the menu focuses on Romagna specialities. Approached by a steep track which winds through much of the establishment's surrounding farmland.

Access
From Bologna: SS 65 for 35km

Sights nearby: La Martina park, country villages, Santuario della Madonna dei Boschi

23

B&B ABBAZIA

Sig.ra Balestra
Via San Rocco, 7
40050 Monteveglio (BO)
Tel. 051 6701024 – Fax 051 6701835
clcandel@tin.it

47/73€

Closed 7-14 Jul, 20 Aug-3 Sep • 3 double rm • No restaurant • Garden, no dogs

The privilege of staying in a medieval village.

Monteveglio is a classic medieval village, panoramically situated in the Apennines yet only 20km from the regional capital (Bologna). Occupying a typical stone built house, this establishment has four rooms of various sizes, two of which share a bathroom. There is a pleasant breakfast room, and an attractive garden bordering the woodland in which to lounge during the day. The hamlet also has a trattoria serving local specialities.

Access
From Bologna: SS 569 for 11km, then left onto the SP 27 for 4.5km

Sights nearby: Castle and abbey

24

VILLA BELFIORE

Fam. Bertelli

Via Pioppa, 27
44020 Ostellato (FE)
Tel. 0533 681164 – Fax 0533 681172
info@villabelfiore.com – www.turismoruralebelfiore.it

75-85/ 90-100€

Open all year • 18 double rm • Half board €70-85 • Menu €25-30 • Parking, swimming pool, garden, no dogs • Jam and medicinal plants for sale

The many rugs which provide warmth and decoration throughout.

The tranquillity of the countryside has an ever more elusive quality so in demand from city dwellers, namely silence. Villa Belfiore also offers efficient service, impeccable cleanliness and an orderly ambience. The rustic yet elegant furnishings are stylish, enhancing the public areas and rooms alike. The restaurant serves genuine Romagna cuisine and home made pasta, while the swimming pool is a welcome feature during the summer months.

Access

From Ferrara; SS 16 for 5km to join Ferrara-Ravenna superstrada for 25km to Ostellato exit

Sights nearby: Ferrara: cathedral, Castello Estense, Palazzo Schifanoia, Palazzo dei Diamanti, Casa Romei

25

VANDELLI

Sig. Vandelli

Via Giardini Sud, 7
41026 Pavullo nel Frignano (MO)
Tel. 0536 20288 – Fax 0536 23608
info@hotelvandelli.it – www.hotelvandelli.it

48-65/65-85€

Open all year • 18 single rm, 21 double rm • Half board €55-70 • Menu €20-40 • Parking, no dogs in the restaurant

We most liked

The surprising value for money.

Roughly equidistant from Reggio Emilia, Modena and Bologna, Pavullo is around 700m up among the woods and valleys of the Frignano district, the ideal backdrop for a holiday away from the hustle and bustle of contemporary life. Owned by Signor Vandelli, this hotel is on the town's main street and is distinctive for the quality of its furnishings. The lobby has fine wood panelling, the public areas are spacious and well laid out, and the tastefully decorated rooms have many personal touches.

Access

From Modena: SS 12 for 37km

Sights nearby: Modena: cathedral, Galleria Estense, Palazzo Ducale

26

AL VECCHIO CONVENTO

Sigg. Raggi e Cameli

Via Roma, 7

47010 Portico di Romagna (FC)

Tel. 0543 967014 – Fax 0543 967157

info@vecchioconvento.it – www.vecchioconvento.it

50/73€

Closed 12 Jan-12 Feb • 3 single rm, 13 double rm • Breakfast €8.50; half board €74 • Menu €26-40 • No dogs in the restaurant • Horse riding, bicycle hire

Savouring Romagna specialities beneath the restaurant's imposing stone arches.

The old convent from which this establishment derives its name is barely apparent, having been superseded by a 19C stone palazzo with a well preserved facade and interior with wood and terracotta detail. The impression is one of rustic solidity which is also apparent in the rooms, furnished with late 19C pieces. During the summer months guests can bask in the cool shade of the garden's trees, while in winter the open fireplaces provide warmth and ambience.

Access

From Forlì: SS 67 towards Firenze for 32km

Sights nearby: Forlì: basilica of San Mercuriale, Pinacoteca

27

DEL VESCOVADO

Sig.ra Bergomi

Stradone Vescovado, 1
42100 Reggio nell'Emilia (RE)
Tel. 0522 430157 – Fax 0522 430143
frabergomi@yahoo.com

62/80€

Closed Aug • 6 double rm • No restaurant • No dogs

The sense of being guests rather than clients.

'A home away from home' states the brochure for this B&B, and everything seems presented with this slogan in mind. The rooms are simple, spacious and bright, furnished with period pieces which make for a comfortable family ambience. Breakfast, including home made pastries, can be served in the room or downstairs, and the kitchen is always available for the peckish to fix themselves a snack. Well situated in the city centre, not far from the cathedral which stands out as a masterpiece of Romagna architecture.

Sights nearby: Galleria Parmeggiani, churches of la Ghiara and San Prospero

28

ANTICA TORRE

Sig. Pavesi
Cangelasio Case Bussandri, 197
43039 Salsomaggiore Terme (PR)
Tel. 0524 575425 – Fax 0524 575425
info@anticatorre.it – www.anticatorre.it

40-50/ 80-100€

Closed Dec-Feb • 2 single rm, 6 double rm • Half board €60-70 • Menu €20-30 • Parking, garden, swimming pool, no dogs in the restaurant • Bicycle hire, archery, tasting of cured meat and cheese

The ivy clad stonework of the old farmhouse.

Once the hard labour of convicted criminals was employed in this area to turn milling machinery used to grind salt excavated from locally occurring natural deposits. Times have changed and Salsomaggiore is now a quiet town, best known for the curative properties of its thermal springs. The low hills of the surrounding district, given over to farmland and woods populated by hares, pheasants and squirrels, are another good reason to visit, especially if choosing to stay here, a restored stone tower from where the view takes in fields, with distant mountains in one direction, and the rivers of the great plain in the other.

Access
From Parma: SS 9 for 18km to Fidenza, onto the SS 359 for 6.5km to Salsomaggiore, then right for 8km to Cangelasio, from where signposted

Sights nearby: Salsomaggiore: spas, Palazzo Comunale; Stirone National park

29

SELVA SMERALDA

Sig. Raimondi
Località Selva Smeralda
43050 Sivizzano (PR)
Tel. 0525 520009 – Fax 0525 520009

70€

Closed 1 Nov- 31 Jan • 4 double rm • Half board €50 • Menu €30 • Parking, garden

The crenellated tower which dominates the establishment.

In Emilia, it is not unusual to be able to stay in a 14C castle, since the region's turbulent history saw the construction of many fortresses. What distinguishes this one from the rest, however, is its striking watchtower which, after seven centuries, continues to stand guard, impervious to the passage of time. Delightful surrounding scenery and imposing old walls complete the picture. There are also stables for those who wish to follow in the hoofprints of the feudal knights who were once here.

Access
From Parma: SS 64 for 21km, then left for 6.5km

Sights nearby: Torrechiara: castle

30

LE CASE ROSSE

Sig.ra Savazzi e Sig.ra Gattei
Via Tenuta Amalia, 141
47826 Verucchio (RN)
Tel. 0541 678123 – Fax 0541 678876
info@tenutaamalia.com – www.tenutaamalia.com

62-72€

Open all year • 1 single rm, 6 double rm • No restaurant • Parking, garden, golf • Wine for sale (tasting)

A residence fit for a queen in the heart of the Romagna countryside.

According to legend, this red walled farmhouse set among open fields was visited in the 18C by Caroline of Brunswick, wife of the future British king George IV. Restored in the 19C by the opera singer wife of a politician, this charming residence has subsequently become a pleasant country guesthouse. The ample breakfast of home grown products served here is very much in the rural tradition. Activities include exploring the local area on horseback or excursions to the nearby jewels of artistic heritage, Ravenna and Urbino.

Access
From Rimini: SS 258 for 16km, then left for 2km to Verucchio, left for 2km to Tenuta Amalia

Sights nearby: San Marino: scenery, cliffs

Tauern
Bad Gastein
Tamsweg
Mur
Großglockner
Heiligenblut
Katschberg
Lienz
Spittal
St. Ve
Drau
Dobbiaco
Cortina d'Ampezzo
Pörtsch
Villach
Velden
Tarvisio
Jeseni
Kranjska Gora
Triglav 2863
Bled
FRIULI VENEZIA GIULIA
Tolmin
Cividale
Udine
Nova Gorica
Gorizia
Pordenone
onegliano
Monfalcone
Portogruaro
Grado
Trieste
Piran
Koper
Mestre
VENEZIA
Lido di V.
Opati
Golfo di Venezia
Pazin
Poreč
Chioggia
Plomin
Piave
eviso
elluno
5
6
7
8
1
2
3
4

FRIULI – VENEZIA GIULIA

Friuli Venezia Giulia is a frontier region which defies easy categorising. Once the via Postimia passed through here on its way to the eastern provinces of the Roman Empire. Traces from this era remain, like the mosaics at Aquileia and the early Christian churches at Grado, alongside evidence of later epochs and waves of invasion; the great Lombard works of art at Cividale, Venice's domination during the Renaissance period as evinced by the fortifications of Palmanova, and the central European cosmopolitan feel of Trieste, the great port of the Austro-Hungarian empire. This quality of variety is not specific to the art and architecture; the geography is also disparate, ranging from the snow capped peaks of the Carniche Alps, through gradually softening hills and down into the farmlands of the plain, irrigated by rivers winding towards the Adriatic. The region's excellent cuisine includes fish, filled pasta shapes *(agnolotti),* San Daniele ham and mountain cheeses, best enjoyed with a glass of Tocai or Picolit.

8 establishments

1

LA BOATINA

Sig. Span

Via Corona, 62
34071 Cormons (GO)
Tel. 0481 808124 – Fax 0481 808124
info@paliwines.com – www.paliwines.com

50/70-85€

Open all year • 5 double rm • No restaurant • Garden • Wine for sale

The farmstead with its vineyards bordered by pine trees.

Il Collio is an area where grapes have been grown since time immemorial and the tradition is proudly perpetuated on this farm, its white buildings nestling in the plain at the foot of the Friuli hills. Located in the old hostel, the accommodation is furnished with traditional style pieces. Needless to say, guests are able to savour the estate wines and visit its cellars, where the fragrance of the fermentation process blends with the wood scents of the barrels and casks.

Access
From Gorizia: SS 56 for 11km

Sights nearby: Gorizia: castle, fortified city of Palmanova

2

VENICA E VENICA - CASA VINO E VACANZE

Sig. Venica
Località Cerò, 8
34070 Dolegna del Collio (GO)
Tel. 0481 60177 – Fax 0481 639906
venica@venica.it – www.venica.it

80-90/ 95-105€

Closed 1 Nov-31 Mar • 6 double rm • Breakfast €15 • No restaurant • Parking, garden, swimming pool, tennis, no dogs • Wine for sale (tasting)

The huge beam supporting the ceiling in the lounge area.

Since 1929, the Venica family has been involved in winemaking. Their property covers the slopes of four hillsides, and walking, cycling, tennis and swimming are all available. Authentic hospitality enhance the simple, rustic-style farm accommodation comprising plain yet welcoming rooms, plus a pleasant lounge area with tiled floors, rugs, plenty of woodwork in evidence, and a fine open fireplace.

Access
From Gorizia: SS 56 for 11km, right onto the SS 356 for 2.5km to Brazzano, then right for 9.5km to Via Mernico

Sights nearby: Gorizia: castle; fortified city of Palmanova

3

KOGOJ

Fam. Kogoj
Via Zorutti, 10
34076 Medea (GO)
Tel. 0481 67440 – Fax 0481 67440
kogoj@kogoj.it – www.kogoj.it

40/ 80€

Closed 7-30 Sep • 1 single rm, 4 double rm • No restaurant • Parking, swimming pool, small dogs welcome • Wine for sale (tasting)

The warmth and hospitality of the owners.

This long established winemaking operation only opened its doors as a country guesthouse at the end of the last decade. Since then, the sensitively restored hay barn has provided accommodation in the shape of five comfortable, elegant and welcoming rooms. The property is surrounded by a pleasant garden, beyond which are the attractive vineyards which merit a closer look. The excellent breakfast includes many home made products.

Access
From Gorizia: SS 56 for 11km to Cormons, then left for 5.5km

Sights nearby: Gorizia: castle; fortified city of Palmanova

4

LOCANDA AI CAMPI

Sig.ra Bregant
Via Napoli, 7
34074 Monfalcone (GO)
Tel. 0481 481937 – Fax 0481 720192

46/74€

Open all year • 10 single rm, 4 double rm • Breakfast €7; half board €60 • Menu €20-22 • Parking, garden • Bicycle hire

We most liked

The high degree of comfort in the well equipped accommodation.

Close to the Monfalcone shipyards, where cruise liners and luxury yachts are built, this small establishment has been recently refurbished. It offers well equipped accommodation with a guests-only restaurant for evening dining (next door is another restaurant, also run by the owners, specialising in fish dishes). Friendly, professional management which bodes well for your visit.

Access
From Gorizia: SS 55 for 16km, right for 2km, then right onto the SS 14 for 3km

Sights nearby: Gorizia: castle; Aquileia: basilica, archaeological site

5

SCHNEIDER

Futura & C. Sas

Via Sauris di Sotto, 92
33020 Sauris (UD)
Tel. 0433 86220 – Fax 0433 866310
allapace@libero.it

46/ 70€

Closed 7-28 Jun, 8-22 Nov • 1 single rm, 7 double rm • Half board €52 • Parking, small dogs welcome

The view of the village; traditional buildings surrounded by meadows.

The mountains here have always been a border country between two cultures, and this is evident in Sauris, located in the Carnia district, where the local dialect is of German derivation. For two centuries, the Schneider family have run the Alla Pace inn, next to which a new building has been erected providing eight comfortable and spacious rooms. This is an ideal base from which to explore the local mountain scenery, including Lake Sauris.

Access

From Udine: 6km to join A 23 for 32km to Tolmezzo exit, left onto SS 52 for 27km to Ampezzo, then right for 16km

Sights nearby: Lago di Sauris, valley scenery

6

EDELHOF

Gestione Nuove Iniziative Srl

Via Diaz, 13
33018 Tarvisio (UD)
Tel. 0428 644025 – Fax 0428 644735
info@hoteledelhof.it – www.hoteledelhof.it

80/ 90€

Open all year • 2 single rm, 12 double rm • Half board €65 • Menu €15-30 • Parking, garden

We most liked

The warm ambience of the traditional stube.

Having been completely restored in keeping with the alpine gothic style once prevalent in the region, this hotel has an unusual quality. Particular care has been taken with the rooms, each of which has its own individual feel and decor. A splendid tiled open fireplace in the bar and the stube style dining room add to the mountain ambience.

Access
From Udine: A 23 for 85km to Tarvisio exit, then onto the SS 13 for 2km

Sights nearby: Church of Santi Pietro e Paolo; Fusine Lakes

7

GELINDO DEI MAGREDI

Sig. Trevisanutto
Via Roma, 16
33099 Vivaro (PN)
Tel. 0427 97037 – Fax 0427 97515
info@gelindo.it – www.gelindo.it

35-40/ 70€

Open all year • 4 single rm, 5 double rm • Half board €50-55 • Menu €23-35 • Parking, garden, no dogs • Horse riding, organised trips, fruit, vegetables, apple juice and wine for sale

The Magredi plateau; beautiful riding country in the shadow of the Dolomites.

Riders of all levels of proficiency should make for this rural guesthouse which combines equestrian facilities with a delightful location. Lying at the foot of the Friuli Dolomites, the Magredi is a rich alluvial plateau furrowed by numerous rivers. This establishment offers simple yet well presented accommodation and a family atmosphere. The polenta cutter appearing on the restaurant sign indicates that the emphasis here is on local cuisine. Also worth a visit is the small museum of rural and farm life, perhaps in the company of the friendly proprietor.

Access

From Pordenone: SS 13 for 2km, then left for 19km

Sights nearby: I Magredi landscape; Pordenone: cathedral, Palazzo Comunale, Museo Civico

8

LATARIA DEI MAGREDI

Fam. Trevisanutto

Vicolo Centrico
33099 Vivaro (PN)
Tel. 0427 97322 – Fax 0427 97515
info@gelindo.it – www.gelindo.it/it/lataria.htm

43-46/70-76€

Open all year • 2 single rm, 13 double rm • Half board €50-55 • Menu €21-27 • Parking • Horse riding, organised trips, cured meat and jam tasting, wine and organic produce for sale

The old dairy; transformed from place of work to place of pleasure.

The energy of the Trevisanutto family knows no bounds. Having opened the Gelindo dei Magredi agriturismo, they subsequently restored this adjacent old dairy; almost entirely rebuilt in stone, it now provides elegant and well equipped accommodation. The restaurant serves typical regional cuisine in a relaxed atmosphere and at reasonable prices. Regular evening events are held combining music, gastronomy and entertainment. Sporting facilities are also available, including the stables of the adjoining agriturismo.

Access
From Pordenone: SS 13 for 2km, then left for 19km

Sights nearby: I Magredi landscape; Pordenone: cathedral, Palazzo Comunale, Museo Civico

Arezzo
Città di Castello
Jesi
Gubbio
Siena
Cortona
Perugia
Macerata
Fabriano
Civitanova Marche
Fermo
Montepulciano
Assisi
Chianciano Terme
Foligno
S. Benedetto d. Tronto
Ascoli Piceno
Todi
Spoleto
Orvieto
Teramo
Bolsena
Montefiascone
Terni
Gr. Sasso d'Italia
2914
Viterbo
Rieti
L'Aquila
Tarquinia
Civitavecchia
ROMA
Vaticano
Tivoli
Avezzano
Sulmona
2795
Fiuggi
Sora
Frosinone
Montecassino
Ostia
Albano
Velletri
LAZIO
Cassino
Latina
Anzio
Terracina
Formia
Gaeta
Volturno
NAPOLI
Ponza
Pozzuoli
Ischia
Tevere
Arno
1
2
3
4
5
6
7
8
9
10
11
12
13
14
15
16
17
18

LAZIO

“Est! Est! Est!”, not the battle cry of the emperor Trajan setting forth to conquer new oriental provinces for Rome, but the name of a traditional local wine. 'Traditional' applies across the board in these parts and the visitor is met with the sight of important architectural remains at every turn; ancient monuments, Etruscan necropolises such as those at Tarquinia and Cerveteri, Roman roads impervious to the passage of time which continue to lead to the heart of the Empire. Situated on its famous hills between the Apennines and the sea, Rome stands as custodian of the history and spirit of the western world. Imperial splendour, medieval decadence, the Renaissance and Baroque periods; all have left their mark in the open-air museum that is the city of Rome. Richly decorated patrician palaces, ruined baths, temples and mausoleums come together to create a unique ambience of cultural heritage. A visit to the capital should not be missed, but neither should the other delights of Lazio; its peaceful countryside, the Tyrrhenian coast, the Roman castles by the volcanic lakes, all perfect settings in which to seek tranquillity against a historical backdrop.

18 establishments

1

MIRALAGO

Miralago Sas

Via dei Cappuccini, 12
00041 Albano Laziale (RM)
Tel. 06 9322253 – Fax 06 9322253
info@hotelmiralagorist.it – www.hotelmiralagorist.it

65-70/90-100€

Open all year • 10 single rm, 35 double rm • Half board €70-75 • Menu €30-44 • Parking, garden • Horse riding

The pleasure of dining outside during the summer months.

Stretching out over the slopes of the Albani hills, the Castelli Romani region lies to the south-east of Rome, and is popular with the city's inhabitants, drawn here by its history, architecture, climate and food. This establishment is conveniently located halfway between Albano and Castel Gandolfo, the Pope's summer residence. Visitors are assured of a warm welcome but will be most impressed by the country house atmosphere complete with tapestries, plants and elegant drapes. The restaurant occupies a circular room with fine panoramic views of Lake Albano.

Sights nearby: Villa Comunale, church of Santa Maria della Rotonda, Lake Albano

2

IL CAVALIER D'ARPINO

Sig. Schiavo

Via Vittoria Colonna, 21
03033 Arpino (FR)
Tel. 0776 850060 – Fax 0776 849348
info@cavalierdarpino.it – www.cavalierdarpino.it

35-52/ 50-85€

Closed Nov • 5 single rm, 20 double rm • Half board €35-55 • Menu €18-35 • Parking, garden, no dogs

The plants and flowers which bedeck and aromatise the gardens.

According to legend, Arpino was founded by Saturn, Roman god of agriculture, although military might rather than farming seems to be the original function of the imposing megalithic remains. Many famous people came from here, including Cicero, Marcus Agrippa, and the 16C painter Giuseppe Cesari, known as the Cavalier of Arpino, hence the hotel's choice of name. Set in attractive parkland, this historic building is furnished in tasteful rustic style; family run with a relaxed atmosphere.

Access
From Frosinone: SS 214 for 23km to Isola del Liri, then right for 6km

Sights nearby: Walls, ruins of acropolis, churches of San Michele Arcangelo, Sant'Andrea and Sant'Antonio

3

ROMANTICA PUCCI

Sig.ra Pucci e Sig. Mari
Piazza Cavour, 1
01022 Bagnoregio (VT)
Tel. 0761 792121 – Fax 0761 792121
hotelromanticapucci@libero.it – www.hotelromanticapucci.it

70€

Open all year • 10 double rm • Menu €20-30 • Parking

The tasteful choice of furnishings throughout.

Located in the historic heart of Bagnoregio, this small hotel was opened a few years ago by a couple previously in the fashion business. The care with which its five rooms have been decorated is apparent, each one having its own distinctive style. Antique furniture and wrought iron or wooden four poster beds set the tone. Equally attractive are the formal dining room and the breakfast room, creating by roofing over an internal courtyard. Pets welcome and catered for.

Access
From Viterbo: SS 2 for 16km, right onto the SS 71 for 8.5km, then right for 5.5km

Sights nearby: Civita di Bagnoregio

CERROSUGHERO

Sig. De Parri
Località Cerro Sughero
01011 Canino (VT)
Tel. 0761 437242 – Fax 0761 437242
info@cerrosughero.com – www.cerrosughero.com

50-60/ 60-80€

Open all year • 12 double rm • Half board €48-58 • Menu €20-30 • Parking, garden, swimming pool • Tasting and sale of honey and oil

The home-produced olive oil, the ideal culinary souvenir for friends and family.

Three hundred metres up in the Maremma district on the Tuscany Lazio border, this 210 hectare estate of woodland, pasture and olive groves provides agriturismo facilities in the shape of four farmhouses. The main property has a large, attractive lounge area and a restaurant with characteristic sloping roof. Accommodation takes up the other three buildings; the rooms are spacious and the suites have charming open fireplaces. Families and groups can stay in apartments with kitchen facilities. Guests are free to explore the 10km of footpaths around the property, or they might prefer to lounge by the swimming pool.

Access

From Viterbo: SS 2 for 6.5km then left for 25km to join SS 312 for 12km to Canino, continue for 3km to Cerro Sughero

Sights nearby: Tuscania: churches of San Pietro and Santa Maria Maggiore

5

LA TORRETTA

Sig. Scheda

Via Mazzini, 7
02041 Casperia (RI)
Tel. 0765 63202 – Fax 0765 63202
latorretta@tiscali.it – www.latorrettabandb.com

70/85€

Open all year • 1 single rm, 7 double rm • No restaurant • No dogs • Organised trips, oil tasting

The beauty of the place, which takes the visitor by surprise on arrival.

A winning combination of an English wife, bringing with her the knack of creating a welcoming family atmosphere, and an Italian husband, whose training as an engineer has ensured a very successful restoration (during which original frescoes were uncovered) of this 15C aristocratic residence. Located at the top end of the village, there are fine views from the terrace and from the rooms, which are tastefully decorated in a manner which, if not luxurious, certainly marks them out as being somewhat special.

Access

From Rieti: east for 10km to Contigliano, left for 16.5km to Cottanello, then left again for 10km

Sights nearby: Rieti: cathedral, Palazzo Vescovile, Giardino Pubblico; Convento di Greccio

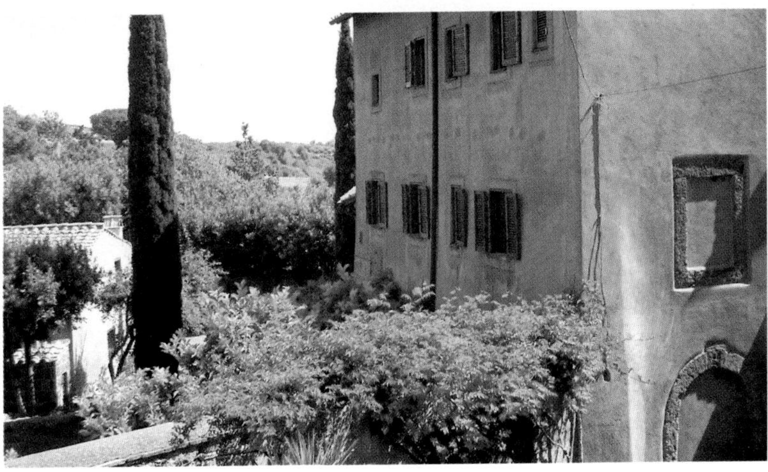

6

BORGO DI CERI

Sig. Cera

Piazza Immacolata, 17-18-19
00052 Ceri di Cerveteri (RM)
Tel. 06 99207208 – Fax 06 99207208
info@borgoceri.it – www.borgoceri.it

65-100€

Closed Nov, Jan, Feb • 4 double rm • No restaurant • Garden, no dogs • Horse riding, bicycle hire, organised trips

The wisteria-covered pergola in the garden.

Ceri is a charming medieval village built on a tufa spur in the middle of one of the largest and most important archaeological areas in Europe. The small square in the heart of the village is a delightfully peaceful oasis, surrounded by well-preserved buildings. With its hanging gardens built against part of the old village walls, this bed and breakfast has two two-bedroomed apartments, both with their own fireplace. The style is rustic, complemented by cosy, individual touches.

Access

From Rome: A 12-SS 1 for 1.5km, then A 12 for 12km to Cerveteri exit, SS 1 for 2km and left for 7km

Sights nearby: Etruscan necropoli

7

CASALE DI GRICCIANO

Sig.ra Ricci

Via Casale di Gricciano, 177
00052 Cerveteri (RM)
Tel. 06 9941358 – Fax 06 9951013
casaledigricciano@casaledigricciano.com – www.casaledigricciano.com

50/ 70€

Closed Jan • 9 double rm • Half board €55 • Menu €25-30 • Parking, swimming pool, no dogs • Horse riding, bicycle hire, tasting and sale of jams, vegetables, oil and wine

The authentic cooking of Signora Romanina.

It is difficult to identify what makes this spot so pleasant. There is the surrounding countryside, a hilly landscape of vineyards and olive groves on the lower slopes of the Tolfa mountains, yet close to the coast. There is the welcome from Stafania and Luca, who have lovingly restored the house and now enthusiastically manage the operation. Then there is the history, the ubiquitous evidence of Etruscan civilisation throughout the locality. All of which add up to make for a delightful stay.

Access

From Rome: raccordo A 12-SS 1 for 1.5km, then onto the A 12 for 12km to Cerveteri exit, left onto SP 14 for 7km to Gricciano

Sights nearby: Etruscan necropoli

8

CASA CIOTTI

Sig.ra Flamini

Via Terni, 14
01033 Civita Castellana (VT)
Tel. 0761 513090 – Fax 0761 599120
info@casaciotti.com – www.casaciotti.com

65/86€

Closed 15 Dec-15 Mar • 10 double rm • Breakfast €7 • No restaurant • Parking, garden, swimming pool • Bicycle hire, archery, spelt and oil for sale

The gardens, planted with fine trees which surround the attractive pink house.

This establishment has multiple personalities: 1) An old post office on the route of the ancient Via Flaminia. 2) The spot where, in 1870, Papal forces stopped the advance of General Cadorna. 3) A 17C farmhouse, strikingly attractive in its simplicity. 4) A delightful place to stay, with a pool set among gardens, olive groves and oak trees.

Access
From Rome: SS 3 for 43km, then left onto SS 11 for 1km

Sights nearby: Cathedral, Rocca (castle)

9

URBANO V

Sig.ra Smafora Bruni, Sig. Bruni, Sig. Cappannella.

Corso Cavour, 107
01027 Montefiascone (VT)
Tel. 0761 831094 – Fax 0761 834152
info@hotelurbano-v.it – www.hotelurbano-v.it

54-60/ 70-80€

Open all year • 4 single rm, 22 double rm • No restaurant • No dogs • Organised trips, tasting and sale of wine, grappa, oil and cakes

The imposing stone vaulting over the entrance.

Laid out around a charming inner courtyard, this restored 17C palazzo is conveniently located in the centre of town. Beyond the impressive doorway there is an interesting old well, bearing witness to the building's rich history, but the real joy of this place is its terrace, providing all round views over the city and out towards the hills and lake Bolsena; the ideal spot to enjoy a bottle of Est! Est!! Est!!!, the well known local wine. The elegant rooms are classically decorated with period furniture and matching fabrics.

Access
From Viterbo: SS 2 for 16km

Sights nearby: Cathedral, church of San Flaviano

10

VILLA IL NOCE

Sig.ra Ponzi
Via Antica, 1
03040 Picinisco (FR)
Tel. 0776 66259 – Fax 0776 66259
villailnoce@email.it

30-40/60-80€

Open all year • 4 double rm • No restaurant • Parking, garden, swimming pool, tennis, no dogs • Horse riding, bicycle hire, tasting and sale of jam, oil and vegetables

The friendly and welcoming ambience prevailing throughout.

Uniquely situated at the head of a valley composed of wooded hillsides and picturesque farmland, this flower bedecked little villa has four rooms ideal for those in quest of the authentic B&B experience. Inside, care has been taken with the decor and the emphasis is on comfort, while outdoors guests can enjoy the garden and swimming pool. The surrounding countryside is the perfect backdrop for gentle strolls, vigorous walks, cycling and fishing.

Access
From Frosinone: SS 214 for 20km, then left for 4.5km to Sora, right onto the SS 267 to Atina, left for 3km, then right for 9km

Sights nearby: Abruzzo National Park

11

A CASA DI GIORGIA

Sig.ra Guastalla

Corso Trieste, 62
00198 Roma (RM)
Tel. 06 8548797 – Fax 06 8548797
gettat@yahoo.it – www.bbacasadigiorgia.it

75-95€

Closed 1-15 Feb, Aug • 5 double rm • No restaurant • No dogs

The genteel ambience of the patrician residence and its well presented accommodation.

On the second floor of a palazzo, in a residential district rich in parks and conveniently located for access by bus to the city centre, this establishment provides accommodation in the shape of four spacious and well kept rooms. Night owls will be pleased to know that room service will provide breakfast whenever required. Prices are competitive compared to other hotels in the area, ideal for those seeking a comfortable place to stay without breaking the bank.

Access

Grande Raccordo Anulare to exit 11-Nomentana

Sights nearby: Mausoleo di Santa Costanza, church of Sant'Agnese fuori le Mura

12

MAXIMUM

Sig. e Sig.ra Rendina

Via Fabio Massimo, 72
00192 Roma (RM)
Tel. 06 3242037 – Fax 06 3242156
bbmaximum@tiscali.it – www.bbmaximum.com

40/ 70-80€

Closed Aug • 3 double rm • No restaurant

We most liked

The convenient location close to the Vatican.

Ranged off an elegant passageway embellished by a series of small arches, the colourful rooms of this B&B have been recently renovated, but the best feature of this establishment is its location, a few hundred metres from the medieval fortress of Castel Sant'Angelo, where Pope Clement VII sought refuge when Rome was sacked, and originally the Emperor Hadrian's mausoleum. Also nearby are the basilica of San Pietro and the Vatican museums, meaning that a large slice of the city's artistic heritage is but a stone's throw away.

Access

Grande Raccordo Anulare to exit 3-Cassia; Metropolitana: linea A, Ottaviano stop

Sights nearby: Musei Vaticani and Sistine Chapel, Basilica of St Peter, Castel Sant'Angelo

13

58 LE REAL DE LUXE

Sig. Pagnanelli

Via Cavour, 58
00184 Roma (RM)
Tel. 06 4823566 – Fax 06 4823566
info@58viacavour.it – www.58viacavour.it

70-100/70-110€

Open all year • 8 double rm • No restaurant • No dogs

The convenient location coupled with the quality of the accommodation.

Via Cavour is one of central Rome's main thoroughfares, linking Via dei Fori to Termini station and passing close to the Colosseum and Santa Maria Maggiore, one of the city's four basilicas. On a nearby street corner stands a typical late 19C patrician residence; occupying its fourth floor, this establishment offers well presented, spacious and comfortable accommodation which is more akin to a hotel than a B&B. The ideal spot for those in quest of a simple and welcoming place to stay in the heart of Rome.

Access

Grande Raccordo Anulare to exit 11-Nomentana; Metropolitana: linea A, Cavour stop

Sights nearby: Church of San Pietro in Vincoli and Michelangelo's Moses; Basilica of Santa Maria Maggiore

14

PRINCIPE SERRONE

Sig. Cacciotti
Via del Serrone, 1
04010 Sermoneta (LT)
Tel. 0773 30342 – Fax 0773 30336
hotelserrone@virgilio.it – www.hotelprincipeserrone.it

40-50/75-85€

Open all year • 6 single rm, 11 double rm • No restaurant • No dogs

The timeless quality of the old buildings.

In the oldest quarter of the medieval village of Sermoneta, close to the imposing Caetani castle, an alley opens up between two houses, a connecting passageway running above it. This heralds the entrance to the Principe Serrone, as if from the pages of a historical novel. Built entirely of stone, with a decorative frieze embellishing the first floor, it has been carefully refurbished inside without detracting from its authenticity. Its rooms and corridors, with wood panelled or cross vaulted ceilings, give the visitor the impression of having travelled back in time.

Access
15km northwest of Latina

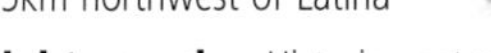

Sights nearby: Historic centre

15

PEGASO PALACE HOTEL

Fam. Franci e Sig.ra Tanini

Via Martano
01016 Tarquinia (VT)
Tel. 0766 810027 – Fax 0766 810749
info@hpegaso.it – www.hpegaso.it

45-60/ 60-80€

Open all year • 48 double rm • Half board €60-85 • Menu €26-36 • Parking, swimming pool, no dogs

The peaceful setting by the sea.

Not far from Tarquinia and the motorway, this modern establishment is strongly Mediterranean in style. The luminous colours employed on the exterior are also used in the spacious rooms, many of which provide sea views. Meat and fish dishes feature on the menu, which draws heavily on the traditional cuisine of the region. The delightful location close to the water's edge is ideal for beach lovers, while those in quest of culture can explore the area's rich Etruscan heritage.

Access
From Viterbo: SS 2 for 12km to Vetralla, right onto the SS 1 bis for 25km, then right for 12km to Marina Velca

Sights nearby: Tarquinia: Etruscan necropoli, Museo Nazionale Tarquinese, church of Santa Maria in Castello

16

LOCANDA DI MIRANDOLINA

Sig.ra Salaparuta

Via del Pozzo Bianco, 40/42
01017 Tuscania (VT)
Tel. 0761 436595 – Fax 0761 436595
info@mirandolina.it – www.mirandolina.it

32-36/62-67€

Closed 10 Jan-15 Feb • 2 single rm, 6 double rm • Half board €51-55 • Menu €22-40 • Honey, vegetables, cheese and oil for sale

The loquat tree, cascading ivy and jasmine.

From here there are fine views over the surrounding countryside, yet this little inn is situated in the historic heart of Tuscania and makes for a pleasant alternative to staying in a hotel. The façade has been colonised by ivy and jasmine, giving off a heady scent when in bloom. A large loquat tree stands in the outdoor area where typical local cuisine is served to guests. The rooms are very simple, yet not without an intimate charm.

Access
From Viterbo: SS 2 for 1.8km, then left for 23km

Sights nearby: Churches of San Pietro and Santa Maria Maggiore

17

DA BENITO AL BOSCO

Sig. Morelli
Via Morice, 96
00049 Velletri (RM)
Tel. 06 9633991 – Fax 06 9641414
benitoalbosco@virgilio.it

55/80€

Open all year • 5 single rm, 45 double rm • Half board €65 • Menu €26-40 • Parking, garden, swimming pool, no dogs • Tasting of oil, wine and regional specialities

The verdant chestnut and pine woods surrounding the swimming pool.

Originally just a restaurant, this establishment now also offers accommodation. It is tucked away among pines and chestnuts growing in a parkland setting which makes for an attractive backdrop, particularly in the evening when the poolside lighting illuminates the scene. The modern rooms are spacious, with wood furnishings and floors. Traditional regional cuisine with plenty of seafood, bought direct from Anzio fish market.

Access
From Rome: SS 7 for 26km

Sights nearby: Colli Albani; lago di Nemi

18

ANTICO PALAZZO FILONARDI

Sig.ra Ferriello
Piazza dei Franconi, 1
03029 Veroli (FR)
Tel. 0775 235296 – Fax 0775 235079
info@palazzofilonardi.it – www.palazzofilonardi.it

61-71/75-85€

Closed 8-31 Jan • 2 single rm, 29 double rm • Half board €65-75 • Menu €24-45 • Parking, no dogs in the restaurant

The hilly landscape of the Ciociaria viewed from the rooms.

The medieval hill settlement of Veroli is located in the heart of the Ciociaria district; constructed in the 19C, this establishment was in use as a convent until 1996. A closed order of nuns still occupies the building next door, and figures in habits may occasionally be glimpsed in the garden. The hotel's previous incarnation as a religious house is evident from its chapel, which remains consecrated. In addition to stunning views, the rooms are delightfully tranquil, a reminder to guests that this was once a place of prayer.

Access
From Frosinone: SS 214 for 5.5km to Il Giglio, then onto the SP 50 for 5km

Sights nearby: Veroli: cathedral and historic centre; abbey of Casamari

Biella
Ivrea
Novara
Treviglio
MILANO
Vercelli
Vigevano
Lodi
Pavia
Chivasso
Casale Monferrato
Cremona
TORINO
Piacenza
Asti
Alessandria
Tortona
Salsomaggiore Terme
Savigliano
Alba
Fossano
LIGURIA
GENOVA
Mondovi
Tende
Savona
Rapallo
Sestri Levante
Finale Ligure
La Spezia
Alassio
Ventimiglia
Imperia
San Remo
Bordighera
Forte dei Marmi
Riviera Ligure
Golfo di Genova
Monaco - Monte-Carlo
d'Azur
Cap Corse
Capraia
St Florent
Cisa
Ticino
Po
Adda
Oglio
Tunis
Barcelona, Palma
Porto Torres
Olbia, Cagliari
Ile-Rousse
Palermo
Bastia
l'Ile-Rousse
Ajaccio
Marseille
Nice
Genova
La Spezia
Livorno

LIGURIA

Imagine a winding road hugging the coastline, above which extend slopes planted with olive groves running up to the tree line, punctuated by little stone built hamlets clinging to hilltops. Such is the landscape of Liguria, a narrow and ancient region separating mountains from the sea. Once one of Europe's great mercantile powers, Genova remains a dynamic commercial powerhouse. Although a major industrial centre, it retains its medieval centre of imposing patrician palaces and criss-crossed by *carugi*, the narrow alleys so characteristic of Liguria. Although most of the coastline is quite developed, some unspoilt strips remain, notably the Portofino promontory between Camogli and Santa Margherita with its paths winding through scrubland, emerging occasionally to provide stunning views. This wild backdrop has influenced the character of the local population, an understated and determined people, the region's cuisine, best exemplified in its fish dishes and its famous pesto sauce, and its wines, most notably Vermentino and Pigato.

7 establishments

1

LA CAMOGLIESE

Sig.ra Rocchetti

Via Garibaldi, 55
16032 Camogli (GE)
Tel. 0185 771402 – Fax 0185 774024
info@lacamogliese.it – www.lacamogliese.it

55-85/ 75-90€

Open all year • 6 single rm, 15 double rm • No restaurant • No dogs • Boat trips

The view over Golfo Paradiso together with the smell of the sea.

This little jewel is located in one of the pearls of the Ligurian riviera; a small, family run hotel which makes for the ideal destination either for a weekend break or a longer stay on the coast. After a recent major refit, the rooms are well presented; the best are those overlooking the bay. Improvements are ongoing; among those anticipated is an expansion of the currently limited public areas.

Access

From Genova: SS 1 for 17km

Sights nearby: Harbour, scenery; San Fruttuoso: abbey

2

CA DU CHITTU

Sig. Nardi
Isolato Camporione, 25
19012 Carro (SP)
Tel. 0187 861205 – Fax 0187 861205
caduchittu@virgilio.it – www.caduchittu.it

58-66€

Open all year • 7 double rm • Half board €44-51 • Menu €21-25 • Parking, garden • Bicycle hire

The authenticity of the cuisine, hospitality and management.

In the delightfully unspoilt Ligurian hinterland, not far from the famous Cinque Terre coastline, woodland dominates the landscape. In the Vara valley, this small white house set in a clearing is run by a dedicated and friendly couple who, in addition to farming organic products, offer accommodation and meals to travellers. Seven rooms, plus campsite space and a restaurant make this a good place to stay, especially for those here to enjoy the rafting and canoeing opportunities of the river Vara.

Access

From La Spezia: SS 1 for 21km to Borghetto di Vara, then SP 566 for 10km, then left for 5km

Sights nearby: Santuario della Cerreta, parish church; Cinque Terre: scenery and trips along the coast

3

LA VALLE

Sig. Musetto

Via delle Colline, 24
19030 Castelnuovo Magra (SP)
Tel. 0187 670101 – Fax 0187 674075
agriturismolavalle@virgilio.it

50/70€

Closed Jan • 1 single rm, 6 double rm • Half board €55 • Menu €20-25 • Parking, garden, no dogs • Tasting and sale of wine and oil

The vineyards and olive groves surrounding the house.

This large yellow house, deep in the Ligurian hinterland, stands close to the border with Tuscany. La Valle is perfect for those looking for a peaceful and relaxing holiday, as well as visitors interested in exploring the area's artistic heritage and attractive coastline. The Lunigiana, an area which borders three different regions, has a rich history and strong local traditions, most of which focus on the land rather than the sea. The agriturismo, situated on the road leading to the village, has comfortable rooms decorated with hand-crafted wooden furniture. Authentic local cuisine (fixed-price menu) accompanied by regional wine makes the restaurant here a must.

Access

From La Spezia: A 15 for 8.5km, then SS 62 for 6km, SP 1 for 4.5km, then left for 3km

Sights nearby: Sarzana: cathedral, Sarzanello fortress; Luni: archaeological site

4

NEGRO

Sig. Negro

Via Canada, 10
18020 Rezzo (IM)
Tel. 0183 34089 – Fax 0183 324800
hotelnegro@libero.it

50/75€

Closed 8 Jan-16 Apr • 4 single rm, 8 double rm • Half board €50-55 • Menu €28-35 • Parking, swimming pool, bowls, no dogs • Bicycles available

The swimming pool, from where there are panoramic views across the countryside.

Cenova is a typical mountain village of the Arroscia valley, deep in the Ligurian hinterland. Most of its houses are stone built, perched on the steep hillside among the cultivated terraces so characteristic of Liguria. The Negro family's hotel is located in a panoramic spot at the very top of the settlement. A wood and stone structure, the building has a natural warmth and friendliness to it. Although simply furnished, the accommodation provides high standards of comfort. The restaurant, also very popular with non-residents, focuses on creative local specialities.

Access

From Imperia: SS 28 for 22km, then left for 5km to Cenova

Sights nearby: Albenga: old town, cathedral and baptistery

5

ROSITA

Sig. Monesiglio
Via Mànie, 67
12024 Finale Ligure (SV)
Tel. 019 602437 – Fax 019 601762
info@hotelrosita.it

40-50/ 65-85€

Closed 7-30 Jan, Nov • 9 double rm • Half board €40-52 • Menu €29-40 • Parking, no dogs in the restaurant • Jam, oil and olives for sale

Gazing at the sea from the bedroom balcony.

Panoramic views over Finale and Varigotti, the tranquillity of the countryside, the silence and coolness of the evening; this hotel is in an excellent location, reached by following the road away from the beach and up into the hills, where a warm welcome awaits from the family management team. All the simply furnished rooms have balconies with sea views, while the restaurant serves Ligurian specialities and fish dishes. For the energetic, mountain bikes are available.

Access
From Savona: SS 1 for 15km to Finale Ligure, then right into Via Mànie

Sights nearby: Finale Borgo: historic centre

6

NUOVA RIVIERA

Sig. Sabini

Via Belvedere 10/2
16038 Santa Margherita Ligure (GE)
Tel. 0185 287403 – Fax 0185 287403
info@nuovariviera.com – www.nuovariviera.com

90/100€

Closed 3 Nov-26 Dec • 1 single rm, 8 double rm • No restaurant • Garden, no dogs

The friendly and welcoming family management.

This early 20C villa evokes the days when the Ligurian coast was a much frequented destination for visitors to Italy, and it remains popular with foreign guests. Run by the Sabini family, the curvilinear building has nine rooms over two floors. These are spacious and some are circular, mirroring the exterior. The decor is simple, but everything is well presented and the atmosphere of friendly hospitality makes guests feel at home.

Access
From Genova: A 12 for 17km to Rapallo exit, right onto SS 1 for 0.2km, then left onto SS 227 for 2.5km

Sights nearby: Promontorio di Portofino; San Fruttuoso: abbey

7

ROBERTO GNOCCHI

Sig. Gnocchi

Via Romana, 53
16038 Santa Margherita Ligure (GE)
Tel. 0185 283431 – Fax 0185 283431
roberto.gnocchi@tin.it

85/100€

Closed 16 Oct-30 Apr • 9 double rm • Half board €70 • Parking, garden, no dogs in the restaurant • Jam, cheese and oil for sale

The view of the gulf of Tigullio, where the coast seems to wrap itself around the sea.

A winding track heads off the main road and up the hill between Santa Margherita and San Lorenzo, leading to two buildings providing accommodation in the form of nine rooms which are simple, bright and furnished with imposing wood pieces. All around are the olive trees which for centuries have been synonymous with the Ligurian landscape, but the greatest attraction of this establishment is its view of the sea. From the terrace, where meals are also served, guests can enjoy the panoramic Tigullio coastline lapped by white crested waves.

Access

From Genova: SS 1 for 23km to San Lorenzo della Costa

Sights nearby: Promontorio di Portofino; San Fruttuoso: abbey

Zug
Einsiedeln
Schwyz
Vierwaldstätter See
Altdorf
Andermatt
St. Gotthard
S. Bernardino
2065
Vaduz
LIECHTENSTEIN
St. Anton
Arlberg
Landeck
Innsbr
Brenner
3774
Ötztaleralpen
Reschen
1507
Silvretta
3312
Scuol
Chur
Rhein
Davos
Graubünden
St. Moritz
Splügen
2113
Piz Bernina
4049
2330
Bormio
Stelvio
2757
Merano
Tonale
1883
Chiavenna
Tirano
Sondrio
Edolo
Madonna di Campiglio
Trento
Locarno
Bellinzona
Lugano
Lago di Como
Adda
Lago Maggiore
Stresa
Bellagio
LOMBARDIA
Regione dei Laghi
Lecco
Como
Varese
Bergamo
Iseo
Riva
Rovereto
Gardone Riviera
Gallarate
Monza
Treviglio
Brescia
Sirmione
Verona
Novara
MILANO
Vercelli
Vigevano
Ticino
Lodi
Oglio
Pavia
Cremona
Mantova
Nogara
Piacenza
Tortona
Parma
Reggio Emilia
Salsomaggiore Terme
Modena
EMILIA
GENOVA
Cisa
1039
BOLOGNA
Savona
Rapallo
Cerreto
1261
Sestri Levante
Carrara
1388
Abetone
La Spezia
1
2
3
4
5
6
7
8
9
10
11
12
13
14

LOMBARDIA

Apart from coastline, Lombardy has everything; mountains, hills, plains, rivers, lakes and cities rich in history. Named after the Lombard invaders who settled here, it was subsequently carved up between city states who for generations engaged in conflict, siding either with the pope or Holy Roman emperor. Eventually Milan emerged as the dominant power, becoming one of Europe's richest and most vibrant centres in the process, and the subject of bitter rivalry between the era's greatest kings and emperors. Today, the city is synonymous with business and industry, but in earlier times it was capital of the Roman Empire and one of the centres of the Renaissance, when Bramante and Leonardo worked here, leaving their legacies in the masterpieces that are Santa Maria delle Grazie and the Last Supper. But Lombardy is also an important agricultural region, its fields in the Po plain growing wheat and maize, and its vineyards producing Franciacorta and Oltrpo Pavese grapes. To the north rise the mountains, with alpine lakes reflecting their steep side shorelines in a spectacular play of dark and light.

14 establishments

1

LOCANDA SANT'ANNA

Fam. Peroni

Via Sant'Anna, 152
22010 Argegno (CO)
Tel. 031 821738 – Fax 031 822046
locandasantanna@libero.it – www.locandasantanna.it

80-94€

Open all year • 9 double rm • Half board €65-75 • Menu €29-37.50 • Parking, garden, small dogs welcome

The greenery of the surrounding woods and fields, a prelude to the panoramic landscape beyond.

An establishment of less than ten rooms, but recently refurbished throughout. The restaurant provides the main focus and takes up most of the ground floor and, during the summer, part of the gardens too, around which are set a number of apartments. The property adjoins the Santuario di Sant'Anna; peace and quiet in abundance combined with panoramic views make this a pleasant place to stay and enjoy the nature, history and traditions of this borderland between Italy's Lake Como and Switzerland's Lake Lugano.

Access
From Como: SS 35 for 2km, then the SS 340 for 18.5km, left for 3km to Sant'Anna

Sights nearby: View of the lake

2

TENUTA CAMILLO

Sig. Nidasio
Località Trognano
27010 Bascapé (PV)
Tel. 0382 66509 – Fax 0382 66509
agrimillo@libero.it

55/70€

Open all year • 6 double rm • Breakfast €5 • Menu €23-40 • Parking, garden, swimming pool, no dogs • Rice for sale and risotto tasting

The bygone atmosphere of this beautiful farmstead.

In 1903, the antecedents of the proprietors Mariolina and Franco established a fine farm here in the classic Lombard tradition. Today its doors are open to guests who may stay in the spacious rooms furnished with original pieces from between the wars. During the summer months the courtyard pool is in operation, bicycles are available for the energetic and creative types can study decorative arts with Mariolina! The restaurant serves classic Lombard cuisine.

Access

From Milan: A 1 for 3km to Melegnano exit, then onto the SP 40 for 2.5km to Carpiano, left for 5km to Trognano

Sights nearby: Chiaravalle: abbey; Milan: cathedral, Castello Sforzesco, basilica of Sant'Ambrogio, Pinacoteca di Brera

3

LOCANDA DEL MEL

Sig. Panzeri

Piazza Vittorio Veneto, 2
23801 Calolziocorte (LC)
Tel. 0341 641296 – Fax 0341 630265
hotel@locandamel.com – www.locandamel.com

58-68/78-88€

Closed 8-26 Aug • 2 single rm, 7 double rm • No restaurant • No dogs

The rooms: well presented, stylish and individual.

What distinguishes this hotel is the accommodation offered here. The individual touches, careful presentation and quirkiness of the top floor rooms provide an excellent solution to those here to enjoy the delights of Lake Como without spending a fortune. The public areas are a little cramped, though, with the exception of the bar, which is large, lively and popular with non-residents as well. Breakfast may be taken in the bedrooms, the bar or on the terrace, and is consistently generous and tasty.

Access
From Lecco: SS 639 for 6km

Sights nearby: Lecco: basilica of San Nicolò, church of Santa Marta, house of Manzoni and other places associated with the writer, view of the lake

4

L'AIRONE

Sig. Dellavalle

Strada per Isola Dovarese, 2
26034 Drizzona (CR)
Tel. 0375 389902 – Fax 0375 381021
info@laironeagriturismo.com – www.laironeagriturismo.com

45/ 60€

Open all year • 1 single rm, 9 double rm • Half board €55-58 • Menu €28-35 • Parking, no dogs in the restaurant • Horse riding, organised trips, bicycle hire, honey and mostarda for sale

The farmland rolling out across the vast plain.

This 19C farmstead has been painstakingly restored with great attention to detail, taking care not to detract from the original architectural features. It is pleasantly situated a little out of town, within the parkland bordering the Oglio river, and its rooms are furnished with period style pieces and fabrics which make for an elegant ambience. The inner courtyard is enlivened by greenery, with plants chosen by the proprietors.

Access

From Cremona: SS 10 for 25km, then left for 0.9km, after Drizzona continue towards Castelfranco d'Oglio

Sights nearby: Canneto sull'Oglio: Doll Museum; Piadena: Museo Antiquarium Platina

5

DOLA B&B

Sig. Papadia

Via Roma, 2/4
21030 Duno (VA)
Tel. 0332 624773 – Fax 0332 624773
info@doladuno.com – www.doladuno.com

50/96€

Closed 10 Jan-10 Feb • 2 single rm, 2 double rm • Half board €65-75 • Menu €20-28 • Garden, bowls • Goats' cheese for sale (tasting)

The wood furnishings in the rooms.

Duno is a hamlet in the Valcuvia, situated between Lake Maggiore and the green valleys of Vresotto, the ideal base from which to enjoy both the pleasures of the lakes and the fragrant forests which cover this part of Lombardy. Occupying a typical country house, this classic B&B is enlivened by the friendliness and enterprise of its proprietors; the charming rooms, some with open fireplaces, make for an intimate ambience, as do the public areas. Visitors wishing to take home a souvenir can acquire one of the numerous home made products available.

Access

From Varese: SS 233 for 10km to Ganna, left for 6km, then left onto SS 394 for 3km and left again for 2.5km

Sights nearby: Laveno: view of Lake Maggiore

6

GAMBARA

Sig. Ciccarello e Sig.ra Massari

Via Campo Fiera, 22
25020 Gambara (BS)
Tel. 030 9956260 – Fax 030 9956271
info@hotelgambara.it – www.hotelgambara.it

45-50/ 65-70€

Open all year • 1 single rm, 12 double rm • Half board €50-55 • Menu €29-38 • Parking

The matching fabrics in the rooms.

Expect a cordial reception from the owners at this small country hotel which is a well managed and efficiently run operation. It has a dozen rooms, all lovingly decorated, with modern bathrooms, while its public areas are somewhat less dazzling. All in all, though, this establishment of early 20C vintage remains a good place to know for both tourists and business travellers, not least because it represents value for money.

Access
From Brescia: A 17 for 21km to Manerbio exit, then 19km to Gambara

Sights nearby: Cremona: Cathedral and baptistery, campanile, Palazzo Fodri

7

LA VILLA

Sig.ra Glunz e Sig. Mellone

Via Regina Ponente, 21
22015 Gravedona (CO)
Tel. 0344 89017 – Fax 0344 89027
hotellavilla@tiscali.it – www.hotel-la-villa.com

60-62/80-92€

Closed 20 Dec-10 Jan • 3 single rm, 11 double rm • Half board €65 • Menu €23 • Parking, garden, swimming pool, no dogs

The spacious and pleasantly laid out terrace garden.

This austere yet elegant building is painted all in white with dark green shutters; down one side runs its large and airy veranda restaurant which opens out onto the garden with inviting pool. Above is a terrace from where guests can admire the fine views over the lake and surrounding mountains. The classically furnished rooms are well proportioned, the public areas thoughtfully laid out and the restaurant specialises in regional cuisine.

Access

From Como: SS 35 for 2km towards Chiasso, then right onto the SS 340 for 49km

Sights nearby: View of the lake, church of Santa Maria del Tiglio

8

ALBERI

Sig.ra Pradella

Lungo Lario Isonzo, 4
23900 Lecco (LC)
Tel. 0341 350992 – Fax 0341 350895
info@hotelalberi.lecco.it – www.hotelalberi.lecco.it

55/75€

Closed 23 Dec-7 Jan • 4 single rm, 16 double rm • Breakfast €8 • No restaurant • No dogs

The contemporary feel coupled with value for money.

Travellers not overly preoccupied with aesthetics yet keen to stay in a place with every modern convenience will like this hotel, and guests wanting beautiful natural surroundings will not be disappointed either. Built in 1998 in a panoramic lakeside setting, this establishment has well equipped accommodation of almost Nordic simplicity. Friendly and efficient family management.

Sights nearby: Basilica of San Nicolò, church of Santa Marta, house of Manzoni and other places associated with the writer, view of the lake

9

IL TELEGRAFO

Sig.ra Milanesi

Via Zuavi, 54
20077 Melegnano (MI)
Tel. 02 9834002 – Fax 02 98231813
info@hoteliltelegrafo.it – www.hoteliltelegrafo.it

57-62/80-82€

Closed Aug • 14 single rm, 20 double rm • Breakfast €8; half board €62 • Menu €33-47 • Parking, no dogs in the restaurant

The lobby, redolent of bygone times.

Close to the beginning of the motorway on the outskirts of Milan, this establishment's name recalls its original purpose when first built in 1861, namely a staging post where travellers could change horses, dine or spend the night. Over the years it has been extended and renovated, but the original character of the place remains. Today it has more than thirty well equipped and modern rooms; below these is its medium sized restaurant, entered via the lobby with large open fireplace.

Access

From Milan: A I for 3km to Melagnano exit, then 2km on the SP 40

Sights nearby: Chiaravalle: abbey; Milan: cathedral, Castello Sforzesco, basilica of Sant'Ambrogio, Pinacoteca di Brera

10

VILLA SAN PIETRO

Sigg. Ducroz

Via San Pietro, 25
25018 Montichiari (BS)
Tel. 030 961232 – Fax 030 9981098
villasanpietro@hotmail.com – www.art-with-attitude.com/villa/san_pietro.html

60/100€

Open all year • 3 double rm • No restaurant • Parking, garden, no dogs • Bicycle hire, wine tasting

The cosmopolitan atmosphere created by the owners.

A rustic-style establishment in the heart of town, easily identifiable on account of its small sign over the door. Guests arriving by car are given a pass allowing access to parking in the internal courtyard. Friendly and efficient management, rooms rich in detail and warmth, and a generous and tasty breakfast. A good alternative to the many commercial hotels which are the norm in the area.

Access

From Brescia: SS 11 for 1.6km, onto the SS 236 for 16km, then left for 1.9km

Sights nearby: Brescia: Loggia, Duomo Vecchio, Via dei Musei, Pinacoteca Tosio Martinengo, Museo della Città

11

CORTE MEDAGLIE D'ORO

Sig. Cobellini

Strada Argine Secchia, 63
46027 San Benedetto Po (MN)
Tel. 0376 618802 – Fax 0376 5879595
cobellini.claudio@virgilio.it – www.cortemedaglidoro.it

40/ 64€

Open all year • 2 single rm, 5 double rm • No restaurant • Parking, garden • Bicycles available, fishing, archery, tasting and sale of honey and jam

The rooms in the old granary.

Once called the King of Rivers, the Po irrigates the vast fertile plain bordering it, which does indeed give it a majestic air. The richness of the local harvests is reflected in the name of this guesthouse; the gold medals referred to were won by the owner's grandfather for his exceptional fruit orchards. Located in the former granary, the pleasant rooms under wooden ceilings make for pleasant accommodation, from where guests can listen to the gentle sounds of living agriculture and the silence of the plain's hot summer afternoons.

Access

From Mantova: SS 10, then right to join SS 482 for 12km, right for 2km, then left onto SS 413, then 5.5km to Quistello

Sights nearby: Mantova: Palazzo Ducale, Palazzo Te, Piazza delle Erbe, churches of San Lorenzo and Sant'Andrea

12

LOCANDA CA' ROSSA

F.lli Ceresini

Via Giuseppina, 20
26037 San Giovanni in Croce (CR)
Tel. 0375 91069 – Fax 0375 312090
locandacarossa@libero.it

60/85€

Closed 23 Dec-5 Jan and 1-15 Aug • 6 single rm, 6 double rm • Menu €30-55 • Parking, no dogs

The spacious, well-kept grounds

This recently opened property comprises an 18C manor house with a large courtyard on one side and an attractive garden on the other. The complex is impressive, with its new interior decor of arte povera furnishings, matching fabrics and modern facilities. The elegant restaurant serves a range of regional and international cuisine. The gym and sauna are welcome additions to the property.

Access
From Cremona: SP 87 for 27km

Sights nearby: Cremona: cathedral and Torrazzo, Museo Civico

13

LOCANDA DEL SOLE

Sig. Milito

Via Ruga del Porto Vecchio, 1
21018 Sesto Calende (VA)
Tel. 0331 914273 – Fax 0331 921759
info@trattorialocandasole.it – www.trattorialocandasole.it

🚹65/🚹🚹80€

Closed 25 Dec-10 Jan • 1 single rm, 6 double rm • Breakfast €5 • Menu €20-35 • No dogs

The genteel simplicity of the restaurant and the rustic charm of the accommodation.

Close to the point from where the waters of Lake Maggiore emerge to provide the source of the River Ticino is the old town of Sesto Calende where, at the junction of two streets in its historic centre, this establishment is located. Behind the rather municipal façade are seven charmingly rustic, well equipped rooms. The pleasant restaurant is elegantly decorated, and serves regional cuisine with particular emphasis on fish fresh from the lake.

Access

From Novara: SS 32 for 33km, then right onto the SS 33 for 4.5km

Sights nearby: Lake Maggiore

14

VILLA FLORA

Sig. Pinciroli
Via Torrazza, 10
22020 Torno (CO)
Tel. 031 419222 – Fax 031 418318

57/73€

Closed Nov-Feb • 20 double rm • Breakfast €9; half board €62 • Menu €23-39 • Parking, garden, swimming pool

The scenic views from the terrace.

Its name suggests a place nestling among lakeside greenery, but there is a lot more to this early 20C establishment, as guests discover when stepping out onto the poolside terrace. From here, there are breathtaking views over the waters of the lake and the villages dotting its verdant shoreline, up to the mountain peaks beyond.

Access
From Como: SS 583 for 6km

Sights nearby: View of the lake; Como: cathedral, town hall, church of San Fedele, basilica of Sant'Abbondio

Ravenna
Cervia
Cesena
Rimini
Riccione
Cattolica
San Marino
Pesaro
Fano
Senigallia
Ancona
Urbino
Sansepolcro
Jesi
MARCHE
Città di Castello
Gubbio
Fabriano
Macerata
Civitanova Marche
Cortona
Fermo
Perugia
Assisi
Ascoli Piceno
S. Benedetto d. Tronto
Foligno
Todi
Spoleto
Teramo
Terni
Gr. Sasso d'Italia
2914
Viterbo
Rieti
L'Aquila
Tevere
ROMA
Mali Lo
2795
1
2
3
4
5
6
7
8
9
10
11
12
13
14

MARCHE

The blend of medieval and renaissance towns, rolling hills, varied coastline, hospitable inhabitants, traditional cuisine and pleasant wines all contribute to this region's unique charm.

The Marche represents central Italy at its best. Its history has left a ubiquitous legacy of art and culture, but the industrious nature of its inhabitants has also made it a manufacturing centre of excellence, most notably in the field of footwear.

In order to fully understand the region, visitors should divide their time between the coast with its seafaring traditions, and the undulating hinterland with its impressive artistic centres including Urbino, Macerata and Ascoli Piceno. The region's capital is Ancona, a charming city and an important Adriatic port which in summer months is besieged by tourists from all over Europe boarding ferries for the Greek islands and Croatia.

14 establishments

1

FIORENIRE

Sig. e Sig.ra Cocci
Contrada Filette, 9
63032 Castignano (AP)
Tel. 0736 821606 – Fax 0736 822117
fiorenire@fiorenire.it – www.fiorenire.it

35-40/ 54-74€

Open all year • 6 single rm, 2 double rm • Half board €42-52 • Menu €16-35 • Parking, garden, tennis • Horse riding, jam, oil and wine for sale

The obvious affection of the owners for the surrounding landscape.

Situated in open country offering 360 degree views over the characteristic Marche hills towards the Apennines to the south and, on clear days, towards the sea to the east, this rose coloured villa is run by Carla and Pompilio Francesco who, having inherited the surrounding farmland and a passion for agriculture, set about restoring the building. With sports facilities and an equestrian centre, this is a great spot for those looking to get back to nature.

Access
From Ascoli Piceno: SS 4 for 14km, then left for 15.5km to Filette

Sights nearby: Ascoli Piceno: Palazzo dei Capitani del Popolo, cathedral, churches of San Francesco and Santi Vincenzo ed Anastasio, Ponte di Solestà

GOCCE DI CAMARZANO

Sig.ra Balducci

Località Camarzano, strada verso Moscano
60044 Fabriano (AN)

Tel. 336 649028 – Fax 0732 628172

goccedicamarzano@libero.it – www.goccedicamarzano.com

50-60/ 70-80€

Open all year • 6 double rm • Breakfast €3 • No restaurant • Parking, garden, no dogs

The frescoes which decorate parts of the first floor.

The versatile Signora Balducci runs not only her family farm, but also this fine establishment occupying an aristocratic 17C villa. The surrounding parkland provides tranquillity and panoramic views of the landscape as it changes with the seasons. The limited public areas are stylish, while the rooms have tasteful wood furnishings, wrought iron beds and modern, spacious bathrooms. Happily, there are no televisions.

Access

From Ancona: SS 16 for 11km, then left onto SS 76 for 58km, right for 2km and right again for 1.5km to Camarzano

Sights nearby: Piazza del Duomo, Piazza del Comune; Grotte di Frasassi

3

LA LUMA

Sig. Bartolini

Via Cavour, 1
62010 Montecosaro (MC)
Tel. 0733 222273 – Fax 0733 229701
info@laluma.it – www.laluma.it

62/ 73-77€

Open all year • 10 double rm • Half board €50-70 • No restaurant • Parking, garden, no dogs • Tasting and sale of jams and cakes

The varied and original interior decor.

This delightful little hotel has been built into the ramparts of the town, using materials from the old wine cellars. The recently constructed accommodation is furnished in period style while the bathrooms are more contemporary in appearance. But the most attractive features of the place are the terrace offering spectacular views over the Marche hills along with the charming breakfast room. There is also a lovely restaurant with stone and brick walls and vaulting.

Access

From Macerata: 6.5km to join Camerino-Civitanova Marche superstrada for 12.5km to Montecosaro exit, continue for 1.5km

Sights nearby: Recanati: Palazzo Leopardi, Museo Civico; Loreto; Santuario della Santa Casa, Pinacoteca

ANTICO MULINO

Sig.ra Cesari

Località Tenna, 2
63047 Montefortino (AP)
Tel. 0736 859530 – Fax 0736 859530
anticomulino@virgilio.it – www.anticomulino.it

40-50/ 55-70€

Closed 7 Jan-15 Apr, 6 Nov-23 Dec • 1 single rm, 14 double rm • Half board €42-50 • Menu €15-20 • Parking, no dogs • Bicycles available, fishing, jam and cured meats for sale

The history of the place, lost in the mists of time.

Deep in the Monti Sibillini natural park, the Antico Mulino sits by the river Tenna, which previously powered its milling machinery, but is today animated by no more than trout and other fish species. The originally fortified main building has an imposing air; accommodation is spread between this and adjacent structures. The rustic-style furnishings go perfectly with the tiled floors and beamed ceilings. Hearty local cuisine is a feature of the restaurant menu.

Access

From Ascoli Piceno: SS 7 for 7km, onto the SS 78 for 23km, then left for 5.5km to Montefortino, continue west 2km beyond the village

Sights nearby: Montefortini: Pinacoteca Civica, churches of S. Agostino and S. Francesco; Monti Sibillini National Park

5

LA GINESTRA

Sig. Mostardi
Contrada Coste
63020 Montelparo (AP)
Tel. 0734 780449 – Fax 0734 780706
info@laginestra.it – www.laginestra.it

50/57-70€

Open all year • 3 single rm, 10 double rm • Breakfast €6.50; half board €52-60 • Menu €21-25 • Parking, garden, swimming pool, tennis, bowls • Horse riding, bicycles available, honey, oil and wine for sale

The sporting activities against a verdant backdrop.

Perched on a panoramic hillside between the Sibillini mountains and the Adriatic, this hotel is the result of a recent project which has restored a number of stone buildings. In addition to the beautiful rural location, guests can enjoy a wide variety of sports facilities; there are six tennis courts, stables, crazy golf, mountain bikes and a swimming pool – great for health and fitness enthusiasts. The relaxing accommodation is simply decorated and furnished in dark wood, while the cuisine focuses on local fish and meat specialities

Access

From Ascoli Piceno: SS 4 towards San Benedetto di Tronto for 6.5km, left for 29km, then right for 3km to Coste

Sights nearby: Ascoli Piceno: Palazzo dei Capitani del Popolo, cathedral, churches of San Francesco and Santi Vincenzo ed Anastasio, Ponte di Solestà

GIARDINO

Sig.ra Rosichini

Via Mattei, 4
61047 San Lorenzo in Campo (PU)
Tel. 0721 776803 – Fax 0721 735323
giardino@puntomedia.it – www.hotelgiardino.it

58/70-75€

Closed 10 Jan-10 Feb • 1 single rm, 17 double rm • Half board €70-75 • Menu €40-60 • Parking, garden, swimming pool, no dogs in the restaurant • Bicycle hire

The blend of tradition and innovation delivered with courtesy and care.

Opened in 1971, this establishment began life as a trattoria with a few rooms, since when it has evolved considerably in terms of both its cuisine (the kitchen operates under the watchful eye of Mamma Efresina, the owner) and accommodation (now a well presented hotel with tasteful and stylish furnishings). The open fireplace in the lobby makes for a welcoming and elegant ambience.

Access

From Pesaro: SS 16 for 25km to Marotta, then right onto SS 424 for 30km

Sights nearby: Fano: Corte Malatestiana, church of Santa Maria Nuova

7

LOCANDA SALIMBENI

Locanda Salimbeni Snc

Strada statale 361
62027 San Severino Marche (MC)
Tel. 0733 634047 – Fax 0733 633901
info@locandasalimbeni.it – www.locandasalimbeni.it

48/65€

Open all year • 9 double rm • Half board €52 • Menu €21-31 • Parking, garden, swimming pool, no dogs • Horse riding, organised trips, tasting of honey, preserved vegetables, olive and cured meat

The Marche heritage evident in the cuisine and the decor.

Originally from San Severino, Lorenzo and Jacopo Salimbeni were artists active in the 14C and 15C. Many of their works remain in the city's churches and museums, and their legacy is celebrated in an art prize which bears their name. Another homage to their creativity is to be found in the restaurant of this establishment, where one of their works is reproduced alongside other landscape scenes. The rooms are furnished with antique pieces and four poster beds.

Access

From Macerata: southwest for 10km to Passo di Treia, then onto the SS 361 for 19km

Sights nearby: San Severino: Piazza del Popolo, cathedral, church of San Lorenzo in Doliolo, Pinacoteca Civica

8

ANTICA ARMONIA

Sig. Colombaroni

Località Scapezzano - Via del Soccorso, 67
60010 Scapezzano (AN)
Tel. 071 660227
anticaarmonia@libero.it – www.anticaarmonia.it

50-60/ 75-85€

Closed 15-30 Oct • 6 double rm • Half board €62-67 • Menu €25-30 • Parking, garden, swimming pool

The centuries-old olive groves surrounding the property.

This recently restored 19C farmhouse is set in its own parkland deep in the Marche hills – look out for the ancient mulberry tree peeping out above the olive groves. The tranquillity of the location is in stark contrast to the hustle and bustle of the coastal resorts. Inside, the atmosphere is relaxing, with open fireplaces, a billiards room and simply furnished accommodation which is ideal for guests seeking a peaceful stay.

Access

From Ancona: SS 16 for 30km, left after Senigallia for 3.5 km to Scapezzano

Sights nearby: Senigallia: Rocca Roverasca, Fontana del Nettuno, Fontana dei Leoni, Palazzo del Duca, cathedral, church of S. Martino

9

BEL SIT

F.lli Manfredi Snc
Via dei Cappuccini, 15
60010 Scapezzano (AN)
Tel. 071 660032 – Fax 071 6608335
info@belsit.net – www.belsit.net

55-70/ 65-85€

Closed Feb • 28 double rm • Breakfast €7; half board €44-67 • Menu €18-40 • Parking, garden, swimming pool, tennis, no dogs in the restaurant • Organised trips, bicycle hire, oil for sale

The tranquillity of this former convent.

In the Marche foothills and still within sight of the coast, this imposing 19C building sits in a verdant location. Once a convent and later a seminary, it is now a sensitively restored hotel. Its change of use from a house of God is evident from the swimming pool and tennis courts; spacious and peaceful accommodation allowing visitors to while away the days in total tranquillity, yet surprisingly close to civilisation.

Access

From Ancona: SS 16 for 30km, left after Senigallia for 3.5 km to Scapezzano

Sights nearby: Senigallia: Rocca Roverasca, Fontana del Nettuno, Fontana dei Leoni, Palazzo del Duca, cathedral, church of S. Martino

10

CASA OLIVA

Sig.ra Polverari e Sig. Fabbri

Via Castello, 19
61030 Serrungarina (PU)
Tel. 0721 891500 – Fax 0721 891500
casaoliva@casaoliva.it – www.casaoliva.it

50/75€

Closed 10-31 Jan • 2 single rm, 13 double rm • Half board €50 • Menu €24-38 • Parking, no dogs in the restaurant • Bicycles available

The views of the Marche hills from the ramparts.

The fortified village of Bargni is situated on Via Flaminia, the old Roman road that heads inland from Fano. As with so many settlements in the Marche, it originated as a lookout post and to this day it retains a forbidding aspect. Sitting at the foot of the village, the hotel has a stone facade with a raised entrance reached by a flight of steps. Inside, the carefully restored building has a spacious restaurant with large windows, and unfussy, well presented and comfortable accommodation.

Access
From Pesaro: SS 16 for 10km, then right for 18km to Bargni

Sights nearby: Rocca, church of Sant'Antonio

11

VILLA FEDERICI

Sig. Guerrieri
Via Cartoceto, 4
61030 Serrungarina (PU)
Tel. 0721 891510 – Fax 0721 891510
info@villafederici.com – www.villafederici.com

63-93€

Closed 8-31 Jan • 5 double rm • Menu €20-45 • Parking, garden, no dogs • Horse riding, bicycles available, organised trips, oil, wine and pasta for sale

The rustic tranquillity of the hillside location among trees.

"Parva domus magna quies", states the brochure (small house, great tranquillity) for this peacefully situated late-17C patrician residence. Far from the hustle and bustle of urban life, the building sits between two copses, partially obscuring it and giving it an air of understated refinement. Inside, the female owner has created an ambience of elegance using antique family pieces to furnish the rooms in a simple rustic style. Fine views of the hillside landscape and the Metauro river running through it.

Access
From Pesaro: SS 16 for 10km, then right for 18km to Bargni

Sights nearby: Rocca, church of Sant'Antonio

12

IL CASOLARE DEI SEGRETI

Fam. Lucamarini

Contrada San Lorenzo, 28
62010 Treia (MC)
Tel. 0733 216441 – Fax 0733 218133
info@casolaredeisegreti.it – www.casolaredeisegreti.it

40/ 60€

Closed 3-19 Nov • 2 double rm • No breakfast • Menu €24-32 • Parking, garden, no dogs in the restaurant

The ambience of an earlier age.

It is difficult to summarise the appeal of this solid rustic establishment, nestling among the undulating Marche hills. One of the attractions is the restaurant with lovely stonework in its arches and passageways, redolent of bygone times and making for a warm ambience. Traditional Marche cuisine is lovingly prepared by Signora Lucamarini using carefully selected produce, a hallmark of good quality.

Access
From Macerata: 9km to Pollenza, then 4.5km to Passo di Treia, 5km to Treia and left to San Lorenzo

Sights nearby: Palazzo Comunale and Civico Museo Archeologico, cathedral, churches of San Michele and Santa Chiara

13

MULINO DELLA RICAVATA

Sig.ra Faggi
Via Porta Celle
61049 Urbania (PU)
Tel. 0722 310326 – Fax 0722 310326
info@mulinodellaricavata.com – www.mulinodellaricavata.com

70-75€

Open all year • 4 double rm • Half board €60-70 • Menu €20-30 • Parking, garden • Fishing, flowers, vegetables and dried flower arrangements for sale

A mill bearing witness to centuries of history on the banks of the Metauro.

Travellers along the banks of the Metauro in the 14C may well have encountered the occasional friar making his way with produce from his convent to this stone built mill. Now as then, it sits among trees by the riverside. A chance to see some old mill equipment, as the mill itself and the little cave with its underground spring, makes the journey all the more worthwhile. The flower bedecked façade also gives the place a certain charm.

Access
From Urbino: SS 73 bis for 16.5km, right onto SP 36 for 1.1km to Porta Celle

Sights nearby: Urbino: Palazzo Ducale, Galleria Nazionale delle Marche, Casa di Raffaello, churches of San Giovanni Battista and San Giuseppe

14

CA' ANDREANA

Sig.ra Loschi e Sig. Ferrari

A Gadana - Località Cà Andreana
61029 URBINO (PU)
Tel. 0722 327845 – Fax 0722 327845
info@caandreana.com – www.caandreana.com

55-70/70-88€

Closed 9-27 Jan, 27 Sep-7 Oct • 6 double rm • Breakfast €6; half board €58 • Menu €27-40 • Parking, garden, swimming pool, no dogs in the restaurant • Organised trips, jams and eggs for sale

The Marche hills and the proximity to Urbino.

The verdant hills of the Marche seem to give colour to the pale stone and roof tiles of this old but well maintained farmhouse. Against this rustic backdrop, the cuisine is surprisingly sophisticated without compromising its authenticity, using carefully selected local produce (home grown wherever possible). During the summer months, meals are served in the cool courtyard, from where guests can survey the peaceful countryside, perhaps before setting off to discover Urbino, the quintessential Renaissance city.

Access
2.5km north-west of Urbino

Sights nearby: Urbino: Palazzo Ducale, Galleria Nazionale delle Marche, Casa di Raffaello, churches of San Giovanni Battista and San Giuseppe

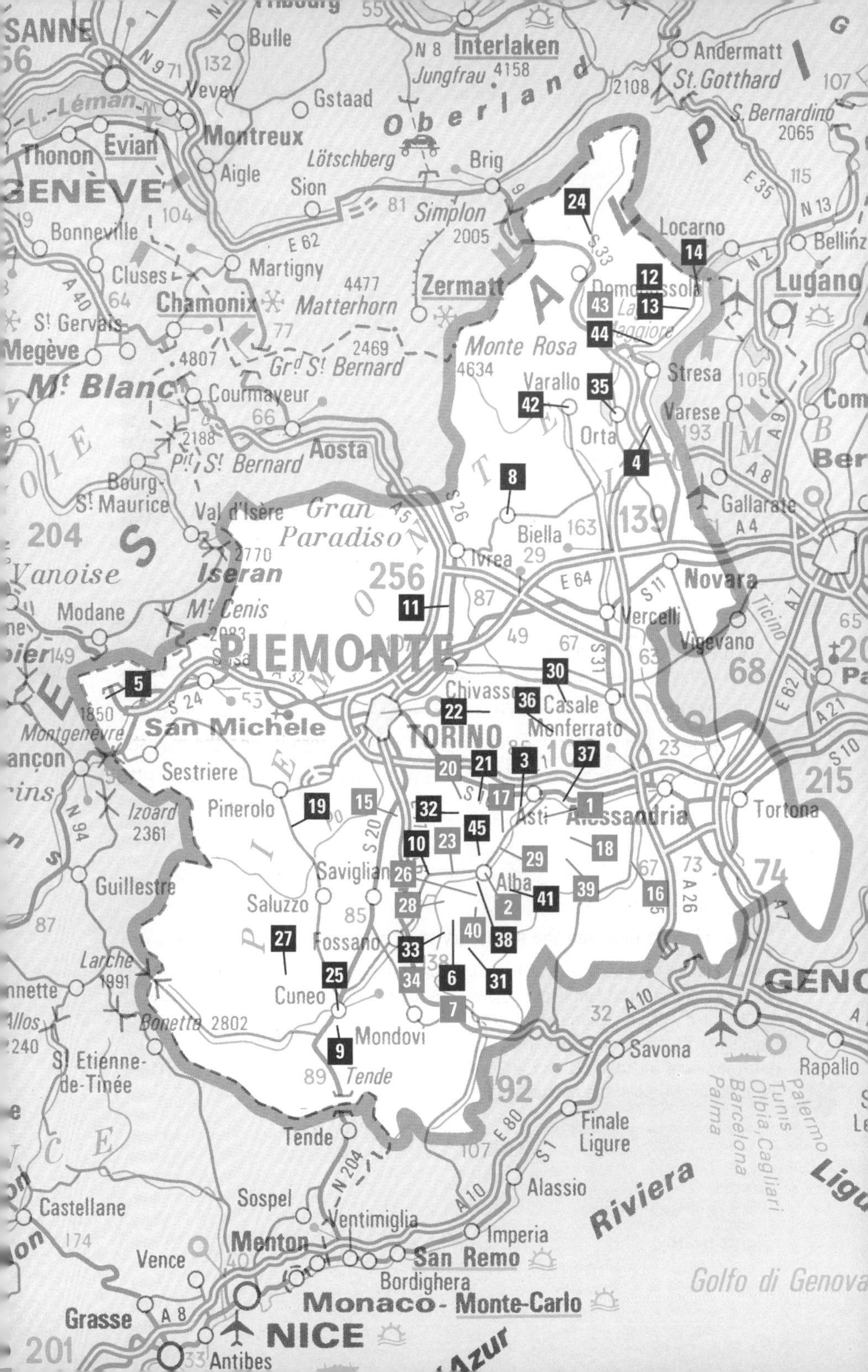

PIEMONTE
Interlaken
Jungfrau 4158
Oberland
Bulle
Vevey
Gstaad
Lötschberg
Brig
Andermatt
St. Gotthard
S. Bernardino
2065
L. Léman
Thonon
Evian
Montreux
Aigle
Sion
GENÈVE
Simplon
2005
Bonneville
Martigny
Cluses
Chamonix
Matterhorn
4477
Zermatt
St Gervais
Megève
Mt Blanc
4807
Grd St Bernard
2469
Monte Rosa
4634
Courmayeur
Aosta
Pit St Bernard
2188
Bourg-St Maurice
Val d'Isère
Gran Paradiso
Iseran
2770
Vanoise
Modane
Mt Cenis
2083
Susa
1850
Montgenèvre
San Michele
Sestriere
Pinerolo
Izoard
2361
Guillestre
Saluzzo
Fossano
Cuneo
Larche
1991
Bonette
2802
Mondovi
Tende
St Etienne-de-Tinée
Sospel
Castellane
Ventimiglia
Menton
San Remo
Bordighera
Imperia
Alassio
Vence
Monaco-Monte-Carlo
Grasse
NICE
Antibes
Riviera
Golfo di Genova
Finale Ligure
Savona
Rapallo
Palermo
Tunis
Olbia, Cagliari
Barcelona
Palma
Locarno
Bellinzona
Lugano
Domodossola
Lago Maggiore
Stresa
Varallo
Orta
Varese
Gallarate
Biella
Ivrea
Novara
Vercelli
Vigevano
Ticino
Chivasso
Casale Monferrato
TORINO
Asti
Alessandria
Tortona
Alba
Savigliano
Pavia
1
2
3
4
5
6
7
8
9
10
11
12
13
14
15
16
17
18
19
20
21
22
23
24
25
26
27
28
29
30
31
32
33
34
35
36
37
38
39
40
41
42
43
44
45

PIEMONTE

Piedmont is a region of mountains and rivers, hemmed in on three sides by the rugged profile of the Alps which gradually soften prior to rising as the foothills of the Apennines, beyond which lie Liguria and the sea. Water rushes down valleys from the spectacular snow capped peaks before joining the majestic river Po, flowing placidly past the farmland and towns which mark the boundaries of the Monferrato district. To the south, between the mountains and the plain, are the hills of the Langhe and the Roero, renowned for their prestigious wines such as Barbera and Barolo, the perfect accompaniment for a typical Piedmontese meat dish. The inhabitants of this land are a reserved and determined people whose forefathers were instrumental in the campaign to unify Italy. For centuries, Piedmont was ruled by Europe's most ancient dynasty, the House of Savoy; although French speakers, it was thanks to their resolve that the unification movement was born. Today, Italy is a Republic and Turin is undergoing a major facelift, but the regal splendour of bygone times is still to be seen at Stupinigi, Venaria and Racconigi, where a succession of state rooms, gardens and fine furnishings survive untarnished.

45 establishments

1

VILLA GIADA-CASCINA DANI

Sig.ra Faccio
Località Dani
14041 Agliano (AT)
Tel. 0141 964120 – Fax 0141 964120
info@andreafaccio.it – www.cascinadani.it

84/105€

Closed 10 Dec-2 Mar • 5 double rm • No restaurant • Parking • Wine for sale (tasting)

The appetising breakfast of home produced bread and jam.

A typical farmstead set among vineyards, on a road that is quiet enough not to spoil the peace and tranquillity enjoyed by guests. Rooms are accessed off the first floor balcony; each one is painted in a different colour. Although simply furnished, the place is well presented, with modern and traditional cleverly blended together. Pleasant public areas, especially the open terrace converted from a former hayloft.

Access
From Asti: SS 231 for 5km, left on the SS 456 for 10km to Agliano, then right for 2.5km to Dani

Sights nearby: Asti: cathedral, church and baptistery of San Pietro

VILLA LA MERIDIANA-CASCINA REINE

Sig. Giacosa
Località Altavilla, 9
12051 Alba (CN)
Tel. 0173 440112 – Fax 0173 440112
cascinareine@libero.it

70/ 85€

Open all year • 5 double rm • No restaurant • Parking, garden, swimming pool, bowls • Bicycle hire, archery, truffle hunting excursions, wine tasting

The views over the old town and, on clear days, the Alps.

Situated on one of the hills outside Alba, this hotel is an attractive mix of genteel refinement and rustic idyll. The accommodation is divided between an old farmhouse and an Art Nouveau villa, on the façade of which is the sundial from which this establishment takes its name. The best rooms are those providing views over the surrounding countryside. Guests may enjoy a reading room, billiards, gym and the opportunity to go truffle hunting with dogs.

Access
From Asti: SS 231 for 25km, past Alba head east 1km to Altavilla

Sights nearby: Alba: medieval historic centre

3

LOCANDA DEL VALLONE

Sig. Lupica

Strada del Vallone, 9
14010 Antignano d'Asti (AT)
Tel. 0141 205572 – Fax 0141 205572
info@locandadelvallone.com – www.locandadelvallone.com

55/75€

Closed 10 Nov-31 Mar • 3 double rm • No restaurant • Parking, swimming pool

Breakfast served under the eaves of the former hen house during the summer months.

Situated among verdant gardens, this is a tastefully restored Piedmontese farmhouse. The limited accommodation is furnished in period style, with equally historic bathrooms to match. The tiled floor is original, dating from the 18C. Altogether more recent, and the only concession to contemporary pleasures, is the swimming pool, a welcome amenity for visitors during the summer months. A gem of a place at a reasonable price.

Access
From Asti: SS 231 for 9km, right for 3km to San Martino Alfieri, then right for 2.5km to Gonella

Sights nearby: Asti: cathedral, church and baptistery of San Pietro

4

IL GIARDINO DI ALICE

Sig. Saporiti
Via Motto Mirabello, 51
28041 Arona (NO)
Tel. 0322 57212 – Fax 0322 57145
info@ilgiardinodialice.com – www.ilgiardinodialice.com

65/95€

Open all year • 1 single rm, 4 double rm • Breakfast €7 • No restaurant • Parking, no dogs • Boat trips, bicycle hire

Enjoying views over the lake from the sunny terrace and the sounds of the woods.

A Northern European feel pervades this establishment, run by a writer and psychoanalyst who turned their backs on decades of city life to settle by the lakeside. Here, surrounded by woodland, peace and tranquillity prevail. The large windows and terrace allow the light to stream in, adding to the ambience of any visit, be it a weekend break or a longer stay. In addition, the unusually lively decor and Lewis Carroll-related touches make this an interesting spot.

Access
From Novara: SS 32 for 33km, then 6.8km on the SS 33, left for 2.5km to Campagna

Sights nearby: Colosso di San Carleone, view of the lake, church of Santa Maria, Rocca

5

LA NIGRITELLA

Sig.ra Scavino
Via Melezet, 96
10052 Bardonecchia (TO)
Tel. 0122 980477 – Fax 0122 980054
info@lanigritella.it – www.lanigritella.it

50-70/78-100€

Open all year • 1 single rm, 6 double rm • Half board €45-98.50 • Parking, garden, no dogs in the restaurant

Breathing in the fresh country air from the bedroom balcony.

Once the owners' family home, this classic mountain residence sits harmoniously in its surrounding countryside. Opened in 1999 after a programme of restoration, this small family run hotel, albeit offering limited public areas, is notable for its attention to detail. There are seven rooms, each with private bathroom and balcony, a bar-restaurant and gardens. Equally suitable for summer holidays or a winter break, being a mere 500m from the ski lifts. Welcome to Bardonecchia!

Access
From Torino: A 32 for 72km to Bardonecchia exit

Sights nearby: Gran Paradiso National Park

CA' SAN PONZIO

F.lli Bianco

A Vergne ovest 3,5 km, via Rittane, 7
12060 Barolo (CN)
Tel. 0173 560510 – Fax 0173 560510
sanponzio@areacom.it – www.casanponzio.com

62-68€

Closed 2-31 Jan • 6 double rm • Breakfast €8 • No restaurant • Parking, garden, bowls • Organised trips, bicycle hire, tasting of jams, cheeses, wine and cakes, hazelnuts for sale

Enjoying the sounds of the countryside from the comfort of the terrace.

Originally built in 1915 and in the hands of the same family ever since, this farmhouse has recently been carefully restored. An unexpected English-style lawn laid out between the hazelnut trees precedes the entrance, located beneath a typical Piedmontese balcony, accessible from some of the rooms. These are furnished in rustic style while those on the top floor have period pieces and are better proportioned. Young management team and guaranteed peace and quiet, bar the odd cockerel and church bell.

Access

From Asti: SS 231 for 25km to Alba, then 9km on the SP 9 and 6km on the SP 3 to Vergne

Sights nearby: Alba: medieval historic centre

7

LA TERRAZZA SUL BOSCO

Sig. Camerano
Via Conforso, 5
12060 Barolo (CN)
Tel. 0173 56137 – Fax 0173 560812
laterrazzasulbosco@tiscali.it – www.barolocamerano.it

60/70€

Open all year • 5 double rm • Breakfast €5 • No restaurant • Parking, garden • Horse riding, bowls, bicycle hire, wine tasting

Being next door to the king of Italian wines.

Barolo is the centre of production for one of Italy's most important wines; opened in 2001, this establishment is next door to the castle, home of the town's wine museum. Occupying an 18C building, it lies along the old town walls and overlooks the countryside beyond. The rooms are simple, furnished with modern pieces and wrought iron beds. A great place to stay for all kinds of visitors, but particularly appropriate for wine buffs.

Access
From Asti: SS 231 for 25km to Alba, then 9km on the SP 9 and 4km on the SP 3

Sights nearby: Alba: medieval historic centre

8

BUGELLA

Sig. Sechi

Via Cottolengo, 65
13900 Biella (BI)

Tel. 015 406607 – Fax 015 405543
info@hotelbugella.it – www.hotelbugella.it

65/ 85€

Open all year • 10 single rm, 14 double rm • Breakfast €5 • Menu €25-40 • Parking, no dogs in the restaurant

The clean, elegant lines of the architecture.

Situated on the outskirts of town, this genteel four storey Art Nouveau villa is a warm and welcoming place to stay, both for tourists visiting Piemonte and business travellers looking for something a little different. Comprising a small lobby, lounge area, rooms and restaurant, this is a colourful, well equipped, comfortable and professionally managed hotel. Plenty of parking for guests.

Sights nearby: Baptistery, basilica of San Sebastiano, church of SS. Trinità, medieval village of Piazzo

9

LA BISALTA

Sig.ra Passerini
Via Tetti Re, 5
12012 Boves (CN)
Tel. 0171 388782 – Fax 0171 388782

55€

Closed 16 Oct-30 Apr • 5 double rm • Breakfast €6; half board €35 • Menu €22-31 • Parking, garden, tennis, bowls, minigolf, no dogs • Bicycles available, snails for sale (tasting)

Snails on the menu for dinner - the owners are passionate about their snail farming operation.

There are countless reasons for staying at this friendly establishment. Dating from 1741, the well restored house sits at the foot of the Alps, and has a tennis court and crazy golf for younger visitors. The rooms are modern and spacious; the two most sought after retain their original 18C tiled floors and brick vaulted ceilings. Perhaps the most unusual feature of the place, though, is its organic snail farming operation; guests wishing to savour the house delicacy may do so in the restaurant.

Access

From Cuneo: SP 21 for 5km to Boves, through the village and continue to Riviora

Sights nearby: Santuario della Madonna dei Boschi; Cuneo: Museo Civico, churches of Santa Chiara and Sant'Ambrogio, cathedral

10

L'OMBRA DELLA COLLINA

Sig. Chiesa

Via Mendicità Istruita, 47
12042 Bra (CN)
Tel. 0172 44884 – Fax 0172 44884
lombradellacollina@libero.it – www.lombradellacollina.it

62/78€

Open all year • 5 double rm • No restaurant • Parking

The proprietor's genuine interest in days gone by.

In the historic centre of Bra, one of Piemonte's gastronomic centres, this charming establishment is set around an internal courtyard at the centre of which stands an imposing fig tree. Originally built in 1768, the building was subsequently embellished with the addition of a typical balcony. The owner's passion for antiques manifests itself not only in the adjoining toy museum, but also in the tasteful choice of furnishings.

Access
From Asti: SS 231 for 40.5km

Sights nearby: Alba: medieval historic centre

11

RESIDENZA DEL LAGO

Sig.ra Ferrari
Via Roma, 48
10010 Candia Canavese (TO)
Tel. 011 9834885 – Fax 011 9834886
info@residenzadelago.it – www.residenzadelago.it

70-73/80-85€

Open all year • 11 double rm • Half board €60 • Menu €29-39 • Garden

The large rooms with open fireplaces and brick vaulting.

At the centre of the triangle formed by Turin, Ivrea and Santhia lies Candia. This is an area still relatively unknown to tourists, despite its natural beauty and artistic heritage. With lakes, hills and castles in its vicinity, this is the ideal base from which to explore the locality; exposed brickwork, vaulted ceilings, open fireplaces and period furnishings make for a characterful ambience. Typical iron balconies look directly onto the garden, while the restaurant serves creative modern cuisine.

Access
From Torino: A 4 for 17km to Chivasso exit, then onto the SS 26 for 13km

Sights nearby: Torino: Cathedral, Palazzo Madama, Palazzo Reale, Museo Egizio, Mole Antonelliana

12

IL CORTILE

Sig. Sgier

Via Massimo D'Azeglio, 73
28821 Cannero Riviera (VB)
Tel. 0323 787213 – Fax 0323 787213
cortilecannero@libero.it – www.cortile.net

73/105€

Closed 1 Nov-14 Mar • 9 double rm • Menu €49-71 • Garden

The central courtyard, from which the establishment takes its name.

Life here revolves around the courtyard, particularly during the summer months, when gourmet meals are served to the many visitors. Surrounding it is the first floor accommodation which Signor Sgier, originally from the Swiss canton of Grigioni, makes available to guests. This is a stylish and tastefully presented establishment, from its carefully selected furnishings to its creative cuisine, which will satisfy the demands of even the most exacting travellers.

Access
From Verbania: SS 34 for 13km

Sights nearby: Lake views; Isole Borromee; Verbania: Pallanza, Villa Taranto

13

SOLE

Sig.ra Comazzi
Via Nuova, 6
28821 Cannero Riviera (VB)
Tel. 0323 788150 – Fax 0323 788150
cristina@albergosole.it – www.albergosole.it

40/ 58-70€

Open all year • 3 single rm, 11 double rm • No restaurant • Parking, no dogs in the restaurant

The colourful flowers which brighten up the balconies.

Close to Cannero Riviera, on the Piedmontese side of Lake Maggiore and not far from the Swiss border, this pleasant hotel is a happy combination of historic appearance and modern convenience. The airy rooms are simply furnished, and almost all have private bathrooms and balconies overlooking the lake. The same view may be enjoyed from the downstairs terrace, where breakfast is served in summer. The friendliness of the family management team makes this a popular place to stay with visitors of all nationalities.

Access
From Verbania: SS 34 for 11km

Sights nearby: Lake views; Isole Borromee; Verbania: Pallanza, Villa Taranto

14

DEL LAGO

Sig. Albertella

Via Nazionale, 2
28822 Cannobio (VB)
Tel. 0323 70595 – Fax 0323 70595
enotecadellago@libero.it – www.enotecalago.com

75/95€

Closed Dec-Feb • 2 single rm, 8 double rm • Breakfast €10 • Menu €40-65 • Parking, garden, no dogs in the restaurant

The ambience of the place, a homage to elegant relaxation.

This large establishment on the main road that runs along the lakeside is renowned principally for its restaurant and wine list. Its accommodation is also of a high standard, with spacious, well presented and elegant rooms. Particularly appealing are its balconies from which visitors can enjoy fine views of the lake, while enjoying a glass of wine in a comfortable armchair. What more could you ask for?

Access
From Verbania: SS 34 for 14km to Carmine

Sights nearby: Santuario della Madonna della Pietà, orrido di S. Anna; lake views; Isole Borromee; Verbania: Pallanza, Villa Taranto

15

MARGHERITA

Sig. Roccia

Strada Pralormo, 315
10022 Carmagnola (TO)
Tel. 011 9795088 – Fax 011 9795228
info@girasoligolf.it – www.girasoligolf.it

70/ 80€

Open all year • 11 double rm • Breakfast €8; half board €65 • Menu €25 • Parking, swimming pool, golf, no dogs in the restaurant • Tasting of regional specialities

The gentle daily rhythm alternating between rounds of golf and relaxation.

A golfer's paradise, with 45 holes over three courses. This large farmstead has transformed itself over recent years, although agricultural traces remain in the form of rabbit farming and the rearing of other small farm animals. The main house has stone floors, brick walls and wooden roof beams; accommodation comprises a dozen rooms and several apartments suitable for longer stays. In addition to the golf club, there is also a restaurant.

Access

From Torino: A 6 for 14km to Carmagnola exit; then left towards Pralormo for 2km

Sights nearby: Torino: Cathedral, Palazzo Madama, Palazzo Reale, Museo Egizio, Mole Antonelliana

16

IL BUONVICINO

Sig. Peverati

Strada Ricaldone di Sotto, 40
15061 Cassine (AL)
Tel. 0144 715228 – Fax 0144 715842
ilbuonvicino@libero.it

30/60€

Closed Aug • 1 single rm, 5 double rm • Menu €15-23 • Parking, garden, no dogs • Bicycle hire, tasting and sale of jam and wine

We most liked

The interesting and surprising nibbles available in the restaurant.

Look out for the barrel on the Ricaldone road which leads to this 19C Monferrato farmhouse, meticulously restored by its owners. Situated in a secluded spot, this is a working winery offering accommodation; six rustic style rooms with many of the original furnishings still in situ. All have a bird theme and painted decor to match; the Turkey and Duck rooms are perhaps the most attractive, the former on the top floor and the latter with open fireplace. The restaurant offers interesting dishes and does not restrict its menu to the local cuisine.

Access

From Alessandria: SS 30 for 22.7km, then right onto Strada Ricaldone di Sotto

Sights nearby: Churches of San Giacomo and San Francesco, the old convent, Palazzo dei Conti Zoppi

17

IL BORGO

Sig.ra Ferrero
Via Trento, 2
12050 Castellinaldo (CN)
Tel. 0173 214017 – Fax 0173 214017
agriturismoilborgo@tiscali.it – www.ilborgoagriturismo.it

50/66€

Open all year • 6 double rm • No restaurant • Parking, no dogs • Wine tasting

The changing view over the hills as the seasons progress.

Castellinaldo is a typical hill village of the Roero district, encircling the walls of a medieval castle. After negotiating sharp bends and steps, the visitor emerges in front of a splendidly restored building, its long history inextricably linked to that of the nearby castle; indeed the whole settlement sprung up here to supply it. Breakfast is served in the brick-vaulted old cellars, and characterful low passageways lead to the rooms, each named after a famous local wine. The attractive furnishings are all in tasteful period style.

Access
From Asti: SS 231 for 16km, then right for 7km

Sights nearby: Medieval castle; Magliano Alfieri: Castello degli Alfieri

18

LA MUSSIA

Sig.ra Ponzio
Regione Opessina, 4
14040 Castelnuovo Calcea (AT)
Tel. 0141 957201 – Fax 0141 957402
info@lamussia.it – www.lamussia.it

35-42/ 60-70€

Closed Jan • 3 single rm, 7 double rm • Half board €50-55 • Parking, swimming pool, tennis • Cheese and wine tasting

We most liked

The remarkable value for money.

A true agriturismo in terms of its competitive prices and simple furnishings, this is not the place for those seeking luxury and ostentation. It is the ideal spot, though, for those in quest of the simple pleasures of rural life and sincere hospitality. All the rooms overlook unspoilt countryside; some are furnished in period style while others are more modern in feel. Livestock and an attractive swimming pool complete the picture.

Access
Asti: SS 231 for 5km to Isola d'Asti, then 12.3km on the SS 456 to Opessina

Sights nearby: Asti: cathedral, church and baptistery of San Pietro

19

LOCANDA LA POSTA

Sig.ra Mignola
Via dei Fossi, 4
10061 Cavour (TO)
Tel. 0121 69989 – Fax 0121 69790
info@locandalaposta.it – www.locandalaposta.it

55-80/ 80-120€

Open all year • 6 single rm, 14 double rm • Half board €55-75 • Menu €15-42 • Cured meat, cheese, tasting and sale of jams and preserved vegetables

The long established and traditional style Genovesio family management.

For five generations the Genovesio family has continued the tradition of hospitality for which this establishment, situated between Pinerolo and Saluzzo, has been renownd since the 18C. The rooms are ranged along the long balcony which overlooks the central courtyard, furnished in period style and offering every modern convenience, including air conditioning. The busy restaurant is particularly animated at the beginning of the summer season, when it hosts a gourmet convention.

Access
From Torino: A 55 for 14km to None exit, then 17km to Pinerolo and left onto the SS 589 for 12km

Sights nearby: Racconigi: Castello Sabaudo; Pinerolo: historic centre

20

CASCINA PAPA MORA

Sorelle Bucco
Via Ferrere, 16
14010 Cellarengo (AT)
Tel. 0141 935126 – Fax 0141 935444
info@cascinapapamora.it – www.cascinapapamora.it

35-40/60-70€

Closed Jan-Feb • 5 double rm • Half board €50-60 • Menu €20-30 • Parking, garden, swimming pool, no dogs • Horse riding, bicycles available, jam, wine and organic produce for sale

The English country house feel of the top floor accommodation.

This early 20C Piedmontese farmhouse is situated in open countryside with organic farming on all sides. It is named after the man who first built the place, the great-grandfather of the current owners, the Bucco sisters. The warm welcome here makes it a popular place to stay; there are five rooms, gardens with a little lake, table tennis and mountain biking, plus a small restaurant offering home grown fruit and vegetables and classic Piedmontese cuisine. Simple, authentic atmosphere.

Access
From Asti: SS 10 for 18km to Dusino San Michele, then left for 7km

Sights nearby: Monta: Castello dei Morra, Santuario dei Piloni

21

GARIBALDI

Sig. Vaudano

Via Italia, 1
14010 Cisterna d'Asti (AT)
Tel. 0141 979118 – Fax 0141 979118

35/60€

Closed 15-31 Jan, 15-31 Aug • 3 single rm, 4 double rm • Half board €45 • Menu €25-30 • Parking, small dogs welcome • Mostarda for sale

The restaurant, a perfect blend of history, local tradition and Piedmontese cuisine.

Was Garibaldi born here? Did he stay here, pass through, or fight a battle here? The answer sadly is no. The hotel was, however, founded by one of his followers in the last quarter of the 19C, and today it is a charming place to stay and absorb a little history, especially in its restaurant. The atmosphere is pleasant, characterful and unique, largely thanks to the efforts of Signor Vaudano and his family who have managed the place for more than half a century. The accommodation is less remarkable, but comfortable nonetheless.

Access
From Asti; SS 10 for 3.5km, then left for 17km

Sights nearby: Castle; Monta: Castello dei Morra, Santuario dei Piloni

22

LOCANDA MARTELLETTI

Fam. Dezzani
Piazza Statuto, 10
14023 Cocconato (AT)
Tel. 0141 907686 – Fax 0141 600033
info@locandamartelletti.it – www.locandamartelletti.it

55/ 95€

Open all year • 3 single rm, 3 double rm • Menu €20-30 • Parking, garden • Tasting and sale of regional specialities

Breakfast served in the delightful hanging garden with fine views over the hills.

At the top of the village, located on the square where the town hall stands, this 18C structure was built on the foundations of a 13C castle, traces of which are still visible inside. Although the original occupants, the noble Martellati family, are long gone, the building's history is very much in evidence from the wine cellars to the four old wells. These days, however, the rooms are very comfortable. The first floor restaurant is laid out over three elegant but intimate rooms.

Access
From Asti: SS 458 for 29km, then right for 2km

Sights nearby: Asti: cathedral, church and baptistery of San Pietro

23

ANTICO CASALE MATTEI

Sig.ra Valfrè
Via Cristoforo Colombo, 8
12040 Corneliano d'Alba (CN)
Tel. 0173 619920 – Fax 0173 619920
antico.casale.mattei@inwind.it

47/67€

Open all year • 4 double rm • No restaurant • Parking, garden

The original 19C wrought iron or wooden beds.

In the 18C the Mattei family built this fine farmhouse, with a typical Piedmontese balcony overlooking the inner courtyard. The property has been passed down through the generations to today's owners, who have converted it to offer superb accommodation without compromising the original structure. The simple rustic style, period furnishings, and excellent breakfast incorporating local produce add up to make this an attractive place to stay.

Access
From Asti: SS 231 for 24km, right onto the SP 29 for 2.5km, then left for 3.5km

Sights nearby: Alba: medieval historic centre

24

EDELWEISS

Sig. Facciola
Località Viceno
28862 Crodo (VB)
Tel. 0324 618791 – Fax 0324 600001
info@albergoedelweiss.com – www.albergoedelweiss.com

40/70€

Closed 13-31 Jan, 3-21 Nov • 9 single rm, 21 double rm • Half board €40-55 • Menu €21-31 • Parking, swimming pool, no dogs in the restaurant • Tasting of cured meats

The sports and leisure facilities.

In recent years, this classic mountain hotel 1000m up has undergone a hugely successful transformation both in terms of accommodation and service, making for a vastly improved place to stay and to eat. Today it is perhaps the liveliest of the Ossola area's establishments, popular with regulars and newcomers alike. Recently an indoor pool, sauna and gym have been opened, yet prices continue to be reasonable.

Access
From Verbania: SS 34 for 12km, onto the A 26 for 4km, then onto the SS 33 for 23.5km, right for 9.5km to Viceno

Sights nearby: Stresa: view of Lake Maggiore, Villa Pallavicino

25

CUNEO HOTEL

Sig.ra Allasina

Via Vittorio Amedeo II, 2
12100 Cuneo (CN)
Tel. 0171 681960 – Fax 0171 697128
albergosiesta@tin.it – www.albergosiesta.com

50-60/ 70-80€

Open all year • 10 single rm, 11 double rm • Breakfast €5 • No restaurant

The peaceful location: a short walk from Piazza Galimberti.

Cuneo is a classic backwater of provincial Italy, offering a stress free existence and life lived on a human scale. Historic palaces, churches, gateways, piazzas, cafés and gastronomic delights make this a great spot for those seeking total relaxation. This appropriately named hotel is popular with business travellers and tourists alike. Friendly family management, modern accommodation and comfortable public areas.

Sights nearby: Cuneo: Museo Civico, churches of Santa Chiara and Sant'Ambrogio, cathedral

26

LA BRICCOLA

Sig.ra Olivero

Via Farinetti, 9
12055 Diano d'Alba (CN)
Tel. 0173 468513 – Fax 0173 468513
labriccola@virgilio.it – www.labriccola.com

45-50/ 70-80€

Closed Jan • 4 double rm • Half board €60-70 • Menu €20-26 • Parking, garden • Wine for sale (tasting)

The fine views over vineyards from the rooms.

While her parents continue to tend their vines and hazel groves, wine expert Ivana has for some years run this establishment, a recently restored hundred year old farmhouse occupying a splendid location among the vines. The trattoria style restaurant has plenty of atmosphere with chandeliers, and bacchanalian frescoes, and accommodation is provided in four themed rooms: Diana, Cupid, Bacchus and Venus, the last of which has a four poster bed.

Access

From Asti: SS 231 for 29km to Alba, onto the SS 29 for 1km, then right onto the SP 32 for 2.5km

Sights nearby: Parish church; Alba: medieval historic centre

27

CAVALLO BIANCO

Sig.ra Belliardo
Piazza Manuel, 18
12025 Dronero (CN)
Tel. 0171 916590 – Fax 0171 916590
cavallo-bianco@libero.it – www.ilcavallobianco.com

35/56€

Open all year • 7 single rm, 11 double rm • Half board €40 • Menu €22-30

The owners' collection of items on display.

This attractive building is located in the centre of Donero, a charming town in the province of Cuneo. Situated in a side street away from the traffic, its interior is filled with ephemera (principally textiles and gramophones) and antiques. The best rooms are on the first floor; some retain their original frescoes. Up on the second floor, the accommodation is more modern but provides romantic views over the rooftops. Classic local fare and pizzas in the restaurant.

Access
From Cuneo: SS 22 for 18km

Sights nearby: Ponte del Diavolo, church of Santi Andrea e Ponzio, Loggia del Grano; Valle Maira: scenery

28

LA CASCINA DEL MONASTERO

Sig. Grasso

Cascina Luciani, 112/a - Fraz. Annunziata
12064 La Morra (CN)
Tel. 0173 509245 – Fax 0173 500861
info@cascinadelmonastero.it – www.cascinadelmonastero.it

75-80/ 85-100€

Closed 15 Dec-15 Jan • 10 double rm • No restaurant • Parking, garden, small dogs welcome • Bicycle hire, fishing, wine tasting

The splendid breakfast room, decorated with country furnishings.

This establishment dates from around 1600, when it was built as a dependant monastic farmstead growing grapes. Since then it has seen many come and go, including Pope Pius VII who in 1804 crowned Napoleon emperor, but its winemaking activities have continued without interruption. Staying here in October is particularly pleasant, when the grape harvest is in full swing and guests have a grandstand view of the action. Inside, great attention to detail is evident thanks to the passionate management of Guiseppe and Velda, who also oversaw the building's meticulous restoration. The play area and little lake will appeal to younger visitors.

Access

From Asti: SS 231 for 28.5km, then continue for 6km before turning right towards La Morra for 2km to Annunziata

Sights nearby: Alba: Medieval historic centre

29

CASCINA SAN BERNARDO

Sig.ra Raballo
Via Adele Alfieri, 31
12050 Magliano Alfieri (CN)
Tel. 0173 66427 – Fax 0173 66427
info@cascinasanbernardo.com – www.cascinasanbernardo.com

65-70/75-80€

Closed 15 Dec-30 Jan • 6 single rm, 6 double rm • No restaurant • Parking, garden, no dogs

The manor-style association between the house and its surrounding landscape.

Built in 1887 and subsequently sold to the family which continues to own it today, this building has been carefully restored and is the archetypal patrician residence, with an imposing brick entrance and a setting providing stunning views over the hills and villages of the Roero district. The charming breakfast room is the former tool store although in summer, breakfast is taken outside to a backdrop of fruit orchards. The comfortable rooms have imposing wrought iron beds and modern bathrooms.

Access
From Asti: SS 231 for 18km, then right for 1.9km

Sights nearby: Castello degli Alfieri; Castellinaldo: castle

30

CA' DUBINI

Sig. Dubini

Via Roma, 17
15015 Mombello Monferrato (AL)
Tel. 0142 944116 – Fax 0142 944928
info@cadubini.it – www.cadubini.it

45€

Closed 1-20 Aug • 4 double rm • No restaurant • Parking • Tasting of regional produce

The harmonious period furnishings.

In the heart of the tranquil Monferrato area and conveniently placed for excursions into the surrounding countryside and the hills around Turin, Asti and Alessandria, Mombello is a typical farming village part of which extends across a wooded hill. Once resplendent with vines, just a few vineyards survive nowadays; those that do produce an excellent, high-quality Barbera wine. Ca' Dubini is the perfect base from which to explore this fascinating region. The property is an old farmstead whose stylish public rooms are furnished with period pieces and traditional terracotta floors. The bedrooms here are simple, yet elegant.

Access

From Alessandria: A 26 for 29km to Casale Monferrato exit, SS 31 for 4km, then SS 457 for 10km and SS 590 for 8km

Sights nearby: Vezzolano: Abbey

31

IL GRILLO PARLANTE

Sig. Clerico

Frazione Rinaldi 47, Località Sant'Anna
12065 Monforte d'Alba (CN)
Tel. 0173 789228 – Fax 0173 789228
info@piemonte-it.com – www.piemonte-it.com

49-55/60-70€

Open all year • 6 double rm • Breakfast €8 • No restaurant • Parking, garden, small dogs welcome

The ideal atmosphere in which to enjoy country life.

The outlying property of a small hamlet reached by a dirt track, this colourful hotel's isolated setting is the perfect location from which to enjoy the Langhe countryside. Everything here is fresh and new, including the young management team. Simple yet tasteful furnishings in keeping with the rustic setting. Wonderful views from the breakfast area and some of the rooms, particularly in the morning.

Access
From Asti: SS 231 for 25.5km, then 17km on the SP 9 to Sant'Anna

Sights nearby: Historic centre

32

BELVEDERE

F.lli Triverio

Vicolo San Giovanni, 3
12046 Montà (CN)
Tel. 0173 976156 – Fax 0173 975587
info@albergobelvedere.com – www.albergobelvedere.com

65/90€

Closed 7-15 Jan, 26 Jul-7 Aug • 10 double rm • Half board €70 • Menu €20 • Parking, garden, no dogs • Wine for sale (tasting)

The excellent value for money.

In the heart of the Roero district, less well known than the Langhe yet equally attractive, this establishment set among vineyards and fruit orchards is an excellent base from which to explore the area. In a quiet hillside location on the outskirts, Emilia and Marco Triverio offer accommodation which is unusually spacious, decorated in late 19C local style. The restaurant occupies a charming room, and in summer also spills out onto a delightful terrace covered by oak trees.

Access

From Asti: SS 10 for 3.5km, onto the SP 58 for 21km to Canale, then right onto the SS 29 for 1.2km

Sights nearby: Castello dei Morra, Santuario dei Piloni

33

B&B ABBAZIA IL ROSETO

Sig.ra Demichelis

Via Roma, 38
12060 Novello (CN)
Tel. 0173 744016 – Fax 0173 744016
info@abbaziailroseto.com – www.abbaziailroseto.com

60/70-75€

Closed Jan • 6 double rm • No restaurant • Parking, garden, no dogs

The spectacular view of Monviso from the balcony of room 3.

Located on the road heading into Novello, this 15C abbey was once renowned for its rose garden. Much has changed over the years although the building retains a great deal of its original charm. Six rooms are available to guests; all have open fireplaces and tastefully selected period style furnishings (rugs, wrought iron beds and wooden furniture). Breakfast is served in the characterful surroundings of the brick built former wine cellars.

Access
From Cuneo: SS 564 for 48km

Sights nearby: Bra: historic centre

34

IL NOCCIOLETO

Sig.ra Rigoni
Località Chiarene, 4
12060 Novello (CN)
Tel. 0173 731323 – Fax 0173 731251
info@ilnoccioleto.com – www.ilnoccioleto.com

40/ 70€

Closed Jan • 1 single rm, 7 double rm • Half board €42 • Menu €24-30 • Parking, garden, swimming pool • Bicycle hire, hazelnuts and wine for sale

The children's area of the garden.

Set deep in the countryside, this attractive building provides comfortable spacious accommodation and pleasant grounds. A former barracks, it opened as an agriturismo a few years ago, following a sensitive restoration project. Vineyards and hazelnut trees surround the property, and there is a garden with swimming pool. Traditional Langhe cuisine in the restaurant, with home made pasta and a wide selection of meat dishes.

Access
From Asti: SS 231 for 25km to Alba, onto the SP 9 for 10km, then onto the SP 3 for 9km to Novello, right for 2.5km to Chiarene

Sights nearby: Alba: medieval historic centre

35

LA CONTRADA DEI MONTI

Fam. Ronchetti
Via dei Monti, 10
28016 Orta San Giulio (NO)
Tel. 0322 905114 – Fax 0322 905863
lacontradadeimonti@libero.it – www.orta.net/lacontradadeimonti

90/110€

Closed Jan • 9 single rm, 8 double rm • No restaurant • Garden, small dogs welcome

The room with sloping wood roof.

The village of Orta has a charm of its own, with its old centre of alleys and historic buildings, and stunning views over the mountains, the lake and the magical island of San Giulio. Located in the heart of Orta, this elegantly genteel and comfortable hotel is close to the picturesque Piazza Motta. Breakfast is served in an attractive room with beamed ceilings and stone walls, while the lobby has an open fireplace with comfortable armchairs and sofas.

Access
From Novara: SS 229 for 45km

Sights nearby: Palazzotto, Lago d'Orta, Isola di San Giulio, Sacro Monte d'Orta

36

RELAIS IL BORGO

Sig. Firato e Sig.ra Comollo

a Cioccaro, Via Biletta, 60
14030 Penango (AT)
Tel. 0141 921272 – Fax 0141 923067
fabiofirato@virgilio.it – www.ilborgodicioccaro.com

100€

Closed 20 Dec-15 Jan • 12 double rm • Breakfast €10; half board €110 • Menu €50-60 • Parking, garden, swimming pool, no dogs in the restaurant

Enjoying the scenery of hillsides and farms from the comfort of a poolside lounger.

This farmstead has been comprehensively restored with due respect to the region's architectural heritage; beyond the lobby is a small courtyard encircled by a balcony giving access to the rooms. Each of these is named after a plant species, and the elegance of the furnishings and attention to detail compare favourably to the area's most distinguished hotels. The public areas are thoughtfully laid out (TV room, library, meeting room), and the courtyard has an unusual circular swimming pool and garden furniture.

Access
From Asti: SS 457 for 18km, then right for 2km to Cioccaro

Sights nearby: Asti: Cathedral, church and baptistery of San Pietro

37

VILLA CONTE RICCARDI

Sig. Mondino

Via al Monte, 7
14030 Rocca d'Arazzo (AT)
Tel. 0141 408565 – Fax 0141 408565
villacontericcardi@libero.it – www.villacontericcardi.it

40-54/ 70-90€

Open all year • 5 single rm, 27 double rm • Half board €55-65 • Menu €20-55 • Parking, garden, swimming pool, tennis, golf, no dogs in the restaurant • Organised trips and walks

The elegant façade of this villa against the parkland backdrop.

It comes as no surprise to learn that this house was once a bishop's residence. The whole building has an air of noble refinement, its bricks laid to create horizontal and vertical banding which divides the facade into symmetrical blocks, surmounted by a small angular tower. The decoration of the rooms differs according to the floors on which they are situated; modern on ground level, classical on the first floor, and an intimate atmosphere with floral wallpaper under the eaves on the second floor. Situated in attractive parkland, providing a relaxing atmosphere in which to stroll beneath the trees.

Access

10km southeast of Asti

Sights nearby: Asti: Cathedral, church and baptistery of San Pietro

38

CASCINA TOETTO

Sig.ra Rubello
Località Toetto, 2
12060 Roddi (CN)
Tel. 0173 615622 – Fax 0173 620002
info@cascinatoetto.it – www.cascinatoetto.it

50/70€

Open all year • 2 single rm, 3 double rm • No restaurant • Parking, garden • Bicycle hire

The aroma of grilled meats wafting across the verdant garden.

The Roddi plain lies among Piemonte's Langhe hills, close to the spot where the tributary waters of the Talloria flow into the Tanaro river. Built in 1939, this farmstead was recently restored to provide accommodation in the shape of five welcoming and spacious rooms furnished in period style. To the front of the two buildings which make up this establishment (the farmhouse and the former hay barn) are the well kept gardens, offering barbecue facilities and archery. A good base from which to discover the area's gastronomic delights.

Access
From Asti: SS 231 for 28.5km, then right for 2.5km

Sights nearby: Castle; Alba: medieval historic centre

39

LE DUE CASCINE

Sig. Assenza Parisi

Regione Mariano, 22
14050 San Marzano Oliveto (AT)
Tel. 0141 824525 – Fax 0141 829028
info@leduecascine.com – www.leduecascine.com

40/ 70€

Open all year • 10 double rm • Half board €55 • Menu €15-20 • Parking, garden, swimming pool, small dogs welcome • Organised trips, jam, wine and home grown produce for sale

The cuisine and the wines; contrasting elements despite their shared heritage.

Assisted by their husbands, the two sisters who inherited this establishment run a sixteen hectare farm dedicated to winemaking. In addition to their agricultural activities, they offer accommodation in the 'new' farmhouse, the rooms accessed directly from a single balcony typical of Piedmontese domestic architecture. The traditional Monferrato cooking uses mostly home grown produce, transformed into cuisine which strongly reflects the area's rural heritage.

Access

From Asti: SS 531 for 5km, left onto SS 456 for 13km, then right for 6km to Regione Mariano

Sights nearby: Asti: Cathedral, church and baptistery of San Pietro

40

LE ARCATE

Sig.ra Manzone

Località Gabutto, 2
12050 Sinio (CN)
Tel. 0173 613152 – Fax 0173 613152
learcate@yahoo.it – www.agriturismolearcate.it

62€

Closed 8 Jan-15 Feb • 8 double rm • Half board €48-50 • Menu €15-25 • Parking • Tasting and sale of honey, hazelnuts and wine

The view from the picture windows of Monviso, beyond vineyards and hazelnut groves.

Situated on the banks of the river Talloria downstream from Alba, Sinio is a village of medieval origin, dominated to this day by its castle standing guard over the road heading south. From the large arched windows, guests enjoy spectacular views of the undulating hills rolling to the horizon, the stark profile of Monviso rising in the distance. Traditional Piedmontese cuisine features prominently in the restaurant; dishes such as bagnacauda, vitello tonnato and brasato are all naturally accompanied by fine wines from the Langhe or Roero.

Access

From Asti: SS 231 for 25km to Alba, onto the SP 9 for 7.5km, then onto the SP 30 for 5.8km, left for 3.7km to Gabutto

Sights nearby: Alba: medieval historic centre

41

CASA BRANZELE

Sig. Bianco

Via Cappelletto, 27
12050 Trezzo Tinella (CN)
Tel. 0173 630000 – Fax 0173 630907
info@casabranzele.com – www.casabranzele.com

50-80/75-90€

Closed 7-31 Jan • 5 double rm • No restaurant • Parking, garden

Wandering among the hazelnut groves with the hillside views beyond.

Ideal for visitors seeking a peaceful hotel in the Langhe countryside, this fine 19C country residence has been comprehensively restored by its current owners, a friendly young couple who are psychologists by training. They are not the only people to have been charmed by this building sitting among vineyards and hazelnut groves. It has five simple yet charming rooms, some of which retain an old Piedmontese-style upper level. Also worthy of note is the excellent breakfast comprising local products.

Access
From Asti: SS 231 for 10km, then left for 17km

Sights nearby: Alba: Historic medieval centre

42

SACRO MONTE

Comune di Varallo

Località Sacro Monte, 14
13019 Varallo (VC)
Tel. 0163 54254 – Fax 0163 51189
albergosacromonte@libero.it

43-55/75-85€

Closed Nov-Mar • 3 single rm, 21 double rm • Half board €47-57 • Menu €25-45 • Parking, garden, no dogs in the restaurant

The tranquillity of this former pilgrims' hostel.

Overlooking the Sacro Monte, a pilgrimage site of national importance, from which it derives its name, this establishment has a long history. Founded in 1594 at the behest of the local bishop to provide shelter for pilgrims, it has been restored to offer up to date accommodation without detracting from its original charm. The delightful restaurant has an open fireplace, wood flooring and antique tools decorating its walls; the cuisine it serves has a strong regional identity.

Access
From Novara: SS 299 for 56km to Varallo, then right for 4km to Sacro Monte

Sights nearby: Sacro Monte

43

IL MONTEROSSO

Fam. Minotti

Via Cima Monterosso, 30
28922 Verbania (VB)
Tel. 0323 556510 – Fax 0323 519706
ilmonterosso@iol.it

30-40/60-75€

Closed Jan, Feb • 1 single rm, 8 double rm • Half board €50-58 • Menu €20 • Parking, garden • Horse riding , bicycle hire, tastings of jam and cured meat

The view of the lake from the house, set among trees.

A ring of forested peaks surrounds the peaceful waters of the lake, making for fine views from the imposing stone tower of this 19C house. The accommodation offers total tranquillity, interrupted only by the occasional lowing of cattle or neighing from the adjacent stables, where horses may be hired for exploring the surrounding woodland.

Access

From Verbania: SS 34 towards Casale for 5km, then right for 0.7km to Cima Monterosso

Sights nearby: Lake views; Isole Borromee; Verbania: Pallanza, Villa Taranto

44

AQUADOLCE

Sig.ra Elisabetta Bartolucci

Via Cietti, 1
28922 Verbania Pallanza (VB)
Tel. 0323 505418 – Fax 0323 557534
info@hotelaquadolce.it – www.hotelaquadolce.it

65-80/75-105€

Closed 15 Jan-28 Feb • 1 single rm, 12 double rm • No restaurant • No dogs

The views from the rooms on the upper floors.

A small gem in the centre of the old town, facing the lakefront in the elegant Verbano district. Far from the fashionable hustle and bustle of Stresa, but still facing the Isole Borromee, this 19C hotel has recently undergone sensitive renovation. Almost all the guestrooms have views of the lake and are furnished in arte povera style. A copious buffet breakfast is served in a light and spacious room next to reception. Aquadolce attracts a mix of Italian and foreign guests who are admirably taken care of by the young and enthusiastic staff.

Sights nearby: Lake views, Isole Borromee, VillaTaranto

45

DI VIN ROERO

Sig. Grasso

Piazza San Martino, 5
12040 Vezza d'Alba (CN)
Tel. 0173 65114 – Fax 0173 658111

42/52€

Open all year • 4 double rm • Half board €30-40 • Menu €20-30 • Garden

The finest traditions of the Roero, namely good food and wine, united under one roof.

Given the area's reputation for producing fine red and white wines, this establishment's choice of name is unsurprising. Located among the Cuneo hills, the ambience is friendly and simple, with the walls painted a lively yellow throughout. Irresistible Piedmontese cuisine with particular emphasis on Roero specialities.

Access

From Asti: SS 231 for 20km, then right for 8km

Sights nearby: Castle ruins; Castellinaldo: medieval castle; Magliano Alfieri: Castello degli Alfieri

PUGLIA

In recent years, this region has experienced a reawakening of interest on the part of independent minded travellers. The attractions of its seaside resorts, particularly those of the Gargano peninsula and the south coast between Otranto and Gallipoli, most notably Santa Maria de Leuca, have played a large part in this, but visitors are increasingly heading inland to discover the delights of the real Puglia among its extensive olive groves. In addition to its natural beauty, the region's rich cultural heritage is remarkably evenly distributed, making some of its smaller towns just as interesting as the big cities. Thus, while the streets and alleys of Bari and Lecce clearly deserve exploration, so the lesser centres of Trani, Barletta, Lucera and Ostuni are also guaranteed to surprise and inspire those who seek them out. Other important landmarks include the *trulli* of Alberobello and Frederick II's castles.

Puglia's cuisine has also grown in reputation over the last few years. Drawing upon excellent natural produce, this simple fare is best savoured at one of the hundreds of little festivals held across the region, mainly in the summer months.

7 establishments

Vasto
Tremiti
Termoli
177
S 16
A 14
Vieste
Promontorio del Gargano
300
1055
E 55
S. Severo
Manfredonia
Lucera
137
Foggia
S 17
2
A 14
49
S 16
S 90
Barletta
Trani
Molfet
Cerignola
111
Canosa
Andria
Ariano Irpino
E 842
A 16
70
Bitonto
PUGLIA
123
243
Melfi
105
Altamura
50
Avellino
37
S 655
Matera
Salerno
Potenza
A 3
107
144
S 407
E 847
Amalfi
Battipaglia
Paestum
262
S 18
227
205
302
Sapri
M. Pollino
2248
E 45

Bari
Durrës
Bari
S 16
E 55
84
5
Fasano
3
111
Brindisi
Martina Franca
S 100
S 7 - E 90
S 7
215
4
S 16
69
39
S 7ter
Taranto
Manduria
88
Lecce
Igoumenítsa
Pátra
45
Otranto
S 16
7
Gallipoli
6
1
Golfo di Taranto
C. Sta Maria di Leuca

1

MASSERIA MACURANO

Sig. Lugli
Contrada Macuran, 134
73031 Alessano (LE)
Tel. 0833 524287
macurano@masseriamacurano.com – www.masseriamacurano.com

40/ 80€

Closed 1 Nov-16 Apr • 4 double rm • Menu €15-20 • Parking, garden, no dogs • Organised trips, bicycles available, oil for sale

The charming high vaulted ceilings.

Situated in the southernmost part of the Salento, this 16C fortified farmhouse is roughly equidistant from the Adriatic and Ionian coasts. Sensitively restored without detracting from the original features, the building is a classic example of the domestic architecture prevalent in this far flung corner of the peninsula. The owner is a sculptor, originally from Modena, and the simply furnished rooms are remarkable for their size. Homely cuisine focusing on local dishes.

Access
From Lecce: SS 16 for 30km to Gagliano al Capo exit; then onto SS 275 for 27km to Alessano, from where signs lead to Macurano

Sights nearby: Grotta Zinzalusa; Otranto: Castello Aragonese, cathedral, church of San Pietro

2

PIANN DE NIJ

Fam. Gallucci

Bosco Comunale, località Piano delle Noci
71020 Faeto (FG)
Tel. 0881 973014 – Fax 0881 973014

25-30/50-60€

Open all year • 1 single rm, 15 double rm • Half board €40-45 • Menu €15-35 • Parking, garden, no dogs in the restaurant

The airiness of the rooms, cool even on the hottest summer days.

Faeto is notable for being Puglia's highest place at 886m, and the surrounding woodlands are popular with city dwellers from Bari and Foggia who come here to escape the worst of the summer heat. Well placed to offer hospitality to visitors, this simple establishment is closer to a mountain refuge in style than a hotel. Informality and simple modern furnishings are the order of the day, and traditional Apulian cuisine prevails in the restaurant.

Access

From Foggia: SS 17 to Lucera exit, then onto the SS 109 to Troia, then right for 18km to Piano delle Noci

Sights nearby: Troia: Cathedral

3

MASSERIA NARDUCCI

Sig. Narducci
Via Lecce, 131
72016 Montalbano di Fasano (BR)
Tel. 080 4810185 – Fax 080 4810185
agriturismo_narducci@yahoo.com – www.agriturismonarducci.it

70/90€

Open all year • 9 double rm • Half board €50-60 • Menu €30-45 • Parking, garden, no dogs • Tastings of jam, oil and rosolio liqueur

The charming and welcoming dining room.

Part of the historical fabric of the landscape, this 19C building began as a post office and retains the typical characteristics of the region's farmhouses, namely functionality and simplicity. Today it is an oasis of peace and tranquillity, sited among gardens and surrounded by the Apulian countryside. Produce grown in the neighbouring fields can be purchased directly, or savoured in the restaurant, a gem of a place serving local specialities.

Access

From Brindisi: SS 379 for 41km to Speziale exit, continue for 4km to SS 16, right for 1.2km

Sights nearby: Brindisi: Castello Svevo, Roman column, Piazza Duomo, church of Santa Lucia and San Giovanni al Sepolcro

4

CASTELLO

Sig.ra Scianaro

Piazza Vittorio Emanuele II, 2
72023 Mesagne (BR)
Tel. 0831 777500 – Fax 0831 777500
info@hotel-castello.com – www.hotel-castello.com

45-50/68-80€

Open all year • 12 double rm • No restaurant

The robust architecture typical of Norman Puglia.

Around the year 1400 a small Franciscan convent was built in Mesagne, an austere and solid building archetypal of the age. Following the suppression of the monastic houses in the Napoleonic era, the main building became a barracks in 1809, and it was not until 1922 that it came into private hands and was converted into a hotel. Today it is a solid, well presented establishment, the ideal base from which to discover the region (close to the railway station).

Access
From Brindisi: SS 7 for 13km

Sights nearby: Tempietto di San Lorenzo, churches of SS. Annunziata and dell'Immacolata, Santuario del Carmine

5

LE CASEDDE

Sig.ra Lacenere
Strada Provinciale 239
70015 Noci (BA)
Tel. 080 4978946 – Fax 080 4978946
info@lecasedde.com – www.lecasedde.com

50/57€

Open all year • 5 double rm • Breakfast €5; half board €52 • Menu €21-23 • Parking, garden, tennis, bowls, no dogs • Organised trips and jams, oil and wine for sale

The unique experience of spending the night in a trullo.

A genuine agriturismo where simplicity goes hand in hand with hospitality. Accommodation comes in the form of trulli, the well known characteristic dwellings of the Puglia region, decorated in a contemporary style and offering a comfortable ambience. A few other rooms and the public areas are in a larger building which has an imposing open fireplace. Strategically located in the centre of an area teeming with places of interest, and 20km from the sea.

Access
From Bari: SS 100 for 39km to Gioia del Colle, then left onto the SS 604 for 13km

Sights nearby: Alberobello: trulli district

6

A CASA TU MARTINU

S.M.A.V. Immobiliare Srl

Via Corsica, 97
73057 Taviano (LE)
Tel. 0833 913652 – Fax 0833 913652
casatumartinu@tiscali.it – www.acasatumartinu.it

45/80-95€

Closed 14 Sep-14 Oct • 11 double rm • Half board €60-70 • Menu €18-27 • Garden, no dogs • Organised trips

The delightful garden illuminated at night.

One of the best places in the Salento, located in the historic heart of Taviano near the church of Santa Lucia. A classic 18C patrician palace, its simple façade is whitewashed to reflect the glare of the scorching sun. Well presented accommodation with period style furnishings, but the real gem here is the charming courtyard garden, a typical feature of the palaces of southern Italy, where the lucky few could relax in total privacy from the public eye.

Access
From Lecce: SS 101 for 37km, then onto the SS 274 for 7km

Sights nearby: Gallipoli: castle, cathedral, church of la Purità

7

MASSERIA GATTAMORA

Sig.ra Baldassarre

Via Campo Sportivo, 33
73020 Uggiano la Chiesa (LE)
Tel. 0836 817936 – Fax 0836 814542
baldassarre@woow.it – www.gattamora.it

40-55/70-100€

Closed Jan • 2 single rm, 9 double rm • Half board €72 • Menu €25-35 • Parking, garden, no dogs • Sailing trips, bicycle hire

The coloured Lecce stone in the vaulted ceilings.

Situated on the outskirts of the village, this long 19C farmhouse has a whitewashed façade. Inside the look is altogether more striking; a vast structure, the walls of local stone supporting the vaulted roof. In the restaurant are two rows of columns supporting star vaults giving the appearance of a church rather than a converted stable block. The same style is in evidence in the rooms, their bare walls of hewn stone possessing an unusual charm.

Access
From Lecce: SS 16 for 30km to Maglie exit, towards Otranto for 9km, then right for 5km

Sights nearby: Otranto: Castello Aragonese, cathedral, church of San Pietro

Bonifacio
Bouches de Bonifacio
Sta Teresa Gallura
Maddalena
Palau
Asinara
Propriano Genova
Golfo Aranci
Civitavecchia
1
7
Tempio Pausania 63
Olbia
Porto Torres
S 199
Sassari
25
95
S 597
S 125
Siniscola
Alghero
Ozieri
S 131
S 131d
2
229
110
Bosa
192
Nuoro
G N A
Macomer
286
6
Monti del Gennargentu
Tirso
SARDEGNA
Arbatax
Genova Civitavecchi
Oristano
Laconi
S 131
Guspini
94
Iglesias
Muravera
5
S. Pietro
3
Carbonia
4
Cagliari
S. Antioco
Genova
Civitavecchia
Napoli
Palermo
Trapani
Tunis

SARDEGNA

Nuraghic evidence suggests activity on the island as early as 1800 BC, from which point onwards Sardinia was subject to successive conquests by maritime powers, including the Phoenicians, Romans, Vandals, Byzantines, Saracens, Pisans, Genoese, Spaniards and Austrians. Traces of their presence are strewn across the island, but most notably in the coastal towns. Inland, the beautiful but wild landscape has been more resistant to conquest.

Today, Sardinia is known throughout the world for its stunning coastline and archipelagos, which every summer draw huge numbers of visitors, including many big spenders. Despite this, it is still possible to avoid the famous resorts and instead seek out an unspoilt corner of natural paradise.

The cuisine is worthy of special mention: specialities include *carasau* (soft-doughed bread), *sebadas* (round doughnuts) and *papassinos* (desserts). Worthy of mention also are the Vermentino (white) and Cannonau (red) wines as well as the myrtle liqueur.

7 establishments

1

IL MUTO DI GALLURA

Sig. Serra
Località Fraiga
07020 Aggius (SS)
Tel. 079 620559 – Fax 079 620559
info@mutodigallura.com – www.mutodigallura.com

45/80€

Open all year • 1 single rm, 12 double rm • Half board €70 • Menu €16-35 • Parking, garden, swimming pool, no dogs • Horse riding, bicycles available, cheese and wine tasting

The heritage conserved in the choice of name.

In the mid 19C, a feud between the families of two young lovers resulted in more than 70 deaths around Aggius. To this day, local folklore recalls the muto di Gallura (the 'Gallura mute'), a hitman who has become a figure of romantic nostalgia. The spirit of the district is best discovered by walking or riding through the countryside, a timeless landscape as venerable as any Sardinian tradition.

Access

From Sassari: SS 131 towards Oristano, left onto the SS 597 for 5km, then left onto the SS 672, onto the SS 127 for 15km, then left to Fraiga

Sights nearby: Golfo dell'Asinara; Arcipelago della Maddalena National Park

SA PISCHEDDA

Sig. Piscedda

Via Roma, 8
08013 Bosa (NU)
Tel. 0785 373065 – Fax 0785 372000
asapischedda@tiscali.it – www.hotelsapischedda.it

35-70/ 45-85€

Open all year • 9 single rm, 9 double rm • Breakfast €7; half board €49-69 • Menu €30-40 • Parking, garden • Sailing, water skiing

The unusual interior, with frescoes and a strong Mediterranean feel.

Named after the owner (the term means a type of basket in local dialect), this establishment is a slice of the real Sardinia, where the island's sense of identity is alive and well. Situated in the centre of Bosa, one of the prettiest towns in the area, it occupies a 19C palazzo. This building also hosts a permanent exhibition of works of art by the painter Eugenio Scheler, whose frescoes adorn the lobby and some of the rooms, making a stay here an even more memorable experience.

Access
From Nuoro: SS 292 for 56km to Suni, then left for 6.5km

Sights nearby: Castello di Serravalle, Torre dell'Isola Rossa, churches of San Pietro and Santa Maria del Mare

3

BELLAVISTA

Sig.ra Tregosti

Via Sottotorre, 7
09011 Calasetta (CA)
Tel. 0781 88971 – Fax 0781 88211
tregomar@tiscali.it – www.calasettabellavista.it

55-61/84-94€

Closed 4 Nov-15 Dec • 2 single rm, 10 double rm • Half board €73-80 • Menu €30-50 • Garden, no dogs

We most liked

Watching the sun go down over the island of San Pietro.

This is not the place for those few unmoved by Sardinia's culture of cuisine and the sea. This little hotel has a simple façade and is attractively situated on a low hill above the beach with views over the island of San Pietro, separated by a narrow strip of water from the peninsula of Sant'Antioco. The restaurant has two appealing features, namely its terrace and the traditional Sardinian cuisine, including some interesting cheeses.

Access

From Cagliari: SS 130 for 50km to Domusnovas, left for 21km to Santa Maria del Flumentepido, then left onto the SS 126 for 29km

Sights nearby: Ruins and necropoli of Sulcis; Sant'Antioco: basilica and catacombs

4

SU MERIAGU

Sig.re Laconi e figli
Via Rimini, 1
09045 Quartu Sant'Elena (CA)
Tel. 070 890842 – Fax 070 890842
sumeriagu@tiscali.it – www.sardegnasud.it

50/70-85€

Open all year • 3 single rm, 5 double rm • Half board €55-70 • Menu €10-35 • Parking, garden, no dogs • Wine for sale

The pride in all things Sardinian, especially matters culinary.

Sant' Andrea is a small settlement on the road which runs east from Cagliari along the gulf of Quartu. The hotel is close to the sea and derives its name from a local term meaning a shaded grazing area. Inside, the modern decor has a tasteful personal feel. Two pleasant rooms; one small and cosy with open fireplace, the other larger and circular with a single central column supporting the ceiling beams. The island's traditional crafts are evoked in the choice of decorative items.

Access
From Cagliari: SP 17 towards Villasimius for 15km to Sant'Andrea

Sights nearby: Cagliari: Museo Nazionale Archeologico, cathedral, towers of San Pancrazio and l'Elefante

5

HIERACON

Arches Srl

Corso Cavour, 32
09014 Carloforte (CA)
hotelhieracon@tiscali.it – www.hotelhieracon.cjb.net

45-57/ 68-98€

Open all year • 3 single rm, 15 double rm • Breakfast €4; half board €60-75 • Menu €22-40 • Garden, no dogs

Enjoying the cool mornings beneath the garden's palm trees.

Hieracon was the Greek name for the island of San Pietro, and although this former private residence does not date back to ancient times, it has some history to it. The façade is in the decorated style of the early 20C, its austere upper storey profile broken up by floral detail surrounding the windows. There is a well planted inner courtyard garden where breakfast may be taken; the seafront is a stone's throw away, while the port and centre of town are also easily reached.

Access

By ferry from Portovesme di Portoscuso or Calasetta

Sights nearby: Coastline and scenery of Sardegna and the island of Sant'Antioco

6

ANTICA DIMORA DEL GRUCCIONE

Sig.ra Belloni

Via Michele Obinu, 31
09010 Santo Lussurgiu (OR)
Tel. 0783 552035 – Fax 0783 552036
info@anticadimora.com – www.anticadimora.com

35-38/70-76€

Closed 7-31 Jan • 3 single rm, 5 double rm • Half board €57-60 • Menu €25-30 • Small dogs welcome

The family's love of nature

Situated at an altitude of 500m in the Parco Naturalistico del Sinis-Montiferru, Santu Lussurgiu is a typical inland medieval village, located 30km from the sea, and is an ideal base for visitors wishing to explore this lesser-known part of Sardinia. The Antica Dimora is a stone mansion whose architecture shows clear evidence of Spain's former influence over the island. An imposing doorway leads to the internal courtyard, which is the perfect spot in which to sit and relax, surrounded by greenery and attractive climbing plants. The well-appointed rooms are discreetly comfortable, while the restaurant serves a selection of genuine Sardinian dishes.

Access

From Oristano: SS 388 for 24km

Sights nearby: San Leonardo di Siete Fuentes: church and seven springs

7

DEPALMAS PIETRO

Sig. Depalmas
Località Preddu Nieddu
07040 Stintino (SS)
Tel. 079 523129

23-28/46-56€

Open all year • 2 single rm, 4 double rm • Breakfast €3.50; half board €41-46 • Menu €25-30 • Parking, garden, no dogs in the restaurant

Views of the sea to both east and west.

This establishment was a restaurant until recently enhanced by the addition of simple, welcoming accommodation from where guests may enjoy the tranquillity of their surroundings. The emphasis remains very much on food; most of the meat is reared by the proprietor and often cooked over the open fire in the dining room. Ideally situated near the famous beach at Pellosa, on the Stintino peninsula from where there are views of the gulf of Asinara and the Sardinian sea.

Access
From Sassari: SGC 131 for 15km to Porto Torres, then right for 15km to Pozzo San Nicola, right for 10km, then left for 2km

Sights nearby: Sassari: Museo Nazionale Sanna, cathedral; Saccargia: church of SS. Trinità

SICILIA

Lying at the very heart of the Mediterranean, Sicily is a historical chronicle. Greeks, Romans, Arabs, Normans, Spaniards and French have left their mark here, among its incredibly varied landscape and extraordinarily hospitable people. From the alleys of Ortigia to the summits of its volcanic peaks, on its protected beaches, and in its little mountain villages perched on rocky outcrops, there is infinite variety which never fails to surprise the visitor. The numerous archipelagos skirting the island are especially popular with those who love the sea.

Sicily's cuisine is justly renowned, and the mere mention of a few of its dishes should get mouths watering. Specialities include *arancini di riso* (rice balls), *pasta alla Norma* (with aubergines, tomatoes and ricotta cheese), *sarde a beccafico* (sardines), *cannoli* (filled with ricotta and candied fruit) and *cassata* (partly-iced cream cake), ice cream and *granite*. Needless to say, these specialities are best accompanied by a glass of the local wine: Alcamo, Etna Rosso, Malvasia delle Lipari, Moscato di Pantelleria and Marsala to name but a few.

10 establishments

Ustica

Cagliari
Genova
Livorno
Napoli

PALERMO

Cagliari
Tunis

6
Monreale

Erice
Trapani
Egadi
104
Alcamo
A 19
47
Cefa
A 20
Marettimo
10
Segesta
Termini
Imerese
A 19
271
Favignana
E 932
Marsala
104
72
126
66
Castelvetrano
A 29
S 189
Mazara d. Vallo
E 90
S 115
Sciacca
Caltanissetta
94
S 640
73
E 931
Canicattì
Agrigento
80
S 115
Licata

S I C I L I A

Pantelleria (I)

Isole Lipari
Stromboli
Salina
Vulcano
Vibo Valentia
Gioia Tauro
Messina
Milazzo
Villa S. Giovanni
Reggio di Calabria
Locri
Barcellona Pozzo di Gotto
Taormina
M. Etna
3340
1847
SICILIA
Acireale
Catania
Piazza Armerina
Lentini
Caltagirone
Siracusa
Ragusa
Modica
Noto
C. Passero
S 280
240
S 106
S 113
S 114
S 115
S 417
A 3
A 18
A 19
A 20
E 45
E 90
231
153
1
2
3
4
5
7
8
9

1

TENUTA DI ROCCADIA

Sig. Vacirca
Contrada Roccadia
96013 Carlentini (SR)
Tel. 095 990362 – Fax 095 990362
info@roccadia.com – www.roccadia.com

49-68/74-96€

Open all year • 20 double rm • Half board €62-87 • Menu €20-35 • Parking, garden, swimming pool, no dogs in the restaurant • Tasting and sale of cheese, oil, jam and liqueurs

The home grown produce, ripened in the Sicilian sun.

No corner of Sicily is without traces of the island's long history, and this district is no exception. This agriturismo is located in an archaeological area where excavations have revealed an ancient necropolis. Today's landscape is agricultural, producing olives and citrus fruits which are used for making jams and liqueurs as well as for immediate consumption. The simple rooms are decorated in rustic style. Activities include swimming, riding and archery.

Access
From Siracusa: SS 14 for 29km, then left for 18km to Roccadia

Sights nearby: Parco archeologico di Leontinoi

LA VECCHIA PALMA

Sig. e Sig.ra Calvino

Via Etnea, 668
95128 Catania (CT)
Tel. 095 432025 – Fax 095 431107
info@lavecchiapalma.com – www.lavecchiapalma.com

65-70/ 100-110€

Open all year • 1 single rm, 9 double rm • No restaurant • Organised trips

The patrician elegance of this villa in old Catania.

Located on via Etnea, the street which runs through the centre of Catania towards the summit of Mount Etna, this hotel is an elegant 19C villa retaining its original interior layout and small courtyards. The period ambience is especially strong in the rooms, furnished with antique pieces and decorated with frescoes and original stucco work on the ceilings.

Sights nearby: Cathedral, Palazzo Biscari, Badia di Sant'Agata, Via Etnea, Via Crociferi, Teatro antico

3

BAGLIO SAN PIETRO

Baglio San Pietro Sas
Via panotto - Contrada San Pietro
94014 Nicosia (EN)
Tel. 0935 640529 – Fax 0935 640651
info@bagliosanpietro.com – www.bagliosanpietro.com

38/76€

Closed 5 Mar-27 Mar, 13-27 Nov • 9 double rm • Half board €56 • Menu €16-24 • Parking, garden, swimming pool, no dogs • Organised trips, bicycles available, tasting and sale of honey, cheese, oil and wine

The flavours and colours of the Sicilian countryside.

Surrounded by leafy oak and hazel trees and grazing sheep, this stone walled farmstead is composed of a 17C main house and farm workers' hovel with inner courtyards. The restaurant is in the old hay barn and serves simple fare incorporating genuine local products grown under the Sicilian sun, a far cry from the elaborate dishes of city hotels.

Access
From Enna: SS 121 for 20km, then onto the SS 117 for 24km

Sights nearby: Cathedral, church of S. Maria Maggiore, ruins of castle

4

CASA MIGLIACA

Sig. e Sig.ra Allegra
Contrada Migliaca
98070 Pettineo (ME)
Tel. 0921 336722 – Fax 0921 391107
info@casamigliaca.com – www.casamigliaca.com

110€

Open all year • 8 double rm • Half board €70 • Parking, garden, bowls, no dogs • Oil for sale

The view from the courtyard over the ancient ruins of Alesa to the azure sea beyond.

Close to Pettineo, the entrance to this property is flanked by pillars, beyond which a dirt track winds through olive trees. After 100m or so it reaches this 17C olive press, entirely surrounded by peaceful farmland which to this day is engaged in cultivation of the olive, the true symbol of the nations of the Mediterranean. Olive processing remains the principal activity of this establishment, although for some years it has also offered accommodation, allowing guests to enjoy stunning views over the valley to the shores of the Tyrrhenian.

Access
From Palermo: A 19 for 45km, onto the A 20 for 18km to Cefalù exit, then onto the SS 113 for 25km, right for 5.5km

Sights nearby: Castle ruins, historic centre

5

L'ANTICA VIGNA

Sig.ra Zuccarello

Località Montelaguardia
95036 Randazzo (CT)
Tel. 095 924003 – Fax 095 923324

60-70€

Open all year • 10 double rm • Half board €50-60 • Menu €18-22 • Parking, garden, tennis, no dogs • Organised trips, bicycles available, oil and wine for sale

The view of Mount Etna, a sleeping giant dominating the horizon.

Randazzo is on the road leading from the sea to the island's hinterland, running from the parkland of the Nebrodi in the north to that of Etna in the south. Not far from the town, this agriturismo blends into a surrounding landscape shaped by centuries of volcanic activity. From the low white farmhouse, guests can explore the countryside, in which it is easy to imagine bygone times of feudal farming activity, when the wider world beyond Sicily's shores would have been unknown to the population.

Access

From Catania: A 18 for 29km to Fiumefreddo exit, then join SS 120 for 23km to Montelaguardia

Sights nearby: Etna National Park

TRANCHINA

Fam. Tranchina
Via A. Diaz, 7
91014 Scopello (TP)
Tel. 0924 541099 – Fax 0924 541099
pensionetranchina@interfree.it

47-57/72-92€

Open all year • 6 single rm, 4 double rm • Half board €55-70 • No dogs

The location in a typical old Sicilian village.

This small family run guesthouse is in the heart of Scopello, a small village surrounded by the scrubland that characterises the local landscape, on a rocky outcrop from where there are fine views out over the gulf of Castellammare and the verdant craggy hills of Sicily. Simple accommodation which is well presented, and courteous service from the owners.

Access
From Trapani: SS 187 for 30km, then left for 4.5km

Sights nearby: Scenery of the golfo del Castellamare, Riserva Naturale dell Zingaro

7

DOLCE CASA

Sig.ra Regolo

Via Lido Sacramento, 4
96100 Siracusa (SR)
Tel. 0931 721135 – Fax 0931 721135
contact@bbdolcecasa.it – www.bbdolcecasa.it

40-50/70-80€

Open all year • 1 single rm, 10 double rm • No restaurant • Parking, small dogs welcome • Tasting of jams and cakes

Walking among the garden's palm trees in the cool evenings.

Here is a real B&B in the English tradition, the result of the experiences of the proprietor's daughter, who after several years in the UK decided to convert this large family home into accommodation for guests. The house is surrounded by spacious gardens, almost a park in fact, where various exotic plant species are grown. The large well presented rooms have a family ambience, as does the bright and airy lounge, supported by arched structures, a pleasant spot in which to while away the time. Within easy reach of the sea and Syracuse with its famous archaeological remains.

Access

From Siracusa: SS 115 for 5km, then left into Via Lido Sacramento

Sights nearby: Archaeological site, Museo Archeologico Regionale, Latomia dei Cappuccini, Ortigia, cathedral

8

GUTKOWSKI

Sig.ra Pretsch

Lungomare Vittorini, 26
96100 Siracusa (SR)
Tel. 0931 465861 – Fax 0931 480505
info@guthotel.it – www.guthotel.it

55-70/80-100€

Open all year • 3 single rm, 22 double rm • No restaurant

The setting; the sea to the front and history on all sides.

The island of Ortigia is Syracuse's original site of settlement, a Greek colony which became one of the most powerful cities in the Mediterranean under its famous tyrant Dionysos. Even today, the evidence of those times remains in the form of the extensive archaeological remains which successive generations have not succeeded in erasing. Many people have been captivated by their charm including the English lady who, together with a local friend, runs this B&B in an old fisherman's house. The accommodation is very simple, but the views of the sea and the convenience of its location make this a place well worth knowing about.

Sights nearby: Archaeological site, Museo Archeologico Regionale, Latomia dei Cappuccini, Ortigia, cathedral

9

LA PERCIATA

Sig. Monello
Via Spinagallo, 77
96100 Siracusa (SR)
Tel. 0931 717366 – Fax 0931 717412
perciata@perciata.it – www.perciata.it

50-72/70-92€

Open all year • 1 single rm, 9 double rm • Half board €58-69 • Menu €25-35 • Parking, garden, swimming pool, tennis, no dogs • Horse riding, jams for sale (tasting)

The contrasting colours of the vegetation and the rocky scenery.

Set at the foot of a small and rugged hill where the Mediterranean scrub clings to the bright white stones. The modern main building with swimming pool is partially hidden by trees which separate it from the stables and surrounding farmland. A mere 11km from Syracuse, this is a good alternative to staying in town. Among the local sights to be discovered are the Monello caves, where the calcareous stone has been gradually eroded by water action down the ages.

Access
Fom Siracusa: SS 115 for 14km to Spinagallo road

Sights nearby: Archaeological site, Museo Archeologico Regionale, Latomia dei Cappuccini, Ortigia, cathedral

10

BAGLIO FONTANASALSA

Sig.ra Burgarella

A Fontanasalsa - Via Cusenza, 78
91100 Trapani (TP)
Tel. 0923 591001 – Fax 0923 591001
fontanasalsa@hotmail.com – www.fontanasalsa.it

60-65/95-100€

Open all year • 2 single rm, 7 double rm • Half board €75-85 • Menu €25-35 • Parking, garden, swimming pool • Bicycles available, tasting and sale of oil and wine

The olive groves and the citrus trees: two symbols of Sicily.

Phoenicians, Greeks, Romans, Arabs, Normans, Angevins, Aragonese.... the list of peoples who have enriched Sicily's history with their monuments and works of art is a lengthy one. Few things have remained unchanged down the ages, but one of them is the olive, the cultivation of which dominates the landscape between mount Erice and the sea. Fontanasalsa is a long established farm which recently diversified into providing accommodation in the shape of seven rooms with rustic wood furnishings and wrought iron beds. The cuisine focuses on local dishes, and in summer may be enjoyed outdoors. Good standards of service from a management team running this place for love rather than money.

Access

From Trapani: SS 155 for 10km

Sights nearby: Paceco: Chiesa Madre and church of the Rosario

Rovigo
Parma
Ferrara
Salsomaggiore Terme
Reggio nell'Emilia
Modena
Comacchio
EMILIA
BOLOGNA
Ravenna
Cisa
Imola
Faenza
Forlì
Cervia
Cesena
Carrara
Massa
Abetone
Raticosa
Pistoia
Prato
Montecatini Terme
Forte dei Marmi
Viareggio
Lucca
Bagno di Romagna
Pontassieve
Pisa
Empoli
FIRENZE
Livorno
San Gimignano
Arezzo
Sansepolcro
Città di Castello
Volterra
Siena
Gubbio
Cecina
Cortona
Montepulciano
Perugia
TOSCANA
Capraia (I)
Chianciano Terme
Piombino
Follonica
Portoferraio
Elba
Orvieto
Todi
Grosseto
Bolsena
Montefiascone
Pianosa (I)
Viterbo
Tarquinia
Civitavecchia
ROMA
Po
Reno
Arno
Ombrone
Tevere
La Spezia
1
2
3
4
5
6
7
8
9
10
11
12
13
14
15
16
17
18
19
20
21
22
23
24
25
26
27
28
29
30
31
32
33
34
35
36
37
38
39
40
41
42
43
44
45
46
47
48
49
50
51

TOSCANA

Florence, Siena, Arezzo, Lucca... Tuscany has so many cities of beauty, memories of them can be evoked by many a visitor years after seeing them. Breakfast in Siena's Piazza del Campo, a morning stroll to Florence's Uffizi museum, a picnic in the woodlands of the Casentino, an early afternoon walk across Chianti's hillsides followed by a dip off Elba's rocky shores, a relaxing thermal bath at Montecatini, an aperitif watching the sun set over the Ponte Vecchio, and a splendid *fiorentina* steak for dinner... such would be a perfect day in Tuscany. With a whole week's holiday, visitors can enjoy a more relaxed itinerary, taking in some of the less well known sites, the incredibly varied countryside, and of course the excellent food and wine. The many who will find it difficult to leave will understand the reasons behind the "Chianti-shire" phenomenon.

51 establishments

1

RONDINELLI

Sigg. Ragnini
Località i Rondinelli, 32
58031 Arcidosso (GR)
Tel. 0564 968168 – Fax 0564 968168

50/ 70€

Open all year • 11 double rm • Breakfast €7; half board €60 • Menu €20-25 • Parking, bowls, no dogs • Horse riding, tasting and sale of oil, fruit and walnuts

Riding through the woods.

The façade of this 19C building reflects the history of this area, its austere functionality suggesting a fertile yet unforgiving landscape, in which gentle foothills give way to the rugged Amiata mountains, and chestnut woods provide the district with its colour and aromas. This establishment offers simple but welcoming hospitality; the spacious rooms contrast with the more limited public areas where the lounge area and dining room merge into one. Most important, however, is the surrounding natural beauty of the landscape, providing a stunning backdrop for visitors to explore.

Access

From Grosseto: SS 322 for 9km towards Scansano, left to Cinigiano, right to Monticello Amiata, right for 7km, right for 7km to I Rondinelli

Sights nearby: Maremma National Park; Grosseto; historic centre, archaeological museum

CASA VOLPI

Sig. Volpi

Via Simone Martini, 29
52100 Arezzo (AR)
Tel. 0575 354364 – Fax 0575 355971
posta@casavolpi.it – www.casavolpi.it

65/ 90€

Closed 5-13 Aug • 1 single rm, 11 double rm • Breakfast €8 • Menu €20-32 • Parking, garden, no dogs • Oil and red wine for sale

The fine view of Arezzo across the verdant parkland.

The medieval backdrop of the centre of Arezzo is readily visible from the windows of this 19C aristocratic residence situated in parkland. The view and surrounding greenery are far from the only features of this hotel. Its 15 stylish, well furnished rooms offer charming accommodation, the public areas and restaurant are elegant and, during the warmer months, guests may dine under a pergola in the garden. An excellent base from which to discover the district's numerous great works of art by Piero della Francesca and others.

Sights nearby: Cathedral, churches of San Francesco, San Domenico, Santa Maria alla Pieve, Santa Maria delle Grazie

3

LA TORRE DI PONZANO

Sig. McAuley e Sig.ra Coppi

Strada di Ponzano, 8
50021 Barberino Val d'Elsa (FI)
Tel. 055 8059255 – Fax 055 8071102
torre_di_ponzano@hotmail.com – www.ponzano.wide.it

89-99€

Open all year • 6 double rm • No restaurant • Parking, garden, no dogs

The Anglo-Italian management, giving the place a style unique in the area.

This part of Tuscany was once the battlefield where the armies of Florence and Siena would regularly meet to resolve their differences. On the ridge of a hill once stood a Florentine farmstead which was destroyed by the Sienese. Of that original structure only the tower remains. This houses one of the rooms, the rest being in the 16C farmhouse next door. Rustic elegance, with the emphasis on quality rather than ostentation.

Access

From Florence: SGC Firenze-Siena for 17km to Tavarnelle Val di Pesa exit, then onto the SS 2 for 10km to Ponzano

Sights nearby: San Gimignano: towers, Collegiata, Palazzo del Popolo, church of Sant'Agostino

LE GRETI

Sig. Nardini
Via privata le Greti
52011 Bibbiena (AR)
Tel. 0575 561744 – Fax 0575 561808
legreti@libero.it

39-46,50/72,50-77,50€

Open all year • 7 single rm, 9 double rm • No restaurant • Parking, garden, swimming pool, small dogs welcome

Breakfast served against a backdrop of green fields and blue sky.

The wooded landscape of the Casentino is being rediscovered by independent minded travellers looking to get off the beaten track, and the area has much to see and admire. At its very heart, Bibbiena is ideally situated to act as a base from which to explore the district's varied charms. In a panoramic location, this establishment is comfortable and relaxing, with a swimming pool that is particularly welcome on hot summer days.

Access

From Arezzo: SS 71 for 37km to Soci

Sights nearby: Arezzo: Cathedral, churches of San Francesco, San Domenico, Santa Maria alla Pieve, Santa Maria delle Grazie

5

CASA PALMIRA

Sig.ra Fiorini

Località Feriolo-Polcanto via Mulinaccio, 4
50032 Borgo San Lorenzo (FI)
Tel. 055 8409749 – Fax 055 8409749
info@casapalmira.it – www.casapalmira.it

60-65/80-85€

Closed 20 Jan-10 Mar • 1 single rm, 5 double rm • No restaurant • Parking, garden, no dogs • Bicycle hire

Reading a book in a comfortable armchair, bathed in natural light from the skylight.

England or Tuscany. Although not quite in Chiantishire, the tasteful style in which this property has been restored and furnished evokes the culture of the English country house. Also evident, though, are strong links to the area's rich history; the oldest part of the building, originally a hay barn, date from the 12C. On the ground floor are the public areas including bar and open kitchen where breakfast is served, while upstairs are the rooms, each individually designed and incorporating furniture collected by the owner.

Access

From Florence: SS 302 for 15km to Feriolo

Sights nearby: Fiesole: Cathedral, convent of San Francesco, archaeological site

CASA RANIERI

Sig.ra Ranieri

Podere la Martina
53023 Campiglia d'Orcia (SI)
Tel. 0577 872639 – Fax 0577 872639
naranier@tin.it

50-60/70-80€

Open all year • 7 double rm • Half board €60-75 • Menu €25-30 • Parking, garden, swimming pool, bowls, small dogs welcome • Horse riding, oil for sale

Riding through the glorious Tuscan countryside.

The period furnishings in the rooms and the covered riding school are but two of the many attractions of this place, transformed from a simple farm into an agriturismo retaining strong links with its heritage. The frills of hotel luxury are absent; instead a characterful rustic elegance pervades. During the summer months guests can cool off in the pool, sited in a panoramic spot with fine views over the green hills of the Orcia valley. Traditional Tuscan cuisine in the restaurant, which also lays on cookery courses.

Access

From Siena: SS 2 for 52km, then right for 5km

Sights nearby: Historic centre, Rocca

7

GHIACCIO BOSCO

Sig.ra Olivi e Sig. Rinaldi
Strada della Sgrilla, 4
58011 Capalbio (GR)
Tel. 0564 896539 – Fax 0564 896539
info@ghiacciobosco.com – www.ghiacciobosco.com

50-65/ 75-110€

Open all year • 15 double rm • No restaurant • Parking, swimming pool, garden

The charming bathrooms.

Far from the typical atmosphere of the Maremma, with its butteri cowboys and rural traditions, the village of Capalbio has long been a fashionable retreat for Italy's political and cultural elite. An attractive village, surrounded by countryside and yet close to the sea, it is now home to the Ghiaccio Bosco agriturismo, which offers elegant accommodation to satisfy the most demanding clientele. Uniformed staff, green lawns reminiscent of England, a swimming pool, comfortable guest rooms and a friendly management all add to the elegant atmosphere.

Access
From Grosseto: SS 1-E 80 for 31km, SS 74 for 8km, then right for 14km

Sights nearby: Promontorio dell'Argentario

8

VILLA CRISTINA

Sig. Landini
Via Fiorentina, 34
53011 Castellina in Chianti (SI)
Tel. 0577 741166 – Fax 0577 742936
info@villacristina.it – www.villacristina.it

50-57/70-73€

Closed 9 Jan-12 Mar, 8 Nov-26 Dec • 5 double rm • No restaurant • Parking, garden, small dogs welcome

The tower room, providing a unique perspective on the surrounding landscape.

This early 20C villa is conveniently located close to the centre of Castellina; a private house for most of its history, it retains its quirky residential layout. The rooms are simple yet well equipped, and to the rear is a terrace garden which is perticularly pleasant early in the day or after dusk. Good, generous breakfasts are served to prepare visitors for days exploring Chianti country.

Access
From Siena: SGC Firenze-Siena for 3.5km to Castellina in Chianti exit, then onto the SS 222 for 22km

Sights nearby: Siena: Palazzo Pubblico, Piazza del Campo, cathedral, churches of San Domenico and Sant'Agostino

9

OSTERIA DEL VICARIO

Sig. e Sig.ra Borchi
Via Rivellino, 3
50052 Certaldo (FI)
Tel. 0571 668228 – Fax 0571 668228
info@osteriadelvicario.it – www.osteriadelvicario.it

70/100€

Open all year • 8 double rm • Half board €80 • Menu €50-60 • Garden • Tasting of pastries and fresh pasta

The charming restaurant terrace.

This is Boccaccio country; the great writer was born in Certaldo, a hill town where cars are forbidden and the atmosphere of the Middle Ages still prevails. It is at its busiest in July, when it hosts a theatre festival. Whatever time of year, this is the ideal hotel in which to stay; a characterful ambience with much woodwork in evidence, period furnishings, fine views and a warm welcome.

Access
From Florence: SGC Firenze-Siena for 16.6km to Tavernelle exit, then the SS 2 for 7.5km, right for 7.5km to join Vico Val d'Elsa, continue for 6.5km

Sights nearby: Palazzo Pretorio, Boccaccio's house, church of San Jacopo

10

LA CASA TOSCANA

Sig. Valeriani

Via Ermanno Baldetti, 37
53043 Chiusi (SI)
Tel. 0578 222227 – Fax 0578 223812
casatoscana@libero.it – www.valerianigroup.com/casat.htm

70-90/80-100€

Closed 15-30 Jan • 1 single rm, 5 double rm • No restaurant • Wine tasting

Breakfast on the terrace, among the perfumes of the flowers.

This tastefully restored palazzo in the centre of Chiusi is a gem; a limited number of rooms, each individually furnished and all bright and charming, with elegant modern bathrooms. At the rear is a planted terrace overlooking the church of San Francesco. A perfect base from which to explore the borderlands between Tuscany and Umbria, especially given the excellent road and rail links.

Access

From Siena: SS 326 for 50km, onto the A 1 for 24.5km to Chiusi exit, then onto the SS 146 for 2.5km

Sights nearby: Archaeological museum; Città della Pieve: cathedral, church of Santa Maria dei Servi, Oratorio di Santa Maria dei Bianchi

11

CASA LUCIA

Sig.ra Formisano
Località Corsignano Vagliagli
53019 Corsignano (SI)
Tel. 0577 322508 – Fax 0577 322510
info@casalucia.it – www.casalucia.it

69-74/ 76-86€

Open all year • 14 double rm • Breakfast €5 • No restaurant • Parking, garden • Bicycle hire

The accommodation housed in the old kiln.

This establishment has twelve simple rooms in two old buildings which have successfully retained their historic charm. The first is a converted barn, its rustic heritage evident in its tiled ceilings and wooden supports. The second is particularly unusual, a former kiln retaining its original ceiling complete with blackened brick tiles. Ideally situated in open countryside yet conveniently close to Siena.

Access
From Siena: SS 422 for 4km, then right for 4km to Corsignano

Sights nearby: Siena: Palazzo Pubblico, Piazza del Campo, cathedral, churches of San Domenico and Sant'Agostino

12

FATTORIA DI CORSIGNANO

Sig.ra Gallo
Località Corsignano - Vagliagli
53010 Castelnuovo Berardenga (Siena)
Tel. 0577 322545 – Fax 0577 322407
info@tenutacorsignano.it – www.tenutacorsignano.it

60-80/ 70-90€

Open all year • 10 double rm • Breakfast €8 • No restaurant • Parking, garden, swimming pool • Organised trips, bicycle hire, tasting and sale of wine, oil and grappa

The large swimming pool in the grounds.

Situated in the southern Chianti region, in the splendid district of Castelnuovo Berardenga, the Fattoria di Corsignano is an attractive farmstead which specialises in the production of wine and olive oil. Guests stay in three buildings housing a total of ten apartments, each of which is equipped with kitchen, elegant rooms and antique furniture. The peaceful location, panoramic views and the friendly, efficient staff combine to offer a holiday in true Chianti style.

Access
From Siena: SS 222 north for 4km, then 8km towards Vagliagli

Sights nearby: Siena: Piazza del Campo, cathedral, Palazzo Pubblico

13

GENESIO

Sig. Cocon e Sig. Consales
Via XXVII Aprile, 9
50129 Firenze (FI)
Tel. 055 496208 – Fax 055 473118
hotelgenesio@tiscali.it

35-70/60-110€

Open all year • 15 double rm • No restaurant

The elegant breakfast room.

Situated between Piazza Indipendenza and Piazza San Marco, a stone's throw from San Lorenzo, this well-maintained small hotel is appreciated by business travellers and tourists alike. Its central location, comfortable rooms and enthusiastic staff combine to offer guests a tranquil base from which to explore the wonders of the city. The guestrooms are adequately spacious, with period furniture, wrought-iron beds and light, colourful fabrics. Excellent value for money.

Sights nearby: Cathedral and baptistry, Palazzo Vecchio

14

MAISON DE CHARME

Sig.ra Hanotel

Largo Fratelli Alinari, 11
50129 Firenze (FI)

Tel. 055 292304 – Fax 055 281014

maisondecharme@estranet.it – www.maisondecharme.it

50-68/ 70-98€

Open all year • 1 single rm, 5 double rm • No restaurant

The proximity to the railway station and the city centre.

Travellers arriving by train will be pleased to avoid a long walk with luggage on arrival at this B&B, situated just across the square from the station and close to the church of Santa Maria Novella. The fourth floor accommodation (access by lift) is modern and functional. No breakfast but every room has a kettle.

Sights nearby: Churches of Santa Maria Novella and San Lorenzo, Palazzo Medici-Riccardi, cathedral and baptistery

15

RELAIS IL CAMPANILE

Sig. Botticelli

Via Ricasoli, 10
50122 Firenze (FI)
Tel. 055 211688 – Fax 055 2675989
relaiscampanile@tiscali.it – www.relaiscampanile.it

48-80/75-98€

Open all year • 2 single rm, 4 double rm • No restaurant

The proximity to the city's artistic highlights.

This Florentine B&B occupies the first floor of a fine 17C palazzo, offering comprehensively equipped modern accommodation and good service, but its greatest asset is its location. On descending the stairs and emerging into the street, guests are presented almost immediately with the subtle hues of the north front of the city's greatest architectural jewel, the cathedral of Santa Maria del Fiore.

Sights nearby: Cathedral and baptistery, Galleria degli Uffizi, Palazzo Vecchio, churches of Santa Maria Novella and San Lorenzo

16

RESIDENZA GIULIA

Sig.ra Sicari
Via delle Porte Nuove, 19
50144 Firenze (FI)
Tel. 055 3216646 – Fax 055 3245149
anna@residenzagiulia.com – www.residenzagiulia.com

50-80/ 68-95€

Open all year • 6 double rm • No restaurant

Enjoying the delightful views of the hills over breakfast.

Situated on the fifth floor, this B&B close to Santa Maria Novella station has stunning views over the Florentine hills. With this scenic backdrop, guests can enjoy breakfast served in the room; the accommodation is simply furnished and well presented by the friendly and helpful young management.

Sights nearby: Churches of Santa Maria Novella and San Lorenzo, Palazzo Medici-Riccardi, cathedral and baptistery

17

RESIDENZA HANNAH E JOHANNA

Sig.ra Gulmanelli e Sig.ra Arrighi

Via Bonifacio Lupi, 14
50129 Firenze (FI)
Tel. 055 481896 – Fax 055 482721
lupi@johanna.it – www.johanna.it

50/85€

Open all year • 2 single rm, 9 double rm • No restaurant • No dogs

The friendly welcome in this unusual and elegant establishment.

The choice of hotel is key to the success of a holiday and its ambience is often one of the most memorable aspects that guests recall long after returning home. The friendly atmosphere of this small establishment makes it feel more like a private house than a city hotel. Situated in an old palazzo with an austere façade (and inner courtyard providing parking), the interior is surprisingly welcoming. Great attention to detail is evident in the elegant rooms, which are tastefully furnished and intimate in feel.

Sights nearby: Cathedral and baptistery, Palazzo Medici-Riccardi, convento and Museo di San Marco, churches of San Lorenzo and Santa Maria Novella

18

RESIDENZA JOHANNA

Sig.ra Gulmanelli

Via Cinque Giornate, 12
50129 Firenze (FI)
Tel. 055 473377 – Fax 055 473377
cinquegiornate@johanna.it – www.johanna.it

85€

Open all year • 6 double rm • No restaurant • Parking, no dogs

The successful combination of domesticity and elegance.

This establishment stands out among the city's hotels on account of its traditional ambience. An informal yet courteous welcome awaits guests; the intimate and refined interior shows great attention to detail, creating a genteel elegance unmatched in the city at this price. This hotel's quality and the competence of its management make it a place well worth knowing.

Sights nearby: Fortezza da Basso, convento and Museo di San Marco, churches of Santa Maria Novella and San Lorenzo, convento di Fuligno

19

LE RESIDENZE JOHLEA

Sig.ra Gulmanelli

Via Sangallo, 76/80
50129 Firenze (FI)
Tel. 055 4633292 – Fax 055 4634552
johlea@johanna.it – www.johanna.it

70/ 95€

Open all year • 2 single rm, 10 double rm • No restaurant • No dogs

The views over Florence dominated by the Duomo.

Occupying two recently restored 19C buildings, each of which has six rooms, this establishment has well presented interiors which have been tastefully furnished and decorated in pastel colours. The rooms are warm and welcoming in a homely way. Spectacular views from the terrace over the city, especially Brunelleschi's dome which towers over the surrounding buildings and is particularly impressive when bathed in the setting sun's rays.

Sights nearby: Cathedral and baptistery, Palazzo Medici-Riccardi, convento e Museo di San Marco, churches of San Lorenzo and Santa Maria Novella

20

IL GIARDINETTO

Sig. Mercadini

Via Roma, 151
54013 Fivizzano (MS)
Tel. 0585 92060 – Fax 0585 92060

26/46,50€

Closed 4-30 Oct • 7 single rm, 10 double rm • Breakfast €3.70; half board €41.50 • Menu €16 • Garden, no dogs

The blend of historic backdrop and contemporary comfort.

Since 1882, this establishment has provided accommodation for travellers crossing the Apuan Alps here in Fivizzano, a historic crossroads between the regions of Emilia, Liguria and Tuscany. The tradition of hospitality which has developed over the years is jealously guarded, and guests may be sure of a warm welcome. Portraits of famous visitors decorate the walls, a fitting archive chronicling the distinguished heritage of this venerable hotel.

Access

From La Spezia: A 15 for 16.2km to Aulla exit, onto the SS 62 for 1km to Aulla, then left onto the SS 63 for 16km

Sights nearby: La Spezia: Museo Lia

21

BORGOLECCHI

Sig. Borsotti

Via San Martino, 50
53010 Lecchi (SI)
Tel. 0577 746903 – Fax 0577 746814
caltur@tiscali.it – www.borgolecchi.com

70-95/80-120€

• 6 double rm • No restaurant • Parking

The attractive combination of grey stone and verdant olive groves.

Located in a charming stone-built village on the so-called castle route, a series of lookout posts originally built to protect Siena from Florentine incursions. Here in Borgolecchi, the tower dates from 1100 while the hotel is situated on the main street; its public areas are simple and its rustic style rooms have attractive furnishings and modern bathrooms. Almost all have terraces giving onto the tranquil hillside.

Access

From Siena: SS 408 for 20km, then left for 1.7km

Sights nearby: Radda in Chianti: castle ruins, church of San Niccolò, Palazzo del Podestà

22

GALEAZZI

Fam. Galeazzi
Località Spinicci, 250
58010 Marsiliana (GR)
Tel. 0564 605017 – Fax 0564 605017
info@agriturismogaleazzi.com – www.agriturismogaleazzi.com

40-50/50-65€

Open all year • 1 single rm, 8 double rm • No restaurant • Parking, garden, swimming pool, no dogs • Bicycles available, fishing, archery, asparagus, oil and wine for sale

The tranquil experience of fishing among the olive groves.

This establishment is very much a working farm, and the agricultural backdrop makes for a relaxing ambience. Although an undistinguished modern building, everything is very clean and tidy, with the simple furnishings in mint condition. Facilities include a fine swimming pool, and a small lake providing carp and tench fishing.

Access
From Grosseto: SS 1 for 31.5km to Albinia, then left onto the SS 74 for 14km to Spinicci

Sights nearby: Promontorio dell'Argentario; Orbetello: cathedral, fortifications

23

POGGIO TORTOLLO

Sig.ra Paggetti

Località Poggio Tortollo
58014 Manciano (GR)
Tel. 0564 620209 – Fax 0564 620949
poggiotortollo@hotmail.com – www.poggiotortollo.it

40-45/65-75€

Closed 10 Jan-10 Feb • 1 single rm, 4 double rm • No restaurant • Parking, garden, swimming pool • Organised trips, bicycles available, honey and oil for sale

The direct access to the rooms from outside.

Passionately run by Signora Poggetti, this small agriturismo has consistently improved over the years, making it a comfortable place to stay. Simplicity is the key here, entirely in keeping with the rural setting. The building is surrounded by greenery, being part of a farm which has fine views over fields, woodland and hills. Guests can lounge by the pool or explore the area on mountain bikes. A perfect base from which to discover the Maremma, and close to the thermal baths at Saturnia.

Access

From Grosseto: 36km to Albinia, SS 74 for 29km to Manciano, right onto the SP 32 for 4km to Poggio Tortollo

Sights nearby: Promontorio dell'Argentario; Orbetello: cathedral, fortifications

IL QUERCIOLO

Sig. Fani

Località Badicorte Via Bosco Salviati, 5
52010 Marciano della Chiana (AR)
Tel. 0575 845000 – Fax 0575 845000
info@ilquerciolobadicorte.com – www.ilquerciolobadicorte.com

80/ 100€

Closed Jan, Feb • 4 double rm • Breakfast €4 • No restaurant • Parking • Bicycle hire, jam tasting and oil and wine for sale

The period washbasins in some of the rooms.

The origins of this farmhouse date back to the 13C, although its present appearance owes much to structural alterations undertaken in the 19C. Recent renovation work has carefully highlighted many of the building's architectural features. In addition to the drawing rooms, fireplaces, wooden beams and stone arches, the bedrooms are striking for their refined period furniture and original ornaments dating from the mid-19C to the Belle Epoque period of the early 20C, all of which belonged to the owner's family. The house is surrounded by an attractive garden, with the hills, olive groves and sunflower fields of the Valdichiana in the distance.

Access

From Arezzo: E 78 for 9km, SS 327 for 10km, then right for 3km

Sights nearby: Monte San Savino: Castello di Gargonza, church of Santa Maria delle Vertighe

25

VECCHIO MULINO

Sig. Ciulli
Viale Italia, 10
50050 Montaione (FI)
Tel. 0571 697966 – Fax 0571 697966
info@hotelvecchiomulino.it – www.hotelvecchiomulino.it

35-50/ 75-90€

Open all year • 3 single rm, 10 double rm • No restaurant • Parking, garden, small dogs welcome • Horse riding, bicycle hire

The stonework in evidence throughout.

Montaione is a delightful village equidistant (60km) from Florence, Siena and Pisa, set in a landscape remarkable for both its natural beauty and rich history. Built into the old ramparts, this hotel today shows little trace of its original function; all the milling machinery is long gone, replaced by characterful accommodation in the form of fifteen fine rooms, furnished with antique pieces and wrought iron beds. Panoramic views, family management, a garden and small breakfast room complete the picture.

Access

From Florence: SGC Firenze-Pisa-Livorno for 27km to Empoli exit, onto SS 429 for 14.5km to Castelfiorentino, then right for 10km

Sights nearby: Convento di San Vivaldo

26

IL GIGLIO

Sig. Machetti

Via Soccorso Saloni, 5
53024 Montalcino (SI)

Tel. 0577 848167 – Fax 0577 848167

info@gigliohotel.com – www.gigliohotel.com

60/ 90€

Closed 7-28 Jan • 3 single rm, 9 double rm • Breakfast €6.50; half board €70 • Menu €27-38 • Parking • Organised trips, jam for sale (tasting)

The delightful backdrop provided by the surrounding scenery.

Everything required for a Tuscan break is here; a historic setting, family management, lobby with open fireplace, restaurant laid out over two intimate rooms, and accommodation in the shape of a dozen attractive rooms with wrought iron beds and luxurious marble baths, all within the walls of a fine 16C palazzo with wood beamed ceilings.

Access

From Siena: SS 2 for 26km, then right for 11km

Sights nearby: Rocca, Palazzo Comunale; Sant'Antimo: abbey

27

IL PODERUCCIO

Sig. Girardi

Via Poderuccio, 52
53020 Sant'Angelo in Colle (SI)
Tel. 0577 844052 – Fax 0577 844150
poderuccio.girardi@virgilio.it

85€

Closed 1 Dec-17 Apr • 6 double rm • No restaurant • Parking, garden, swimming pool, bowls, no dogs • Oil, grappa and wine for sale

We most liked

The attractive garden filled with colourful flowers.

With its panoramic location near the vineyards, this agriturismo is perfect for wine enthusiasts who wish to tour the Montalcino area, which is renowned for its high-quality Brunello wines. The house is simple and classical in style, with a harmonious and symmetrical appearance. Surrounded by a green meadow and a delightful garden carefully tended by the owners, the property also boasts a swimming pool situated slightly away from the house to ensure a quiet and peaceful stay for guests. The rooms are furnished with rustic pieces which perfectly match the overall flavour of the property.

Access

From Siena: SS 2 for 29km, then right for 21km to Sant'Angelo in Colle

Sights nearby: Montalcino: historic centre, Rocca; Sant'Antimo: abbey

28

LOGGE DEI MERCANTI

Sig.ra Capecchi
Corso Sangallo, 40/42
52048 Monte San Savino (AR)
Tel. 0575 810710 – Fax 0575 810710
info@loggedeimercanti.it – www.loggedeimercanti.it

50-60/85-95€

Open all year • 3 single rm, 7 double rm • No restaurant • Oil and wine for sale

The unusual breakfast room.

Situated in the historic centre of the village, opposite the 16C loggia from which it takes its name, the old village pharmacy has recently been turned into a hotel. Although the reception rooms are on the small side, the breakfast room, occupying the underground passages that once led to the aqueduct, is both charming and unusual. The new guestrooms offer both contemporary facilities and period furnishings in total harmony with the ambience of the palazzo. The most eye-catching rooms are those adorned with frescoes, as well as the junior suites affording views of the hanging gardens and surrounding countryside. The attractive sign is a reminder of the building's former use as a pharmacy.

Access
From Arezzo: E 78 for 20km

Sights nearby: Castello di Gargonza, church of Santa Maria delle Vertighe

29

ANTICA CASA DEI RASSICURATI

Piccola Società Cooperativa Peperosa

Via della Collegiata, 2
55015 Montecarlo (LU)
Tel. 0583 228901 – Fax 0583 22498
info@anticacasadeirassicurati.it – www.anticacasadeirassicurati.it

45-50/60-75€

Open all year • 1 single rm, 5 double rm • No restaurant

Breakfast, served either in the lounge with open fireplace, or on the patio outside.

Not to be confused the capital of Monaco, the small medieval village of Montecarlo is situated among the olive groves and vineyards of the Lucchesia, offering a rather more understated experience for visitors against the backdrop of its historic Tuscan buildings. This establishment is the ideal spot for those seeking peace, relaxation and unspoilt beauty. Passionately and competently run by an all female team, its lounge is attractive, the rooms elegant and breakfast is enhanced by the inclusion of home made jams and pastries.

Access

From Lucca: SS 435 for 10km, then right for 5km

Sights nearby: Teatro dell'Accademia dei Rassicurati; church of S. Andrea

30

LA NINA

Fam. Lazzareschi

Via San Martino, 54
55015 Montecarlo (LU)
Tel. 0583 22178 – Fax 0583 22178
infolanina@libero.it – www.lanina.it

45/55€

Open all year • 10 double rm • No breakfast • Menu €23-34 • Parking, garden, no dogs • Home-produced oil and wine for sale

The large, elegant and well presented rooms.

This is an attractive yellow house overlooking the countryside from a verdant location on the outskirts of the village of Montecarlo. The excellent accommodation is tastefully furnished, spacious and shows much attention to detail. No breakfast available (although this may be taken in any of the several bars nearby) but there is an adjacent restaurant of the same name offering robust Tuscan cuisine.

Access

From Lucca: SS 435 for 10km, then right for 5km

Sights nearby: Teatro dell'Accademia dei Rassicurati; church of S. Andrea

31

BRENNERO E VARSAVIA

Fam. Bruschetti

Viale Bicchierai, 70/72
51016 Montecatini Terme (PT)
Tel. 0572 70086 – Fax 0572 74459
info@hotelbrenneroevarsavia.it – www.hotelbrenneroevarsavia.it

45-55/75-85€

Closed Dec-Feb • 12 single rm, 42 double rm • Breakfast €8; half board €53-60 • Menu €18-25 • Parking, no dogs in the restaurant • Tasting of cakes and typical Tuscan specialities

The charming service and hospitality shown to guests.

Thanks to the efforts of the Bruschetti family, Montecatini boasts a hotel offering exceptional value for money. The property is continually being improved upon (Internet access is the latest feature) and the well equipped rooms are large with good bathrooms. The guests-only restaurant serves classic Italian cuisine in bright, spacious surroundings. The high standards of service provided by the management should meet the requirements of even the most exacting visitor.

Access
From Pistoia: SS 435 for 13km

Sights nearby: Museo dell'Accademia d'Arte; Montecatini Alto: historic centre

32

VILLA LE MAGNOLIE

Sig. Meucci

Viale Fedeli, 15
51016 Montecatini Terme (PT)
Tel. 0572 911700 – Fax 0572 72885

65-70/ 90-100€

Open all year • 6 double rm • No restaurant • Parking, garden

The top floor room with wooden ceiling, a must for incurable romantics.

Montecatini is a renowned spa town and consequently there are many hotels from which to choose. Those looking for something a little different without wishing to spend a fortune should seek out this establishment, an early 20C Art Nouveau villa run by the Meucci family in a caring and tasteful fashion. There are six charming rooms, plus an attractive lounge and breakfast room. Guests have access to all the facilities of the neighbouring Hotel Michelangelo (gym, swimming pool, tennis court).

Access
From Pistoia: SS 435 for 13km

Sights nearby: Museo dell'Accademia d'Arte; Montecatini Alto: historic centre

33

LE FONTANELLE

Sig. Perna

Località Poderi di Montemerano
58050 Montemerano (GR)
Tel. 0564 602762 – Fax 0564 602762
informazioni@lefontanelle.net – www.lefontanelle.net

78€

Open all year • 11 double rm • Half board €59 • Menu €20 • Parking, garden, small menagerie, no dogs in the restaurant • Fishing

Getting close to the local flora and fauna.

Perfect for those in quest of the unspoilt, this agriturismo harmoniously co-exists with its natural surroundings, which teem with wildlife. Composed of several stone buildings, there are around a dozen rooms in all which are simple yet welcoming. In summer, the guests only restaurant serves its tasty cuisine beneath a delightful gazebo.

Access

From Grosseto: SS 322 for 28km to Scansano, left onto the SS 323 for 2km, then right onto the SS 322 for 22km to I Poderi

Sights nearby: Maremma National Park; Grosseto: historic centre, archaeological museum

34

LE PANARE

Sigg. Minardi
Località Scheta
50035 Palazzuolo sul Senio (FI)
Tel. 055 8046346
lepanare@tin.it – www.lepanare.it

40-50/60-70€

Closed Nov-Apr • 3 double rm • Half board €35-45 • Menu €10-20 • Parking, garden, no dogs in the restaurant • Natural history walks, cured meats for sale

The young and enthusiastic management.

Situated among Tuscany's unspoilt Mugello hills, this old farmstead offers limited but characterful accommodation with wood beamed sloping ceilings, stone walls and rustic furnishings. Meals are served in a dining room dominated by a large open fireplace and a single horseshoe shaped table. An unusual feature of the place is its small collection of arms and armour.

Access

From Florence: SS 65 for 23km, right onto SS 551 for 8km, left onto SS 302 for 13km, left onto SS 477 for 11km to Schene

Sights nearby: Florence: cathedral and baptistery, Galleria degli Uffizi, Palazzo Vecchio, churches of Santa Maria Novella and San Lorenzo

35

SAN LORENZO HOTEL E RESIDENCE

Sig. Puccinelli

Località San Lorenzo 15/24
51017 Pescia (PT)
Tel. 0572 408340 – Fax 0572 408333
s.lorenzo@rphotels.com – www.sanlorenzohotels.com

55/96€

Open all year • 34 double rm • Half board €65 • Menu €28-41 • Parking, garden, swimming pool, no dogs • Bicycle hire

The garden with swimming pool. A fresh and verdant oasis.

This imposing 18C building makes for an unusual place to stay; in use as a paper mill until the 1960s, it has been thoughtfully converted into a well equipped hotel. The charming public areas composed of numerous rooms, including restaurant, are well thought out. The spacious rooms benefit from plenty of natural light and are furnished in rustic style with dark wood pieces incorporating inset stone detail.

Access
From Lucca: SS 435 for 17km

Sights nearby: Historic centre; Collodi: Parco di Pinocchio

36

LA VOLPE E L'UVA-VILLA VANNINI

Fam. Bordonaro

Via di Villa, 6
51030 Villa di Piteccio (PT)
Tel. 0573 42031 – Fax 0573 42551
info@volpe-uva.it – www.volpe-uva.it

45-60/ 70-90€

Open all year • 7 double rm • Half board €63-73 • Menu €40 • Parking, garden, no dogs in the restaurant • Organised trips, tasting of sauces, bread and jams

The restaurant's excellent cuisine.

This attractive pastel painted house occupies an airy location among trees in open countryside around 10km from Pistoia. For some years, it has been equally renowned for its ever more appetising cuisine and its accommodation. Since taking over this establishment, the Bordonaro sisters have reinvigorated it with their innate sense of hospitality; the rooms are particularly welcoming, although some have external bathrooms.

Access
9.5km north of Pistoia

Sights nearby: Pistoia: cathedral and baptistery, churches of Sant'Andrea and San Giovanni Fuoricivitas, Basilica of the Madonna dell'Umiltà

37

CÀ DEL MORO

Fam. Bezzi

Via Casa Corvi, 9
54027 Pontremoli (MS)
Tel. 0187 830588 – Fax 0187 830588
info@cadelmoro.it – www.cadelmoro.it

90-100€

Closed 7-31 Jan • 4 single rm, 20 double rm • Half board €60-70 • Menu €18-35 • Parking, garden, golf practice range, no dogs

The chestnut woods which surround the farm.

Pontremoli is the capital of the Lunigiana, the delightful district bordered by the parkland of the Apuan Alps, the Versilia riviera down to the southern tip of the Ligurian coast, and the Tuscan-Emilian Apennine watershed. Just out of town, this establishment occupies a typical farmstead which has been well restored. The rooms in the former hay barn are tastefully furnished and well equipped. The restaurant is in the old cellars, and in summer guests may dine outside.

Access

From La Spezia: A 15 for 33km to Pontremoli exit

Sights nearby: Castello del Piagnaro, cathedral, churches of San Colombano and the Annunziata

COSTA D'ORSOLA

Sig. Bezzi
Località Orsola
54027 Pontremoli (MS)
Tel. 0187 833332 – Fax 0187 833332
info@costadorsola.it – www.costadorsola.it

86/114€

Closed Nov and Jan • 14 double rm • Half board €58-72 • Menu €20-30 • Parking, garden, swimming pool • Bicycles available, oil for sale

The horses grazing around the house.

This stone built settlement is surrounded by verdant countryside with wooded hillsides rising in the distance. The peace and quiet here is broken only by the rustling of leaves in the breeze and birdsong. Inside, the ambience is tastefully understated and the furnishings simple. Friendly and helpful family management.

Access

From La Spezia: A 15 for 34km to Pontremoli exit, then right onto SP 31 for 0.8km, then left for 0.5km to Costa d'Orsola

Sights nearby: Castello del Piagnaro, cathedral, churches of San Colombano and the Annunziata

39

LA TORRICELLA

Sig.ra Cipriani
Località Torricella, 14 - Ponte a Poppi
52014 Poppi (AR)
Tel. 0575 527045 – Fax 0575 527046
info@latorricella.com – www.latorricella.com

38-45/55-70€

Open all year • 5 single rm, 8 double rm • Half board €42-46 • Menu €17-25 • Parking, garden • Bicycle hire, home made cantucci biscuits for sale

The view from the restaurant veranda.

Offering panoramic views of the Casentino with its woodlands, castle and rich history, including the battle of Campidoglio in which a young Dante Alighieri took part, this long building has a stone and plaster façade which is characteristically Tuscan. Inside, the decor is rustic and entirely appropriate for a country setting; wood beamed ceilings, tiled floors and wrought iron beds. The restaurant is popular among locals, serving traditional Casentino dishes.

Access
From Arezzo: SS 71 for 33km to Bibbiena, then left onto the SS 70 for 5km

Sights nearby: Castle

FATTORIA SOLAIO

Sig.ra Carabba Serafini

Località Solaio
53030 Radicondoli (SI)
Tel. 0577 791029 – Fax 0577 791015
info@fattoriasolaio.it – www.fattoriasolaio.it

65-80/ 75-90€

Closed 7 Jan-15 Mar, 5 Nov-26 Dec • 8 double rm • Menu €10-20 • Parking, swimming pool, no dogs • Oil and wine for sale

The combination of patrician elegance and rustic simplicity.

This agriturismo encapsulates the agricultural history of the Sienese countryside in microcosm. The earliest buildings date from the 15 and 16C, retaining their original simple demeanour which is decidedly rustic. The main house is of a later date, by which time the traditional rural architecture had given way to a more elegant style befitting a patrician residence. Guests can enjoy an ambience little changed since the18C, when the resident gentry would have walked here among their verdant gardens.

Access

From Siena: SS 73 for 24km, then right for 21km to Solaio

Sights nearby: Siena: Palazzo Pubblico, Piazza del Campo, cathedral, churches of San Domenico and Sant'Agostino

41

ARCHIMEDE

Sig. Marziali
Località Ponte di Casalino
50066 Reggello (FI)
Tel. 055 869055 – Fax 055 868584
archimede@val.it – www.ristorantearchimede.it

60/90€

Closed 20-30 Jan • 5 single rm, 13 double rm • Half board €65 • Menu €21-37 • Parking, garden, swimming pool, tennis, no dogs • Bicycle hire, oil and wine for sale

Strolling through the surrounding woodland, a world away from everyday life.

The road from Reggello to Vallombrosa winds over the peaks which separate the Arno valley from the Pratomagno. The surrounding slopes are heavily planted with dark pine woods. Opened in the 1980s, this hotel sits in a roadside clearing; stone built in the local style, it blends well into the landscape. The terrace and swimming pool are pleasantly situated, almost entirely encircled by the trees which stretch out along the hillside.

Access
From Florence: A 1 to Incisa in Val d'Arno exit, then 11km to Regello, then onto SP 86 for 3.5km to Pietrapiana

Sights nearby: San Pietro in Cascia, Sant'Agata in Arfoli; Reggello: historic centre

42

IL CASALE DEL COTONE

Sig. Martelli

Località Cellole, 59
53037 San Gimignano (SI)
Tel. 0577 943236 – Fax 0577 943236
info@casaledelcotone.com – www.casaledelcotone.com

70-75/98-108€

Open all year • 11 double rm • Menu €35 • Parking, garden, swimming pool, no dogs in the restaurant • Oil and wine for sale

The little 17C chapel with its stucco work decoration.

One of Tuscany's most striking landscapes, the countryside around Siena is a characteristic ochre colour. This natural beauty, coupled with the district's tranquillity, makes a country hotel more appealing than staying in town, especially when it is a late 17C farm with its own chapel and hectares of surrounding olive groves and vineyards. This establishment is decorated in period style with antique furniture; around the property peace reigns supreme among the trees, allowing guests to get away from it all.

Access

From Siena: SGC Firenze-Siena to Poggibonsi, join SP 1 for 12km to San Gimignano, continue towards Certaldo for 5km to Cellole

Sights nearby: San Gimignano: towers, Collegiata, Palazzo del Popolo, church of Sant'Agostino

43

FATTORIA POGGIO ALLORO

F.lli Fioroni

Località Ulignano - Via Sant'Andrea, 23
53037 San Gimignano (SI)
Tel. 0577 950153 – Fax 0577 950290
info@fattoriapoggioalloro.com – www.fattoriapoggioalloro.com

76-90€

Closed 6-31 Jan • 10 double rm • Half board €66-75 • Menu €29-36 • Parking, garden, swimming pool, no dogs • Bicycle hire, oil, wine, pasta, honey and saffron for sale

The view of San Gimignano in the distance, like a mirage in the evening light.

To spend time here is to shut the door on the outside world. The view is over the rolling Sienese hills, planted with cereal crops, olive groves and saffron, and dotted with livestock farms. From this landscape, the local cuisine sources its raw materials, the most distinguished of which is the renowned Chianina beef, used for Fiorentina steak. Gazing from the terrace towards the extraordinary skyline of San Gimignano, guests might be tempted to prolong their stay indefinitely.

Access

From Siena: SGC Firenze-Siena to Colle di Val d'Elsa, right onto SS 68 for 15km, then right for 9.5km to Ulignano

Sights nearby: San Gimignano: towers, Collegiata, Palazzo del Popolo, church of Sant'Agostino

44

PODERE VILLUZZA

Sig.ra Crocchini e Sig. Dei
Località Strada, 25
53037 San Gimignano (SI)
Tel. 0577 940585 – Fax 0577 942247
info@poderevilluzza.it – www.poderevilluzza.it

95€

Open all year • 6 double rm • No restaurant • Parking, garden, swimming pool, no dogs • Extra virgin olive oil for sale

The San Gimignano towers dominating the view with the Sienese landscape rolling away in the distance

Built in pale stone, this easily reached farmhouse occupies an isolated position atop a hill. From here the views stretch for miles, encompassing vineyards, olive groves, citrus orchards and the walls of San Gimignano, encircling the town's extraordinary cluster of medieval towers. Inside, this establishment has an ambience of bygone times with wood beamed ceilings and brick arches; the elegant rooms show the feminine touch of the owner, the courteous Signora Sandra.

Access

From Siena: SGC Firenze-Siena to Poggibonsi exit, then SP 1 for 12km to San Gimignano, continue towards Certaldo to Strada

Sights nearby: Towers, Collegiata, Palazzo del Popolo, church of Sant'Agostino

45

LA LOCANDA DEL CASTELLO

Sig.ra Ratti Ravanelli
Piazza Vittorio Emanuele II, 4
53020 San Giovanni d'Asso (SI)
Tel. 0577 802939 – Fax 0577 802942
info@lalocandadelcastello.com – www.lalocandadelcastello.com

100/ 110€

Closed 15 Jan-28 Feb • 6 double rm • Half board €85 • Menu €30-50 • Small dogs welcome

Dining against the stone backdrop of the olive press, wafted by the scent of truffles.

San Givanni d'Asso sits in the ochre scenery of the Sienese countryside, a small medieval village sited in the shadow of one of the many castles which to this day stand guard over the landscape. The white truffle is one of this area's great natural jewels, and this establishment's restaurant, occupying the old olive press, employs it liberally in its cuisine. Two floors up, in a section of the building dating from the 18C, the rooms are colourful and well furnished, demonstrating the owner's feminine touch at work.

Access
From Siena: SS 2 for 2.5km, onto SS 223 for 2.5km to join SS 73 for 1km, then right onto SS 438 for 21km, right for 12km

Sights nearby: Castle; Siena: Palazzo Pubblico, Piazza del Campo, cathedral, church of San Domenico

46

IL RIGO

Sig. Cipolla e Sig.ra Santo
Località Casabianca
53027 San Quirico d'Orcia (SI)
Tel. 0577 897291 – Fax 0577 898236
info@agriturismoilrigo.com – www.agriturismoilrigo.com

66-71/ 88-94€

Closed 10 Jan-13 Feb • 14 double rm • Breakfast €7; half board €72-78 • Menu €15-23 • Parking, garden • Oil, cereals and vegetables for sale

The air of times gone by here and in the surrounding landscape.

The coat of arms adorning this 16C farmhouse is that of the Hospital of Santa Maria della Scala in Siena, once a significant landowner in this area. The landscape has changed little in the intervening years, although a second house of red brick was subsequently built to house the tenant farmers who tilled the surrounding fields. Today, the accommodation these buildings provide is for guests, for whom there awaits unspoilt countryside, well presented rooms and cordial service from the owners, who dine in company with their visitors. Cookery courses are also available, run in a friendly and relaxed style.

Access
From Siena: SS 2 for 20km to San Quirico d'Orcia, then right for 4.5km to Casabianca

Sights nearby: Sant'Antimo: abbey; Pienza: historic centre

47

VILLA CLODIA

Sig. Ghezzi
Via Italia, 43
58050 Saturnia (GR)
Tel. 0564 601212 – Fax 0564 601305
villaclodia@laltramaremma.it

55/ 90€

Closed 1-20 Dec • 2 single rm, 10 double rm • No restaurant • Garden, swimming pool, no dogs

The little garden surrounded by trees and hedgerows.

Situated in the centre of Saturnia, this quiet little hotel has been converted from a private residence. A family atmosphere prevails without compromising the high standards of the place, which has refined touches such as trompe l'oeil wall decoration in some of the rooms, a few of which also benefit from a large terrace, from where the view takes in the ribbon of trees which encircles the house and its lawn (swimming pool).

Access
From Grosseto: SS 322 for 28km to Scansano, left onto SS 323 for 2km, then right onto SS 322 for 19km, left for 7km

Sights nearby: Promontorio dell'Argentario; Orbetello: cathedral, fortifications

48

CASALI DELL'AIOLA

Sig. e Sig.ra Campelli
Località l'Aiola
53010 Vagliagli (SI)
Tel. 0577 322797 – Fax 0577 322509
info@aiola.net – www.aiola.net

80/90€

Open all year • 7 double rm • No restaurant • Parking, garden, no dogs • Honey, vinegar, oil, grappa and wine for sale

Tasting the local produce against the backdrop of the old hay barn.

Here the eternal rivalry between Siena and Florence is evident; the medieval castle which once occupied this site was razed to the ground in the 16C after Siena was defeated by her rival in alliance with the Emperor Charles V. Today, only traces of its imposing boundary walls survive, around which the farm buildings which today make up this agriturismo were subsequently built. The interiors retain a rustic feel with stone walls and wooden roof beams. The old livestock shed has become the breakfast room, while the former hay barn is a relaxing lounge where guests can while away the hours gazing out over the Tuscan hills.

Access
From Siena: SS 422 for 4km, then right for 8.5km to Vagliagli

Sights nearby: Siena: Palazzo Pubblico, Piazza del Campo, cathedral, churches of San Domenico and Sant'Agostino

49

GAVARINI

Sig.ra Folloni

Mocrone - Via Benedicenti, 50
54028 Villafranca in Lunigiana (MS)
Tel. 0197 495504 – Fax 0187 495790
info@locandagavarini.it – www.locandagavarini.it

35-40/ 70-80€

Closed 7-30 Nov • 1 single rm, 6 double rm • Half board €50-65 • Menu €23-38 • Parking, garden • Organised trips, local produce for sale

The brickwork in the dining room with the open fireplace.

Easily reached from either the motorway or the main road, Locanda Gavarini is in the village's medieval quarter, neat the church of San Maurizio. Originally a trattoria, it now also offers accommodation in the form of six new rooms which are comfortable and welcoming. Meals are served in two large rooms, one of which has an open fireplace and imposing brick arches, or outside among the flowers of the garden in summer.

Access
From La Spezia: A 15 for 16.2km to Aulla exit, then 10km on the SS 62 to Villafranca in Lunigiana, right for 4km to Mocrone

Sights nearby: Pontremoli: Castello di Piagnaro, cathedral, churches of San Colombano and l'Annunziata

50

TASSINAIA

Sig. Ciani
Via di Petroio, 15
50058 Vinci (FI)
Tel. 347 8273962
info@tassinaia.it – www.tassinaia.it

🚹60-70/🚹🚹65-75€

Open all year • 5 double rm • No restaurant • Parking, garden, no dogs

Echoes of Leonardo against the backdrop of the countryside.

It is likely that Leonardo frequented these parts before going on to dazzle the great courts of the Renaissance with his creative genius. Vinci has dedicated a museum to its most famous son which display many models from his vast oeuvre. The landscape is little changed from the 15C, as guests may observe from the terrace of this B&B occupying an 18C house with tile and wood sloping roof. The rustic style interior is in keeping with the tone of the building, with a fine pietra serena open fireplace in the breakfast room, hewn from the same stone in which Brunelleschi and Michelangelo worked.

Access
From Florence: SGC Firenze-Pisa-Livorno to Empoli exit, then left for 2.4km to Empoli, right towards Vinci for 7km to Petroio

Sights nearby: Castle and Museo Leonardiano, birthplace of Leonardo

51

VILLA RIODDI

Sig. Scudellari
Località Rioddi - Strada Monte Volterrano
56048 Volterra (PI)
Tel. 0588 88053 – Fax 0588 88074
info@hotelvillarioddi.it – www.hotelvillarioddi.it

68-93€

Closed 15 Jan-2 Mar, 3 Nov-27 Dec • 13 double rm • No restaurant • Parking, garden, swimming pool, no dogs

The timeless atmosphere of this former post house.

During the period of the Grand Duchy of Tuscany, this 15C building was a post house. Five centuries later it is a peaceful hotel, benefiting from rooms with chestnut furniture, and boasting vaulted ceilings in the former coach house that now makes up the public area. The passage of time has not diluted the charm of this ancient building which is surrounded by extensive gardens and has panoramic views of the Etruscan walls of Volterra and the Cecina valley.

Access

From Siena: SGC Firenze-Siena to Colle Val d'Elsa exit, then onto the SS 68 for 27km to Volterra, then on the SP Monte Volterrano to Rioddi

Sights nearby: Cathedral and baptistery, Piazza dei Priori, Museo Etrusco Guarnacci, Pinacoteca

Garmisch-Partenkirchen
Reutte
Seefeld
Schwaz
Zell
Imst
Anton
Innsbruck
Mayrhofen
Landeck
A L P E N
Großglock
Brenner
1374
Ötztaleralpen
3774
Scuor
Reschen
1507
Vipiteno
Brunico
Bressanone
Dobbiaco
Merano
Cortina d'Ampezzo
Stelvio
2757
Bolzano
2239
Pordoi
Dolomiti
ALTO ADIGE
TRENTINO
ALTO ADIGE
Tonale
Ora
Madonna di Campiglio
Trento
Belluno
Feltre
Riva
Lago di Garda
Rovereto
Conegliano
Bassano del Grappa
Gardone Riviera
Brescia
Treviso
Vicenza
Sirmione
Verona
Mestre
Padova
Lido
Monselice
Nogara
Piave
E 45-60
A 22
S 38
S 47
E 45
S 53
E 70
A 27
A 4
1
2
3
4
5
6
7
8
9
10
11
12
13
14
15
16
17
18
19
20
21
22
23
24
25
26
27
28
29
30
31

TRENTINO-ALTO ADIGE

At dusk, when the sun's rays turn the landscape pink, the Dolomites cease to be inanimate rock and come alive, as captured in countless pictures of the Val di Fassa, Valgardena or the Val Badia. The road winding down from the peaks towards the plain takes in many spots of historical importance; the Holy Roman Emperor passed by here on his way to negotiate with the Italian city states, the German bishops gathered here to participate in the Council of Trent following Luther's reforms, and here Otzi, the mummified herdsman from 3000 BC was found, now on display in Bolzano's archaeological museum. To this day, the region remains a meeting place between cultures, the German and Ladin speaking minorities being the most notable. Historical and cultural diversity has resulted an impressive artistic heritage, encapsulating both the Italianate style of Trento's cathedral and the austere northern style of the cathedrals of the Bolzano area. Its cuisine also reflects this variety of influences: strudel, knödel and Müller-Thurgau contrast with Marzemino d'Isera, carne salada and "strangolapreti".

31 establishments

1

ALPENROSE

Fam. Alfreider

Strada Agà, 20
39033 Corvara in Badia (BZ)
Tel. 0471 836240 – Fax 0471 835652
garni.alpenrose@rolmail.net – www.garnialpenrose.com

28-41/50-80€

Closed May, Nov • 1 single rm, 4 double rm • No restaurant • Parking, no dogs

The friendly management style and ambience.

On the border of Alto Adige and the Veneto, Corvara is situated in one of the most spectacular and charming parts of the Dolomites. A break here offers something for everyone, be it walking through woodland and meadows, or the excitement of skiing; either way the scenery is beautiful. What better base from which to discover the area than this small, pleasant B&B, with a family atmosphere and enjoying a quiet, sunny location?

Access

From Bolzano: SS 12 for 20km to Ponte Gardena, then 9km to join the SS 242, continue for 13.5km, then left onto the SS 243 for 12km

Sights nearby: Scenery towards the Sella range and the Sassongher

CIASA MONTANARA

Sig. Bernardi

La Villa - Strada Plaon, 24
39030 Badia (BZ)

Tel. 0471 847735 – Fax 0471 844920

ciasa@montanara.it – www.montanara.it

30-35/60-70€

Open all year • 1 single rm, 12 double rm • No restaurant • Parking

The combination of traditional style and modern comfort.

The main road through town can get busy in the summer months so this establishment, tucked away up above in the old quarter, enjoys a pleasant location. In addition to its tranquil and panoramic setting, it also offers a comfortable, pleasant ambience and friendly service, making for an unforgettable stay. Built in 1999, this establishment is traditional in style yet incorporates every modern convenience, while its smooth running is assured by the professional management of the Bernardi family.

Access

From Bolzano: follow signs to Brennero, take the Bressanone exit, then near San Lorenzo di Sebato turn right and follow the SP 244 for 20km to Badia

Sights nearby: Scenery; Odle National Park

3

LA CIASOTA

Sig. Rattonara

La Villa - Strada Colz, 118
39030 Badia (BZ)
Tel. 0471 847171 – Fax 0471 845740
laciasota@rolmail.net – www.garnilaciasota.it

37-42/72-82€

Closed 20 Apr-23 Jun, 25 Sep-1 Dec • 2 single rm, 9 double rm • No restaurant • Parking, garden, no dogs

The wooden balconies, decked with colourful flowers in summer.

This large attractive family house has been transformed by a well known local champion skier into a pleasant and welcoming establishment, equally suitable for skiing holidays and summer breaks. Pale pine wood panels cover most of the walls, and the accommodation is full of character and comfortable. The restaurant is also attractive, although its size means that the other public areas are a little cramped. There is a basement gym, and of course the opportunity to have skiing lessons direct from the owner.

Access

From Bolzano: follow signs to Brennero, take the Bressanone exit, then near San Lorenzo di Sebato turn right and follow the SP 244 for 20km to Badia

Sights nearby: Scenery; Odle National Park

4

TAMARINDO

Sig. Bernardi

La Villa - Via Plaon, 20
39030 Badia (BZ)
Tel. 0471 844096 – Fax 0471 844906
tamarindo@rolmail.net – www.tamarindo-lavilla.it

35-40/54-80€

Open all year • 1 single rm, 8 double rm • No restaurant • Parking • Organised trips

The friendly and spontaneous personality of the owner.

This new building is in the old part of town, shrouded in the silence which seems to roll in from the woods to envelop the castle and church. The gregarious nature of the management is surprising, particularly given the reputation of the locals for being reserved. The open terrace offers inspiring views of the valley and surrounding mountains, and is the perfect spot in which to sit with a book and enjoy the sunshine. The spacious rooms have sparklingly modern bathrooms.

Access
From Bolzano: follow signs to Brennero, take the Bressanone exit, then near San Lorenzo di Sebato turn right and follow the SP 244 for 20km to Badia

Sights nearby: Scenery; Odle National Park

5

SCOIATTOLO

Fam. Sartori

Via del Moro, 1
38010 Andalo (TN)
Tel. 0461 585912 – Fax 0461 585980
info@hotelscoiattolo.it – www.hotelscoiattolo.it

49-80/ 68-96€

Closed 6 Apr-19 Jun, 16 Sep-21 Dec • 20 double rm • Half board €50-86 • Menu €26-45 • Parking, no dogs • Bicycles available, tasting of cured meats, cheeses and wine

The comfort and ambience of the honeymoom suite.

Planning a romantic break? Desperate to go skiing? Looking for an alternative to the seaside, somewhere where peace and quiet rules? Then this is the place to go, with just under 30 wood panelled rooms, all spacious and elegant, some of which have four poster beds. In addition, there is a spa, children's games room, restaurant and intimate "stuben" for couples in search of romance.

Access

From Ternto: A 22 for 14km to San Michele all'Adige exit, right onto SS 43 for 8km, then left onto SS 421 for 15km

Sights nearby: Lake Molveno; Adamello-Brenta National Park

6

BAD TURMBACH

Sig. Worndle

Via Rio della Torre, 4
39057 Appiano sulla Strada del Vino (BZ)
Tel. 0471 662339 – Fax 0471 664754
gasthof@turmbach.com – www.turmbach.com

37-40/66-82€

Closed 22 Dec-20 Mar • 1 single rm, 14 double rm • Half board €45-52 • Menu €37-45 • Parking, swimming pool, no dogs in the restaurant • Honey and wine for sale

The classic local cuisine, passionately prepared and served.

Located on a plateau 500m up in the delightful Oltradige district, the town of Appiano sulla Strada del Vino is splendidly located against a backdrop of wine yards and fruit orchards. This simple yet charming hotel has a restaurant with a fine gastronomic reputation. Diners can also enjoy wines produced by the owners themselves.

Access

From Bolzano: SS 4 for 7.5km

Sights nearby: Bolzano: cathedral, Dominican and Franciscan churches, archaeological museum

7

SCHLOSS AICHBERG

Sig. Khuen Belasi

Via Monte, 31
39057 Appiano sulla Strada del Vino (BZ)
Tel. 0471 662247 – Fax 0471 660908
info@aichberg.com – www.aichberg.com

60-65/ 92-100€

Closed 16 Nov-28 Feb • 12 double rm • No restaurant • Parking, garden, swimming pool, no dogs

The vineyards and orchards surrounding the old house.

As the name suggests, this really is a castle with all the features one might expect; crenellated tower, fortified residence, plus some more recent buildings providing the accommodation. Rich in history, this is a remarkable place to stay, even though the interior has recently been renovated. The large gardens and heated pool, plus the hospitality of the owners make for an enjoyable ambience, especially for those in quest of traditional culture and gastronomic delights.

Access
From Bolzano: SS 42 for 7.5km, then right for 2.5km

Sights nearby: Bolzano: cathedral, Dominican and Franciscan churches, archaeological museum

8

LA VECCHIA QUERCIA

Sig.ra Casagrande

Località Masi di Sternigo, 16/1
38042 Baselga di Pinè (TN)
Tel. 0461 553053 – Fax 0461 553053
info@masovecchiaquercia.it – www.masovecchiaquercia.it

42-70,50/ 56-94€

Closed 3-25 Nov • 8 double rm • Half board €30-64 • Menu €22-28 • Parking, garden, no dogs in the restaurant • Jam for sale (tasting)

The relaxing view over the lake.

The 900m high Pinè plateau is a unique spot, a fairytale landscape of peaceful lakes and woodland providing a beautiful backdrop all year round. After a day's walking or sport, there are plenty of tasty local dishes to be savoured. This establishment offers a warm family welcome, extremely reasonable rates, and tranquillity amidst astounding natural beauty. A tonic for any city dweller.

Access
From Trento: after 2km join SS 47, continue for 4km, then left for 12.5km to Masi di Sternigo

Sights nearby: Valley scenery, Lake Serraia and Lake Piazze

9

SAN GIACOMO

F.lli Girardelli

Via Graziani, 1
38060 Brentonico (TN)
Tel. 0464 391560 – Fax 0464 391633
hotels.giacomo@dnet.it

50-70/80-100€

Closed 10-28 Oct • 8 single rm, 26 double rm • Half board €60-80 • Menu €28-35 • Parking, swimming pool, gym, bowls, no dogs • Horse riding, bicycle hire, cheese and wine tasting, honey and potatoes for sale

We most liked

The view over the mountains from the gym.

This hotel will appeal to lovers of efficiency and good organisation. The management here provides the right mix of enterprise and friendliness, as manifestly evident throughout; the well laid out interior, the classic mountain-style decor of the rooms, and most notably the impressive restaurant with painted ceiling panels. Wide range of facilities available to guests.

Access

From Trento: SS 12 for 24km to Rovereto, then right onto the SS 240 for 6km to Mori, then left for 12.5km to San Giacomo

Sights nearby: Church of Santi Pietro e Paolo, Palazzo Eccheli-Baisi; Lake Garda

10

BIRCHER

Sig.ra Mayr Werth

Località Maria Trens
39040 Campo di Trens (BZ)
Tel. 0472 647122 – Fax 0472 647350
info@hotelbircher.it – www.hotelbircher.it

40-45/59-69€

Closed 20 Nov-26 Dec • 4 single rm, 28 double rm • Half board €41-50 • Menu €28-41 • Parking, swimming pool, small dogs allowed in rooms

The warm, generous family hospitality.

Halfway between Bressanone and the Austrian border, 1000m up in the Isarco valley, Campo di Trens is a small village on the edge of woodland, its houses all rigorously adhering to the local architectural style. Enthusiastically run by a family management team (fourth generation), the Bircher hotel has been extensively improved and enhanced, both in terms of decor and facilities which now extend to a covered pool and gym. Generous, mouth-watering buffet breakfast.

Access

From Bolzano: A 22 for 38km to Bressanone exit, then onto the SS 12 for 20km

Sights nearby: Scenery of the Isarco valley and mountains; Vipiteno: historic centre

11

AL VIEL

Fam. Bernard

Streda de Ciampac, 7
38032 Canazei (TN)
Tel. 0462 600081 – Fax 0462 606294
garnialviel@virgilio.it

60-98€

Closed May, Oct-Nov • 12 double rm • No restaurant • Parking, no dogs

The woodwork creating a warm ambience throughout.

Of recent construction, this building has a grey-pink façade and incorporates a great deal of wood in characteristic mountain style. Peacefully located a short walk from the centre and the ski lifts, this hotel has an informal ambience more readily associated with a private house, thanks to the owners' friendly management style.

Access

From Trento: A 22 for 35km to Egna-Ora exit, then onto the SS 48 for 62km

Sights nearby: Scenery towards the Sella range, Catinaccio, Marmolada

ANSITZ FONTEKLAUS

F.lli Gfader

Località Fraina
39043 Chiusa (BZ)

Tel. 0471 655654 – Fax 0471 655045

info@fonteklaus.it – www.fonteklaus.it

42-47/ 70-74€

Closed Dec-Mar • 2 single rm, 7 double rm • Half board €40-52 • Menu €26-47 • Parking, garden, small lake for swimming

Swimming in the lake, with the beautiful panorama of the mountains in view

A fairytale 14C house with red and white shutters and a sloping roof, surrounded by shady fir trees and green sunlit meadows opening out onto some of the best views in the Alto Adige. This is the backdrop against which the Gfader family enthusiastically runs this charming establishment which, in addition to its fantastic location, is noteworthy for its attractive mountain-style decor and its gastronomic delights. The ideal spot for romantic weekends or longer family breaks.

Access

From Bolzano: A 22 for 23km to Chiusa-Val Gardena exit, then left for 3.5km to Fraina

Sights nearby: Historic centre, mountain and valley scenery, monastery of Sabiona

13

UNTERWIRT

Fam. Haselwanter

Località Gudon
39043 Chiusa (BZ)
Tel. 0472 844000 – Fax 0472 844065
info@unterwirt-gufidaun.com – www.unterwirt-gufidaun.com

47/74€

Closed Jan-Mar • 6 double rm • Menu €42-54 • Parking, garden, swimming pool • Tasting of cured meats and preserves, bread and jams for sale

The restaurant, which could not be more typically local in style.

This simple residence is in the pleasant little village of Gudon, not far from the motorway. Surrounded by gardens, it has a pool for those hot summer months. Inside there are seven simple yet comfortable rooms, some with cooking facilities. The restaurant focuses on local specialities, with an interesting and varied menu, and has a cosy feel with antique "stuben" which are characteristic of the local architecture.

Access

From Bolzano: A 22 for 23km to Chiusa-Val Gardena exit, then right for 2km to Gudon/Gufidaun

Sights nearby: Historic centre, mountain and valley scenery, monastery of Sabiona

14

AURORA

Sig. e Sig.ra Tamburini

Località Casina dei Pomi, 139
38082 Cimego (TN)
Tel. 0465 621064 – Fax 0465 621771
graziano@hotelaurora.tn.it – www.hotelaurora.tn.it

28-36/ 54-68€

Open all year • 1 single rm, 18 double rm • Half board €42-48 • Menu €18-30 • Parking, garden, swimming pool, no dogs in the restaurant • Organised trips, fishing, cheese and jam tasting

The infectious enthusiasm of the owners.

Situated 600m up in the Chiese valley, Cimengo is an old town where history is ever present, most notably in the narrow alleys of the Rione quarter with its Venetian style architecture. Located conveniently if not idyllically on a road, this hotel is readily recognisable by its mountain style and painted façade, giving it a chocolate box air. Inside, there is a chalet feel, with a lot of woodwork in evidence, most notably in the top floor rooms and the dining room; renowned for local specialities.

Access

From Trento: SS 45 bis for 16km, then onto the SS 237 for 40km

Sights nearby: Scenery of the Chiese valley; Pieve di Bono castle

15

DEROMEDI

Sig.ra Deromedi
Viale De Gasperi, 118
38023 Cles (TN)
Tel. 0463 423261 – Fax 0463 423261

34-37/57-62€

Open all year • 6 double rm • No restaurant • Garden • Organised trips, honey for sale

The 1950s furniture, once again in fashion.

Apples are the main crop in the Non valley, and they are an ever present feature of the area, along with the towers and castles clinging to the steep hillsides. Cles is the ideal base from which to explore the district, and this hotel, with its high standards of comfort and authentic local ambience of simple, genuine hospitality, is the perfect place to stay.

Access
From Trento: A 22 for 14km to San Michele all'Adige exit, then onto the SS 43 for 26km

Sights nearby: Lake Tovel, Adamello-Brenta National Park

16

KAISERKRONE

Gardenia Srl

Piazza Serra, 3
38025 Dimaro (TN)
Tel. 0463 973326 – Fax 0463 973016
info@kaiserkrone.it – www.kaiserkrone.it

30-60/60-100€

Closed May • 7 double rm • No restaurant

The largest rooms, almost on the scale of an apartment.

In the centre of Dimaro, at the foot of the majestic Sasso Rosso, this hotel is named after the Emperor Franz Joseph who once stayed here. Little has changed since his time. This is a classic Austrian-style building, its façade a light pink, with two tone shutters and a sloping roof. Inside, there is much woodwork in evidence, making for a warm, intimate ambience. The remarkable rooms are spacious and decorated with pale wood furnishings. The public areas, although somewhat cramped, include a bar where the buffet breakfast is served.

Access

From Trento: A 22 for 14km to San Michele all'Adige exit, onto the SS 43 for 32 km, then left onto the SS 42 for 13.5km

Sights nearby: Adamello-Brenta National Park

17

MASO LIZZONE

Fam. Brighenti
Via Lizzone, località Ceniga
38074 Dro (TN)
Tel. 0464 504793 – Fax 0464 504793
info@masolizzone.com – www.masolizzone.com

50-57/78-90€

Closed 20 Jan-28 Feb, 3 Nov-31 Dec • 1 single rm, 4 double rm • No restaurant • Parking, garden, no dogs • Bicycle hire, honey, apples, kiwi fruit, oil and wine for sale

The well equipped kitchen, available to guests.

Water, air, iron, earth and fire. Not mythology or science, but the names of the splendid rooms in this fine country house to the north of Lake Garda, situated in a peaceful spot surrounded by olive groves and vineyards. The accommodation, occupying the first floor, is tasteful and simple. Downstairs is the large vaulted kitchen for the use of guests, a breakfast room and library. There are also seven camping pitches occupying the terraced area.

Access
From Trento: SS 45 bis for 28km, then right for 0.5km to Ceniga

Sights nearby: Riva del Garda: old town, Rocca; Lake Garda

18

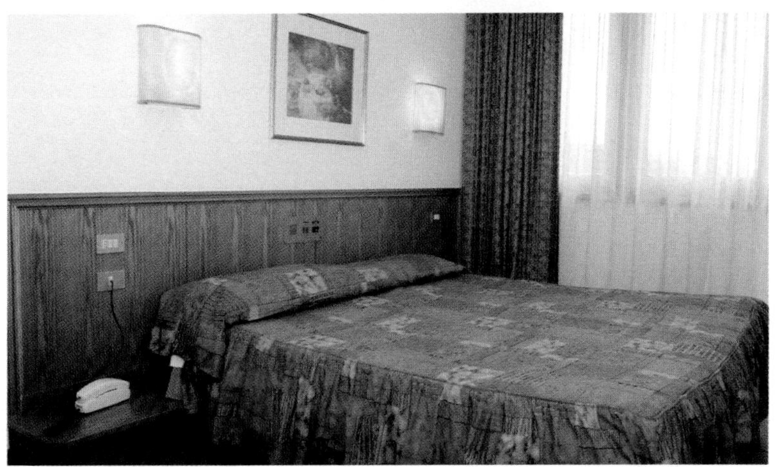

ARCOBALENO

Sig. Tomidandel

Via Cesare Battisti, 29
38010 Fai della Paganella (TN)
Tel. 0461 583306 – Fax 0461 583535
info@hotelarcobaleno.it – www.hotelarcobaleno.it

35-45/60-80€

Closed 1 Nov-8 Dec • 1 single rm, 33 double rm • Half board €35-63 • Menu €15-30 • Parking, gym, no dogs • Bicycles available

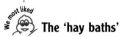

The 'hay baths'

Fai della Paganella sits on a plateau 1000m up, overlooking Trento and the Adige valley. Beautiful landscape, a pleasant climate and plenty of sunshine make this an attractive destination regardless of the season, and this is the perfect place to stay, especially for those looking for relaxation and therapy. Facilities include a gym, solarium, sauna, turkish bath and jacuzzi.

Access

From Trento: A 22 for 14km to S. Michele all'Adige exit, right for 6km on the SS 43, then left for 9km

Sights nearby: Lake Molveno; Adamello-Brenta National Park

19

MASO POMAROLLI

F.lli Franch

Località Maso Pomarolli, 10
38030 Palù di Giovo (TN)
Tel. 0461 684571 – Fax 0461 684570
info@agriturmasopomarolli.it – www.agriturismomasopomarolli.it

40/70€

Closed 11 Jan-15 Feb • 3 single rm, 5 double rm • Half board €50 • Menu €15-20 • Parking, garden, no dogs in the restaurant • Organised trips, bicycle hire, jam, cured meat, cheese and wine tasting

The breathtaking views from some of the rooms.

The Cembra valley with its orchards and terraced vineyards forms the backdrop for this characterful alpine agriturismo, restored and refurbished by the Franch brothers to provide accommodation for around fifteen guests. The rooms have typical wood furniture of good quality; the two most sought after have stunning views. Breakfast and dinner are served in a charming dining room; incorporating home grown ingredients, the cuisine focuses on local specialities and is not to be missed.

Access

From Trento: SS 12 for 8km, then right onto the SS 612 for 5.5km, then left for about 2km to Maso Pomarolli

Sights nearby: Trento: Castello del Buonconsiglio, cathedral, piazza, Palazzo Tabarelli

20

PLONERHOF

Fam. Pohl

Via Peter Thalguter, 11
39022 Lagundo (BZ)
Tel. 0473 448728 – Fax 0473 491220
info@plonerhof.it – www.plonerhof.it

30/54€

Open all year • 2 single rm, 5 double rm • No restaurant • Parking, garden, swimming pool • Jam tasting, fruit for sale

The wooden balconies bedecked with flowers.

This 14C building is not far from the town centre; occupying a sunny and verdant location, it is decorated with typical Tirolese inscriptions in gothic characters which line the staircase and the little dining area. The rooms have a simpler feel, with small but well equipped bathrooms. The swimming pool and garden planted with fruit trees are very welcome features in the summer months.

Access
From Bolzano: SS 42 for 4.5km, right onto SS 38 for 27km, then right for 1km

Sights nearby: Merano: Walks, cathedral, Castello Principesco, Via Portici

21

SITTNERHOF

Sig. Brunner
Via Verdi, 60
39012 Merano (BZ)
Tel. 0473 221631 – Fax 0473 206520
info@bauernhofurlaub.it – www.bauernhofurlaub.it

60-70€

Closed 6 Nov-28 Feb • 5 double rm • No restaurant • Parking, garden, swimming pool, no dogs • Apples, grapes and wine for sale

A bucolic ambience surprisingly close to the heart of Merano.

In a quiet and shady residential street, this agriturismo occupies a splendid building of 11C origin which has undergone numerous alterations down the centuries; today its facade combines dark wood with religiously inspired fresco painting. Inside, the most charming room is the characteristic stube where breakfast is served. The accommodation is less striking and furnished with modern pieces. Around the house is the family vineyard, which guests may visit, and the garden with a splendid swimming pool.

Access
From Bolzano: SS 42 for 4.5km, right onto the SS 38 for 20km, then right for 4.5km

Sights nearby: Merano: Walks, cathedral, Castello Principesco, Via Portici

22

PONTE-BRÜCKENWIRT

Sig. Zanol
Stifstrasse, 2
39040 Novacella (BZ)
Tel. 0472 836692 – Fax 0472 837587
brückenwirt@tin.it

41-45/82-90€

Closed Feb • 3 single rm, 9 double rm • Half board €51-56 • Menu €13-19 • Parking, garden, swimming pool, no dogs

The tranquillity which prevails throughout.

Well situated close to the famous Novacella abbey, this fine 12C building offers traditional local hospitality courtesy of its family management team. Order and cleanliness reign in both the accommodation – the top floor rooms are especially attractive – and the public areas, composed of the bar, restaurant and the characteristic stube. Outside there is a large garden with swimming pool and wooden tables set out under ancient shady trees.

Access

From Bolzano: SS 12 for 3km, then A 22 for 38km to Bressanone exit, onto the SS 49 for 1km, then right onto the SS 12 for 4km, left for 1km

Sights nearby: Bressanone: Cathedral, Palazzo Vescovile

23

CASTEL PERGINE

Sig.ra Neff e Sig. Schneider

Via del Castello, 10
38057 Pergine Valsugana (TN)
Tel. 0461 531158 – Fax 0461 531329
verena@castelpergine.it – www.castelpergine.it

50/100€

Closed 6 Nov-6 Apr • 7 single rm, 14 double rm • Half board €66 • Menu €28-38 • Parking, garden, no dogs in the restaurant

The contemporary artwork exhibited in the garden.

Those wishing to step back in time should choose this hotel for their holiday, a charming medieval castle dating from the 13C which has been well restored and is competently run by Verena and Theo, an enthusiastic couple who were previously a translator and an architect. Gourmets will enjoy the elegant restaurant which serves generous portions of Trentino cuisine and has an excellent wine list.

Access
From Trento: SS 47 for 6km

Sights nearby: Trento: Castello del Buonconsiglio, cathedral and piazza, Palazzo Tabarelli

24

ANTICO BAGNO

Zulian Marcello e C. Snc

Via Antico Bagno
38036 Pozza di Fassa (TN)
Tel. 0462 763232 – Fax 0462 763232
anticobagno@tin.it – www.hotel-anticobagno-terme.com

68-78€

Closed 5 Oct-4 Dec • 15 double rm • Half board €45-76 • Menu €22-35 • Parking, garden, no dogs

The hotel's spa, set on the edge of woodland among mountains.

For centuries, this spot has attracted visitors on account of its sulphurous spring waters and their curative powers. Today the tradition continues thanks to this hotel, founded by the current owner's father, who wanted to create an establishment appropriate for a thermal resort. Pleasantly situated on high ground a little out of town, it is flanked by woods which extend down the slopes, while the view of the village church is enhanced by the backdrop of high mountain peaks beyond.

Access

From Trento: A 22 for 35km to Egna-Ora exit, then onto SS 48 for 52km

Sights nearby: Scenery towards il Catinaccio; Torre di Pozza

25

RIFUGIO FUCIADE

Sig. Rossi
Località Fuciade
38030 Soraga (TN)
Tel. 0462 574281 – Fax 0462 574281

80-84€

Closed 20 Apr-14 Jun, 16 Oct-23 Dec • 7 double rm • Half board €72-74 • Menu €30-45 • No dogs • Jam, cured meat and cheese tasting

The exceptional mountain location.

Keen walkers can reach this establishment on foot through woodland; should the snows have come, a snowmobile will be necessary. Situated nearly 2000m up (1982m, to be specific) the views over the surrounding countryside are stunning, taking in meadows, woods, mountains and sky, with very little else except the odd alpine dwelling in wood and stone. Up here, the world beyond the Dolomites does not impinge at all. In the restaurant, the cuisine is tasty and simple mountain fare, served to guests at solid refectory tables.

Access
From Bolzano: SS 12 for 2km, right onto SS 241, then right to Moena, left onto SS 346, then left to Rifugio Fuciade

Sights nearby: Mountain scenery

26

GEIER

Sig. Geier
Via Chemun, 36
39047 Santa Cristina Valgardena (BZ)
Tel. 0471 793370 – Fax 0471 793370
garni-geier@valgardena.com

60-90€

Closed Dec-Apr • 8 double rm • No restaurant • Gym, no dogs

The high peaks of the Dolomites soaring above the valley.

Travellers passing through Santa Cristina cannot fail to notice this traditional mountain building, its stark white ground floor walls surmounted by the wooden structure of the upper storey and beamed sloping roof. The façade is suggestive of a warm and comfortable alpine residence, and once inside this is confirmed. The accommodation and public areas, including sauna and solarium, are modern yet welcoming in feel, with much pale woodwork in evidence. From the balcony there are fine views of the Dolomites stretching into the distance.

Access
From Bolzano: SS 12 for 20km to Ponte Gardena, then right onto SS 242 for 17.5km

Sights nearby: Odle National Park; scenery around Il Sassolungo

27

VILLA PRA RONCH

Sig.ra Rabanser

Via La Selva, 80
39048 Selva di Valgardena (BZ)
Tel. 0471 794064 – Fax 0471 794064
praronch@valgardena.it

62-98€

Closed Nov, May • 5 double rm • Horse riding, parking, garden, no dogs in the restaurant • Organised trips with mountain guide

The scent of wood from the Tirolese furnishings.

Previously a private house, this charming B&B is in a panoramic location looking out over the surrounding mountains, vast natural watchtowers impervious to time and the elements. Against this rugged backdrop, the traditional architecture of this alpine building is particularly elegant, its stone walls covered in white plaster surmounted by the wooden beams of the upper storey and roof. Inside, woodwork is also prominent throughout; the rooms are variously decorated, but all possess a characteristic style typical of the area.

Access
From Bolzano: SS 12 for 20km to Ponte Gardena, then right onto the SS 242 for 21km

Sights nearby: Odle National Park; scenery around Il Sassolungo

28

MEZZOSOLDO

Sig. e Sig.ra Lorenzi

Località Mortaso
38088 Spiazzo (TN)
Tel. 0465 801067 – Fax 0465 801078
albergomezzosoldo@cr-surfing.net – www.mezzosoldo.it

38-50/ 70-82€

Closed 16 Apr-14 Jun, 26 Sep-4 Dec • 2 single rm, 24 double rm • Half board €40-58 • Menu €28-35 • Parking, no dogs in the restaurant • Organised trips, bicycles available, tasting of produce made from wild herbs

The Trentino heritage evident in the cuisine and the decor.

The Mezzosoldo family have run this establishment for four generations and over a century. The accommodation is furnished with antique pieces which give each room a distinctive style, ranging from rustic to polished mahogany. In the restaurant, diners may choose between four room, one romantic, another rustic, the third like a hay barn and finally the light and airy winter garden style room. An ideal spot for those in search of the real Trentino.

Access

From Trento: SS 45 for 17km to Sarche, right onto the SS 237 for 22km to Tione, then right onto the SS 239 for 8.5km to Mortaso

Sights nearby: Adamello-Brenta National Park

29

ALPENJUWEL

Fam. Köllemann

Località Melago, 102
39020 Vallelunga (BZ)

Tel. 0473 633291 – Fax 0473 633502

info@alpenjuwel.it – www.alpenjuvel.it

59/98€

Closed 10 Jun-1 Jul, 1 Nov-20 Dec • 16 double rm • Half board €43-47 • Parking, swimming pool • Organised trips

Getting away from it all.

This hotel has a traditional white facade with wooden balconies and roof, blending well with the mountain landscape, while the interior has been completely restored. The rustic furnishings and much woodwork make for a welcoming ambience. After a day spent exploring the mountain scenery, guests can enjoy the swimming pool and gym. Signor Köllerman, the proprietor, personally supervises the kitchen – do not hesitate to ask him for menu recommendations.

Access

From Bolzano: SS 42 for 4.5km to SS 38, continue for 97km, then right for 9.5km to Melago

Sights nearby: Alpine scenery, Rifugio Pio IX, Palla Bianca glaciers, source of the River Adige

30

MILLEFIORI

Sig. Mariano
Strada de la Vila 16
38039 Vigo di Fassa (TN)
Tel. 0462 769000 – Fax 0462 769000
info@hotelmillefiori.com – www.hotelmillefiori.com

45/90€

Closed 20 Jun-1 Jul, 4 Nov-4 Dec • 1 single rm, 11 double rm • Half board €55 • Menu €16-30 • Parking, garden, no dogs in the restaurant • Organised trips and climbs, bicycles available

The panoramic view of the Dolomites from the terrace.

Vallonga is a small village on the Passo di Costalunga road, perched on a slope among the woods of the mountain valleys. The hotel is in a sunny and panoramic spot; in summer it is instantly identifiable on account of the flowers which bedeck its wooden balconies. Tiled staircases and corridors lead to the rooms, furnished in alpine style. The owner, Signor Cecco, oversees the kitchen personally and in summer guests are served on the terrace.

Access
From Trento: A 22 for 35km to Egna-Ora exit, then 60km on the SS 48

Sights nearby: Scenery towards Catinaccio

31

KRANEBITT

Fam. Totsch

Val di Vizze - Località Caminata alt. 1441 (Est: 16 km)
39040 Vizze (BZ)
Tel. 0472 646019 – Fax 0472 646088
info@kranebitt.com – www.kranebitt.com

43-54/ 64-88€

Closed 18 Apr-21 May, 30 Oct-25 Dec • 4 single rm, 24 double rm • Half board €36-53 • Menu €30-35 • Parking, garden, swimming pool, no dogs in the restaurant

The mountains which rise skywards from the wooded valley.

Flanked by fir trees, this hotel overlooks a valley dotted with the pale outlines of alpine houses. Recently renovated, it now boasts a health club with sauna, spa bath and solarium. Also on offer are various spa treatments including a hay, algae or milk bath. The overriding attraction however remains the mountains, ideal for winter skiing and summer breaks in one of Italy's most beautiful landscapes.

Access

From Bolzano: SS 12 for 3km, then 59km on the A 22 to Vipiteno exit, then 1.1km to join SS 508, continue for 14km to Caminata

Sights nearby: Scenery; Vipiteno: Città Nuova (New City)

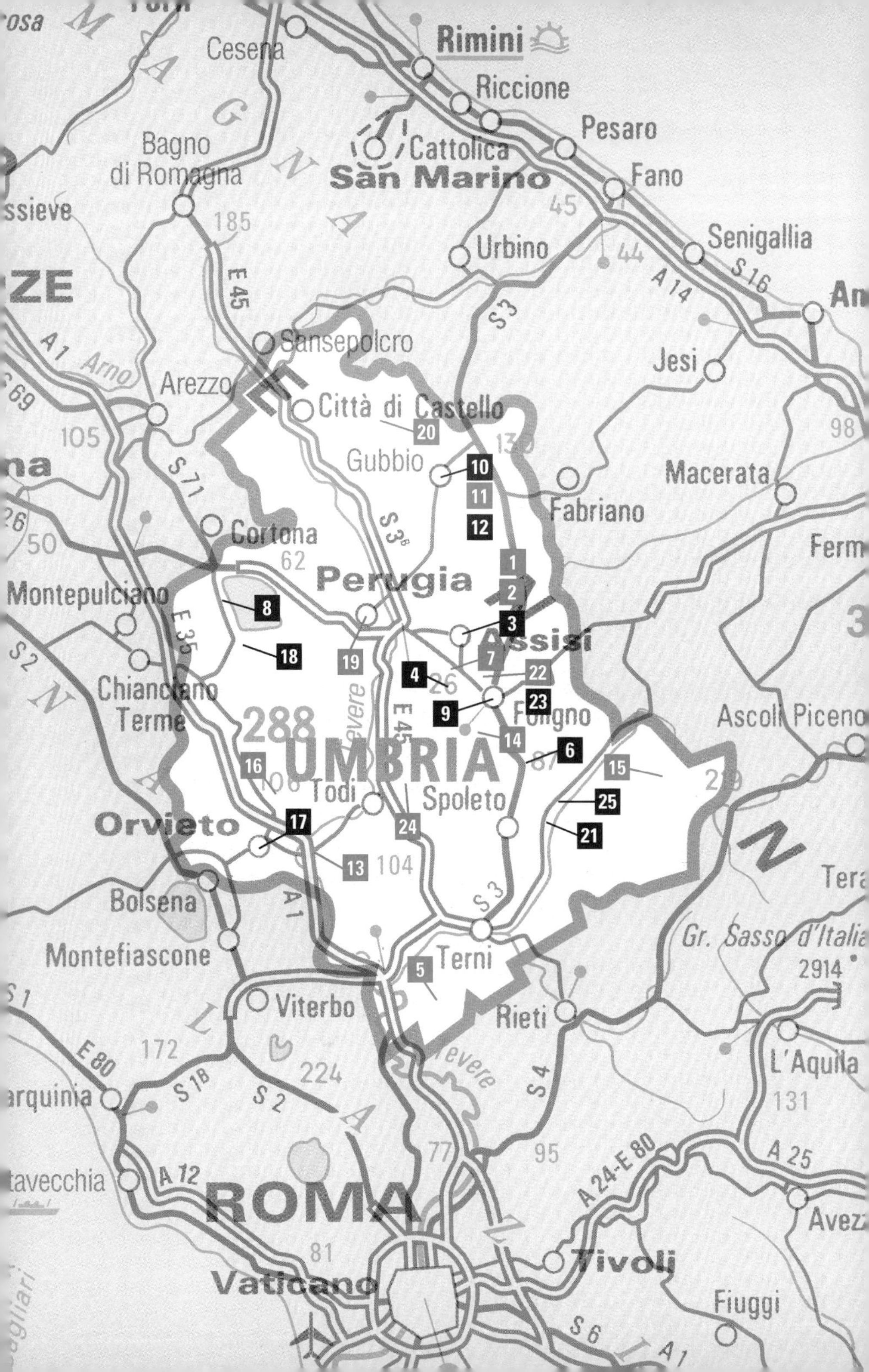

Rimini
Cesena
Riccione
Cattolica
San Marino
Pesaro
Fano
Bagno di Romagna
Urbino
Senigallia
Sansepolcro
Jesi
Arezzo
Città di Castello
Gubbio
Macerata
Fabriano
Cortona
Perugia
Montepulciano
Assisi
Chianciano Terme
Foligno
Ascoli Piceno
UMBRIA
Todi
Spoleto
Orvieto
Bolsena
Terni
Montefiascone
Gr. Sasso d'Italia
2914
Viterbo
Rieti
L'Aquila
ROMA
Tivoli
Vaticano
Fiuggi

UMBRIA

Hilly and lush, Umbria is central Italy's only landlocked region, a fact unlikely to bother visitors given its myriad attractions. Not that water is scarce; it has the large lake Trasimeno, the smaller Piediluco and the river Tiber.

Its gentle scenery and vast pasturelands have been celebrated since Antiquity, and it comes as no surprise that the region has spawned many artists, poets and great men like St Francis of Assisi.

Churches, palaces, streets and squares characterise the historic centres of its cities, such as Gubbio, Orvieto, Spoleto, Spello and Foligno. Its capital, Perugia, sits in a panoramic spot and is one of the most important historical centres as well as being the seat of an ancient and renowned university.

The cuisine includes tasty pasta dishes thanks to the variety of local specialities, almost all of which are meat based. Wine buffs cannot fail to be impressed by the selection available, including Torgiano, Sagrantino di Montefalco and Orvieto.

25 establishments

1

IL GIARDINO DEI CILIEGI

Sig.ra Covarelli
Via Massera, 6
06081 Assisi (PG)
Tel. 075 8064091 – Fax 075 8069070
giardinodeiciliegi@libero.it – www.ilgiardinodeiciliegi.it

80-90€

Closed 8-31 Jan • 8 double rm • Half board €57-65 • Menu €20-30 • Parking, garden, no dogs • Bicycles available, oil for sale

The family atmosphere, making all guests feel at home.

Against the agricultural backdrop of olive growing and wine making, visitors may go walking or cycling, visit local vineyards, or enjoy a game of bowls or table tennis. This is the perfect spot for those seeking a peaceful and relaxing break, cared for by expert hosts. Comfortable rooms, a charming restaurant, and tasteful period style furnishing throughout.

Access
From Perugia: SS 3 bis for 3.5km, then onto the SS 75 for 13km, take the Rivotorto exit and continue for 1.5km to Viole-Capodacqua

Sights nearby: Foligno: Palazzo Trinci; Assisi: Basilica of San Francesco, temple of Minerva, cathedral, church of Santa Chiara

2

MALVARINA

Sig. Fabrizi
Pieve Sant'Apollinare, 32
06081 Assisi (PG)
Tel. 075 8064280 – Fax 075 8064280
info@malvarina.it – www.malvarina.it

52/93€

Open all year • 9 single rm, 9 double rm • Half board €70 • Menu €25-30 • Parking, garden, swimming pool, no dogs • Horse riding, jams and oil for sale, tasting of truffles and cheese

Enjoying the glories of nature from the saddle.

This establishment occupies three buildings surrounded by olive groves, with pool and sun deck for the summer, and stables for those who wish to explore the area on horseback. Situated in a peaceful spot, the place is professionally run with uniformed staff, great attention to detail and fastidious cleanliness. The rustic style rooms are well equipped and the restaurant has a set menu offering home made specialities.

Access

From Perugia: SS 3 bis for 3.5km, then SS 75 for 26km, then SS 3 for 5km toward Nocera Umbra, left for 5km to Capodacqua

Sights nearby: Foligno: Palazzo Trinci; Assisi: Basilica of San Francesco, temple of Minerva, cathedral, church of Santa Chiara

3

IL MANIERO

Sig. Generotti

Via Biagiano, 11
06081 Assisi (PG)
Tel. 075 816379 – Fax 075 815147
ilmaniero@ilmaniero.com – www.ilmaniero.com

52-62/78-96€

Open all year • 5 single rm, 12 double rm • Half board €56-65 • Menu €22-35 • Parking, garden, no dogs in the restaurant

Resting in the cool courtyard on hot summer afternoons.

Also known as the Castello di Biagiano, this fortified building is of medieval origin. Its distinguished past is evinced in its walls, tower and internal courtyard; elsewhere the look is simple and up to date. Open country unfurls in all directions, punctuated by cypresses, pines and oaks, which provide greenery whatever the season. Traditional cuisine in the restaurant, served in the characterful surroundings of the former cellars.

Access

From Perugia: SS 3 bis for 3.5km, SS 75 for 2km, then left into SS 147 for 7km to Biagiano San Fortunato

Sights nearby: Assisi: Basilica of San Francesco, temple of Minerva, cathedral, church of Santa Chiara

POGGIO DEI PETTIROSSI

Sig. Fancelli

Vocabolo Pilone, 301
06031 Bevagna (PG)
Tel. 0742 361744 – Fax 0742 369238
info@ilpoggiodeipettirossi.com – www.ilpoggiodeipettirossi.com

50-70/ 70-93€

Open all year • 29 double rm • Half board €60-71.50 • Menu €25-43 • Parking, garden, swimming pool, no dogs in the restaurant • Vegetables, oil and wine for sale; tasting of typical local produce

Sunbathing by the pool while enjoying the fantastic view.

Those worried about staying in a boarding house pretending to be an agriturismo, or finding themselves sandwiched in a viewless bungalow between a railway line and motorway, can discard their concerns. Here the promotional material is all true; vineyards and olive groves ring the property, the views take in half of Umbria, the accommodation is extremely comfortable, and the situation is perfect, being a short hop from Assisi, Foligno, Spoleto, Perugia, and Bevagna.

Access

From Perugia: SS 317 for 3km then left towards the SS 3 bis, continue to San Martino in Campo exit, then 24km to Bevagna

Sights nearby: Torre Comunale, churches of San Francesco, Sant'Agostino and Santa Illuminata; Bevagna: Roman remains

5

SANTA BRIGIDA

Sig.ra Pannullo

Località Santa Brigida, 3
05032 Calvi dell'Umbria (TR)
Tel. 0744 710386 – Fax 0744 710375
info@bioagriturismo.it – www.bioagriturismo.it

50/75€

Closed Dec-Feb • 4 single rm, 4 double rm • Breakfast €5; half board €65 • Menu €18-25 • Parking, swimming pool, garden • Horse riding, bicycles available, oil for sale

The charming terraced pool with fine views over the valley.

Halfway between Assisi and Rome, Calvi sits on a rocky outcrop at the southernmost tip of the province of Terni, close to the Lazio border. This typical stone built establishment is peacefully located a little out of town; in the main house is the accommodation in the form of rooms and two apartments, while the restaurant is in an adjacent building. The atmosphere is charming, with homely furnishings that are warm yet functional. Also worthy of note are the fine views over the surrounding countryside, and the home made cuisine incorporating meat from animals raised on the adjoining farm

Access

From Terni: SS 3 for 17km, then left for 7km to Santa Brigida

Sights nearby: Narni: Rocca, Ponte di Augusto, Palazzo dei Priori, Palazzo Comunale, abbey of San Cassiano

6

LE CASALINE

Sig. Zeppadoro

Località Casaline
06042 Campello sul Clitunno (PG)
Tel. 0743 521113 – Fax 0743 275099
informazioni@lecasaline.it – www.lecasaline.it

40-50/65€

Open all year • 1 single rm, 6 double rm • Half board €45-55 • Menu €30-40 • Parking, garden • Tasting of cheese and cakes, cured meat and oil for sale

The authentic rural ambience.

Situated 500m up, halfway between Foligno and Spoleto, this building started life as a mill in the 18C before being used as a cowshed in the 19C. Opened as a hotel in 1972, the place retains a strong agricultural feel, with all manner of animals roaming around the perimeter, making for a delightfully rustic setting.

Access

From Perugia: SS 3 bis for 3.5km, then onto the SS 75 for 26km, then 17km on the SS 3, left for 5km to Casaline

Sights nearby: Spoleto: Cathedral, Ponte delle Torri, basilica of San Salvatore, churches of San Gregorio Maggiore and San Domenico

7

LA FATTORIA DEL GELSO

Sig. Rulli Bonaca

Via Bevagna, 16
06033 Cannara (PG)
Tel. 074 272164 – Fax 074 272164
info@lafattoriadelgelso.com – www.lafattoriadelgelso.com

50/80-90€

Open all year • 8 double rm • Half board €65-70 • Menu €25 • Parking, garden, swimming pool • Organised trips, bicycles available, vegetables, oil and wine for sale

We most liked

The lively decorative scheme and well planted garden.

The ideal base from which to explore Umbria's charming towns, this well presented establishment is located just outside the village, and offers pleasant spacious accommodation with personal touches. The owners pride themselves on this haven of peace and quiet, and, in this respect, the hotel is probably not best suited to young families. Situated in a panoramic spot, the pool provides welcome relief during the hot summer months.

Access

From Perugia: SS 3 bis for 3.5km, onto the SS 75 for 19.5km, then right for 9km to Via Bevagna

Sights nearby: Churches of Santa Maria Maggiore and Sant'Andrea

8

LOCANDA POGGIOLEONE

Agrotec Srl

Via Indipendenza, 116/B
06061 Castiglione del Lago (PG)
Tel. 075 959519 – Fax 075 959609
locandapoggioleonel@libero.it – www.locandapoggioleone.it

50-60/ 70-80€

Closed 15 Jan-15 Mar • 2 single rm, 10 double rm • Half board €52-62 • Menu €22 • Parking, garden, swimming pool, no dogs • Bicycle hire, oil and wine for sale

The wrought iron beds, lending a touch of class to the accommodation.

The owner, Signor Luigetti, has fled a white collar existence to fulfill a long standing ambition; ably assisted by his sister, he runs this homely, comfortable establishment with a personal touch. The rooms are furnished in period style, the bathrooms are smart, and the public areas spacious and welcoming, as is the garden with pool, particularly during the summer. The residents-only restaurant specialises in Umbrian and Tuscan cuisine.

Access

From Perugia: SGC Perugia-Bettolle for 29km to Castiglione al Lago exit, onto the SS 71 for 8.8km to Castiglione al Lago, then right for 8km to Pozzuolo

Sights nearby: Lake Trasimeno; Montepulciano: Palazzo Comunale, Palazzo Nobili-Tarugi, cathedral, church of Sant'Agostino

9

VILLA RONCALLI

Sig. Scolastra
Via Roma, 25
06030 Foligno (PG)
Tel. 0742 391091 – Fax 0742 391001

63/85€

Open all year • 2 single rm, 8 double rm • Half board €85 • Menu €40-45 • Parking, swimming pool, no dogs

The sumptuous surroundings of the breakfast room.

Just outside Foligno, this historic residence retains its timeless charm. Surrounded by verdant parkland, it is at its best in summer when the swimming pool is open and guests are served their meals outside. The family management team has created a warm and informal ambience, with a strong feminine touch in evidence in the large and clean rooms. The restaurant is popular with regulars and tourists alike, and serves local dishes which vary according to seasonal availability.

Access
From Perugia: SS 3 bis for 3.5km, then SS 75 for 21km, turn right for 3.5km, once through Foligno continue for 1km to Via Roma

Sights nearby: Cathedral, Palazzo Trinci; Spello: church of Santa Maria Maggiore

10

BOSONE PALACE

Sig. Mencarelli
Via XX Settembre, 22
06024 Gubbio (PG)
Tel. 075 9220688 – Fax 075 9272331
hotelbosonepalace@mencarelligroup.com – www.mencarelligroup.com

70-80/ 100-120€

Closed 10 Jan-1 Mar • 6 single rm, 24 double rm • Half board €76 • Menu €26-50 • Parking, garden • Bicycle hire, tasting and sale of jams, honey and rosolio liqueur

We most liked

The very high ceilings of the rooms.

Situated in the centre of town and close to some of its finest palaces, this is one of Gubbio's most historic hotels. Its beautiful interior has stucco work, staircases, frescoes and other decorative features which would do justice to a film set. Only two of the rooms have frescoes, but all thirty of them are very comfortable. Those in quest of local heritage should book a stay here in mid-May, when the Corsa dei Ceri ('candle race') takes place: three "candles", or ceri, strange wooden poles 4m/13ft tall, each topped with the statue of a saint, are carried through the crowded streets in a frenzied race through the centre of the town and straight past the hotel; an unforgettable experience.

Access

From Perugia: SS 220 for 8.5km, then SS 3 bis for 2km and SS 298 for 27km

Sights nearby: Palazzo dei Consoli, Palazzo Ducale, churches of San Francesco and Santa Maria Nuova

11

LE CINCIALLEGRE

Sig.ra Coffer De Robertis

Frazione Pisciano
06024 Gubbio (PG)
Tel. 075 9255957 – Fax 075 9272331
cince@lecinciallegre.it – www.lecinciallegre.it

48/96€

Closed 15 Dec-15 Mar • 1 single rm, 6 double rm • Half board €65 • Menu €25-40 • Parking, garden, no dogs in the restaurant • Bicycle and quad bike hire, honey, jam and vegetables for sale

The dining room's light and panoramic veranda.

The view from here changes with the seasons, with meadows of daisies in spring, and leaves of every colour in autumn. The house itself is stone built, occupying a delightfully isolated site tucked away in the hills, although guests will be reassured to know that it is well signposted. The warm interior shows great attention to detail; in the dining room, the emphasis is on home grown produce and traditional local recipes.

Access

From Perugia: SS 220 for 8km, then E 45 for 21km to Umbertide exit, then SS 219 for 18km to Pisciano

Sights nearby: Gubbio: Palazzo dei Consoli, Palazzo Ducale, churches of San Francesco and Santa Maria Nuova

12

GATTAPONE

Sigg. Ramacci
Via Beni, 11
06030 Gubbio (PG)
Tel. 075 9272489 – Fax 075 9272417
gattapone@mencarelligroup.com – www.mencarelligroup.com

70-80/100-110€

Closed 8 Jan-8 Feb • 18 double rm • Half board €71 • Menu €26-50 • No dogs • Bicycle hire, tasting and sale of jams, honey and rosolio liqueur

The high ceilings in the guestrooms.

With its enviable position in the heart of the historic centre, this hotel is decorated with an attractive fusion of the traditional and modern. The large entrance hall is furnished with sofas and a television area, while the rustic-style rooms here are well appointed and spacious. The buffet breakfast is served in a vaulted room next to the entrance hall, although in summer guests will want to take advantage of the pleasant outdoor terrace. Good value for money, given the comfort, facilities and location.

Access
From Perugia: SS 220 for 8.5km, then SS 3 bis for 2km and SS 298 for 27km

Sights nearby: Palazzo dei Consoli, Palazzo Ducale, churches of San Francesco and Santa Maria Nuova

13

POGGIO DELLA VOLARA

Sig. Tordi

Via Volara, 1 - Località Volara
05020 Montecchio (TR)
Tel. 0744 951820 – Fax 0744 951820
marco.tordi@libero.it – www.poggiodellavolara.it

55-70/70-80€

Closed Jan-Feb • 6 double rm • Half board €55-62 • Menu €20-25 • Parking, garden, swimming pool • Horse riding, bicycles available, oil and wine for sale

The large and inviting swimming pool, perfect for hot summer afternoons.

Located 400m up, this establishment has fine views over its surrounding hills. This is classic Umbrian scenery, a verdant landscape which invites exploration on foot or by mountain bike. The simple and orderly house is not huge, but comfortably provides accommodation in the form of six rooms, decorated in local style with wooden furniture and wrought iron beds. The guests-only restaurant is overseen personally by the owners and serves traditional Umbrian cuisine.

Access

From Terni: SS 79 for 3km towards Narni, then the E 45 for 10km to Amelia, left onto the SS 205 for 33km to Montecchio, continue for 4.5km to Volara

Sights nearby: Narni: Rocca, Ponte di Augusto, Palazzo dei Priori, Palazzo Comunale, abbey of San Cassiano

14

CAMIANO PICCOLO

Sig. Fabrizi

Località Camiano Piccolo, 5
06036 Montefalco (PG)

Tel. 0742 379492 – Fax 0742 371077

camiano@bcsnet.com – www.camianopiccolo.com

52-73/62-100€

Open all year • 8 double rm • Half board €55-64 • Menu €22-30 • Parking, garden, swimming pool, no dogs • Oil and wine tasting

The gardens, complete with vegetable plot, alongside the swimming pool.

In open countryside, yet only a stone's throw from the walls of Montefalco, this agriturismo is located in a charming little farming settlement. The stone buildings house accommodation in the form of rooms and apartments, public areas and a small guests only restaurant. The tone is no frills simplicity, but entirely adequate given the rustic setting. There are some luxuries, though, including breakfast which in summer is served outside, and the swimming pool with sun umbrellas and loungers, sufficiently distant to ensure that guests are not disturbed.

Access

From Perugia: SS 3 bis for 1km to S.Martino in Campo, then onto the SP 403 for 24km to Bevagna, right onto the SS 316 for 1.3km, then left for 5km

Sights nearby: Torre Comunale, churches of San Francesco, Sant'Agostino and Santa Illuminata; Bevagna: Roman ruins

15

CASALE NEL PARCO DEI MONTI SIBILLINI

Sig.ra Mensurati
Località Fontevena
06046 Norcia (PG)
Tel. 0743 816481 – Fax 0743 816481
agriumbria@casalenelparco.com – www.casalenelparco.com

70-90€

Closed 10 Jan-10 Feb • 13 double rm • Half board €60-80 • Menu €20-40 • Parking, garden, swimming pool, no dogs • Horse riding, bicycles available, rafting, cured meat and cheese tasting

Admiring the natural beauty of the countryside from the saddle.

Opened as an agriturismo at the end of the last decade, this restored farmhouse is situated a little out of town in a panoramic and peaceful spot. It has ten attractive and well presented rooms, while outside there is a large and pleasant garden with swimming pool. Horses may be hired from the neighbouring stables for rides through the countryside. The restaurant serves authentic and tasty cuisine using home-grown organic ingredients.

Access
From Terni: SS 209 for 46km, right onto the SS 320 for 11km to Serravalle, then left onto the SS 396 for 5km to Norcia, left for 1.5km to Fontevena

Sights nearby: Castellina, church of San Benedetto; Monti Sibillini National Park

16

BORGO SAN FAUSTINO

Sig. Perotti

Borgo San Faustino 11/12
05010 Morrano (TR)
Tel. 0763 215303 – Fax 0763 215745
borgosf@tin.it – www.agriturismosanfaustino.it

80-100€

Closed 9-31 Jan • 12 double rm • Half board €50-65 • Menu €20-30 • Parking, swimming pool, no dogs in the restaurant • Horse riding, bowls, bicycles available, tasting and sale of jam, oil and wine

The rustic furnishings in the rooms.

San Faustino is a small farming settlement in the hills outside Orvieto, composed of two picturesque stone buildings which have been painstakingly restored over the years to offer accommodation in the form of a dozen rooms. The setting provides greenery and peace in abundance, while the establishment itself is passionately run by the family management team. In summer the garden and swimming pool come into their own; all year round the restaurant serves dishes incorporating home grown produce.

Access

From Orvieto: SS 71 for 6km, then right for 8km to San Faustino

Sights nearby: Cathedral, Pozzo di San Patrizio, Palazzo dei Papi and Palazzo del Popolo, old town

17

VILLA ACQUAFREDDA

Fam. Vergari

Località Acquafredda
05019 Orvieto Scalo (TR)
Tel. 0763 393073 – Fax 0763 390226
villacquafredda@libero.it

33-48/ 49-68€

Closed 23-27 Dec • 12 double rm • Half board €49 • Menu €13-15 • Parking, swimming pool, garden, no dogs in the restaurant

The ideal location from which to tour the country by car.

This well restored 19C farmhouse has stone detail to its attractive façade. Inside, the functional rooms have modern furnishings in pale wood, while the public areas are well laid out and comfortable, if a little limited. There is a guests only restaurant, and to the rear of the property a spacious garden with swimming pool. Convenient parking in front of the hotel.

Access

From Orvieta exit on the A 1: continue for 1.5km to Orvieto Scalo

Sights nearby: Orvieto: Cathedral, Pozzo di San Patrizio, Palazzo dei Papi, Palazzo del Popolo, old town

18

LE GROTTE DI BOLDRINO

Sig.ra Nicchiarelli
Via Virgilio Ceppari, 30
06064 Panicale (PG)
Tel. 075 837161 – Fax 075 837166
grottediboldrino@libero.it – www.grottediboldrino.com

55-62/70-80€

Open all year • 2 single rm, 9 double rm • Half board €58-63 • Menu €25-35 • Garden • Oil tasting

The characterful restaurant.

Just over 400m up, the well preserved town of Panicale is a classic example of the fortified settlements that characterise the central Italian landscape. Abutting the ramparts, this hotel is entered via a pleasant garden, where meals are served during the summer months. Inside, the public areas (including TV room and games room) are a little limited, but the rooms are spacious and furnished with antiques from the Trento region.

Access
From Perugia: SS 220 for 25km, then right for 4.5km

Sights nearby: Church of San Sebastiano, Lake Trasimeno

19

SAN FELICISSIMO

Sig. Spagnoli

Strada Poggio Pelliccione, 5
06077 Perugia (PG)

Tel. 075 6919400 – Fax 075 6919400

info@sanfelicissimo.net – www.sanfelicissimo.net

60-99€

Open all year • 10 double rm • No restaurant • Parking, garden, swimming pool • Honey and oil tasting

The panoramic and relaxing patio-veranda.

Just outside Perugia yet already deep in the hilly countryside, this classic farmhouse surrounded by olive groves has been tastefully converted into a charming agriturismo. Directly accessed from outside, the rooms are well presented and comfortable, as are the public areas, while the carefully tended garden has a swimming pool. The stunning views extending as far as the eye can see make for an unforgettable backdrop.

Access

5km east of Perugia

Sights nearby: Fontana Maggiore, Palazzo dei Priori, Oratorio di San Bernardino, church of San Pietro, Collegio del Cambio

LA CERQUA

Sig. Martinelli

Località San Salvatore, 27
06026 Pietralunga (PG)
Tel. 075 9460283 – Fax 075 9462033
info@cerqua.it – www.cerqua.it

70-80€

Closed Jan-Feb • 17 double rm • Half board €55-60 • Menu €20-30 • Parking, garden, swimming pool • Horse riding, organised trips, bicycles available, archery, jam and liqueur for sale

The rustic accommodation with wooden ceilings, exposed stonework and open fireplaces.

In an unspoilt natural setting, this establishment is surrounded by stunning Umbrian countryside which retains its beauty on account of the profound commitment to organic farming and ecological principles of those who manage it. This establishment provides simple and genuine hospitality in a largely outdoor setting, offering swimming, riding, country walks and a children's play area. After a day in the fresh air, guests will be more than ready to tuck into the generous and authentic cuisine.

Access
From Perugia: SS 220 for 8.5km, then onto E 45 for 27km to Pietralunga, then left for 2km to San Salvatore

Sights nearby: Gubbio: Palazzo dei Consoli, Palazzo Ducale, churches of San Francesco and Santa Maria Nuova

21

DEL PONTE

Sig.ra Scavolini
Via Borgo, 15
06040 Scheggino (PG)
Tel. 0743 61253 – Fax 0743 61131

55€

Closed 4-28 Nov • 12 double rm • Breakfast €3; half board €55 • Menu €18-40 • Parking, garden, no dogs

The traditional ambience, against the tranquil backdrop of the Nera valley.

Scheggino lies at the foot of two wooded hills separated by the river Nera. Its waters flow gently towards Terni, overlooked by a white tower of medieval origin, all that remains of the village's old fortifications. Around a hundred years old, this inn continues to offer traditional style hospitality, with a fine wood panelled restaurant and comfortable accommodation which has been recently renovated. The cuisine focuses on local dishes and ranges from fresh pasta to trout, but the real gem is the Norcia black truffle.

Access
From Perugia: SS 3 bis for 3.5km, then onto the SS 75 for 26km, SS 3 for 24km, then left for 7km, right onto SS 209 for 3km

Sights nearby: Spoleto: cathedral, Ponte delle Torri, basilica of San Salvatore, churches of San Gregorio Maggiore and San Domenico

22

LE DUE TORRI

Sig. Ciri

Via Torre Quadrano, 1
06038 Spello (PG)
Tel. 0742 651249 – Fax 0743 270273
duetorri@seeumbria.com – www.agriturismoleduetorri.com

62-72€

Closed 9 Jan-11 Feb • 4 double rm • Half board €51-70 • Menu €20 • Parking, garden, swimming pool, bowls, no dogs • Bicycles available, spelt, oil, and wine for sale

The symmetrical severity of the solitary tower.

The imposing tower was once part of a network of fortifications which delineated the territories of Foligno and nearby Rocca Deli. Today's more peaceful times mean that it overlooks nothing more threatening than olive groves, vineyards and these two farmhouses which provide accommodation. Recently renovated, they retain their wood beamed ceilings, tiled floors and atmosphere of rustic simplicity. Guests can enjoy delightful walks through the surrounding farmland, with views over the Umbrian hills towards the white stone outline of Assisi.

Access

From Perugia: 8km to the E 45, follow E 45 for 3km, then onto the SS 75 for 21km, right for 1km

Sights nearby: Churches of Santa Maria Maggiore and Sant'Andrea

23

DEL TEATRO

Sig. Cruciani

Via Giulia, 24
06030 Spello (PG)
Tel. 0742 301140 – Fax 0742 301612
info@hoteldelteatro.it – www.hoteldelteatro.it

60-65/90-100€

Closed 8-26 Nov • 1 single rm, 10 double rm • No restaurant

The splendid views from the breakfast room.

This hotel has the rare distinction of offering well-appointed rooms in a simple, family-run palazzo in the centre of town. The interior follows the irregular layout of the building, making the hotel a maze of corridors, staircases and unexpected nooks and crannies. The reception rooms are on the small side, although this is compensated by the magnificent panoramic views from the top floor, which is used as a breakfast room in summer. With tasteful furnishings, marble bathrooms and parquet floors, the bedrooms are larger than in most mid-category hotels.

Access

From Perugia: 8km to the E 45, then follow E 45 for 3km, then SS 75 for 21km

Sights nearby: Church of Santa Maria Maggiore and Sant'Andrea

CASALE DELLE LUCREZIE

Sig. Adanti

Frazione Duesanti - Vocabolo Palazzaccio
05020 Todi (PG)

Tel. 075 8987488 – Fax 075 8987488

info@casaledellelucrezie.com – www.casaledellelucrezie.com

60-70€

Closed 15-31 Jan • 10 double rm • Half board €50-55 • Menu €20-30 • Parking, swimming pool, no dogs • Bicycle hire, oil and wine for sale

The view of Todi.

This traditional stone farmstead is built in typical Umbrian style. Founded by the Romans, over-run by the Etruscans (an arch remains from this period) and then occupied by the Lucretian nuns in the 13C, the property enjoys a magnificent location deep in the hills, with splendid views of Todi from the bedroom windows. Guestrooms here are new and simply furnished, with modern bathrooms. The restaurant specialises in typical dishes of the region.

Access

From Perugia: 8km to the SS 317, then follow SS 317 for 5km, then E 45 for 28km and SS 488 for 6km

Sights nearby: Piazza del Popolo, Palazzo del Priore and Palazzo del Capitano

25

LA LOCANDA DI CACIO RE

Comune di Vallo di Nera

Località i Casali
06040 Vallo di Nera (PG)
Tel. 0743 617003 – Fax 0743 617214
caciore@tin.it – www.caciore.com

55-60/ 70-75€

Closed Jan and Nov • 8 double rm • Half board €70-80 • Menu €30-45 • Parking, no dogs in the restaurant • Tasting and sale of cheese and cured meat

The local heritage and cuisine.

The castle in this medieval village was once the defensive lynchpin for the entire valley, and many buildings were erected around it to benefit from the protection it offered. Among them was this farmhouse, which has changed little over the last five centuries. But here in the Nera valley, the architecture is not alone in having a long history; the local cuisine has an equally proud heritage. Truffles, barley, lamb and sausages are all standard fare which guests can enjoy in the restaurant, and indeed purchase to take home.

Access

From Perugia: SS 3 bis for 3.5km, then 26km on the SS 75, right for 24km on the SS 3, left onto the SS 209 for 4km, then right for 2.5km

Sights nearby: Spoleto: Cathedral, Ponte delle Torri, basilica of San Salvatore, churches of San Gregorio Maggiore and San Domenico

ontarlier
109
Lac de Neuchâtel
BERN
55
67
126
95
Thun
Yverdon
npagnole
Fribourg
A 6
Suste
E 27-A 12
Bulle
A 8
Interlaken
AUSANNE
156
A 9
71
132
Jungfrau 4158
63
Vevey
Gstaad
Oberland
L. Léman
Montreux
Nyon
Thonon
Évian
Lötschberg
Brig
Aigle
Sion
GENÈVE
83
Simplon
104
9
19
Bonneville
E 62
A 9
2005
S 33
Martigny
E 25
A 40
Cluses
4477
Zermatt
38
64
Chamonix
Matterhorn
Do
St Gervais
77
Monte Rosa
Megève
2469
4810
Grd St Bernard
4634
Varallo
Mt Blanc
Courmayeur
5
2
3
VALLE
Orta
rtville
2188
Aosta
D'AOSTA
béry
Pt St Bernard
E 25
4
Bourg-St Maurice
1
Val d'Isère
Gran Paradiso
A 5
S 26
Biella
163
207
2770
Ivrea
29
Vanoise
E 70
Iseran
251
E 64
87
ean-
urienne
A 43
Mt Cenis
E 70
2083
49
67
alibier
150
Modane
107
S 31
Susa
2556
A 32
Chivasso
S 24
57
Casale
1850
San Michele
Monferrat
ret
Montgenèvre
TORINO
85
Briançon
108
Sestriere
A 21
59
Ecrins
S 10
Pinerolo
N 94
Izoard
2361
Po
Asti
Ales
S 20
E 717 A 6
Savigliano
Alba
Guillestre
Saluzzo
85
87

VALLE D'AOSTA

The woodland and valleys of the Gran Paradiso National Park are a haven for chamois, marmots and ibex, a classic alpine landscape sitting at the head of the long Dora Baltea valley. To the north lies Switzerland beyond the Gran San Bernardo, to the west Mont Blanc marks the border with France, so it comes as no surprise that both Italian and French are spoken here. The region has always been an important crossroads; for many years the local population resisted Roman incursion, but they eventually succumbed. The conquerors founded Augusta Praetoria, today known as Aosta. Monuments from this era were succeeded by many castles in the medieval period, among the finest in Italy. Natural beauty, however, is the overriding attraction of the Val d'Aosta; names such as Courmayeur, La Thiule and Greesney are familiar to lovers of winter sports and alpine ramblers. The local hospitality is best experienced at the dining table, around a fondue accompanied by coffee laced with Genepy, the local liqueur.

5 establishments

1

LA BARME

Sigg. Herren

Località Valnontey, 8
11012 Cogne (AO)

Tel. 0165 749177 – Fax 0165 749213

labarme@tiscali.it – www.hotellabarme.com

46-65/ 70-100€

Closed Oct-Nov • 3 single rm, 13 double rm • Half board €45-60 • Menu €21-43 • Garden, no dogs • Organised trips, bicycle hire, cheese and wine tasting

The mountains, a striking backdrop to any visit.

Peace and quiet reign supreme in the little village of Valnontey, deep in the Gran Paradiso national park. This 18C building has been sensitively restored and reborn as a hotel providing comfortable accommodation without compromising its classic architectural style. The main section houses the smart public areas, namely the restaurant, games room and sauna. The well presented rooms have pine furnishings and are simple yet attractive. Sun lovers can bask all year round in the spacious sun-lounge.

Access

From Aosta: SS 26 for 6km, onto the SS 507 for 19km to Cogne, then right for 3km to Valnontey

Sights nearby: Gran Paradiso National Park

2

LOCANDA DELLA VECCHIA MINIERA

Sig. Gregorini

Frazione Rey, 11
11010 Ollomont (AO)
Tel. 0165 73414 – Fax 0165 73414
info@locandavecchiaminiera.it – www.locandavecchiaminiera.it

74-100€

Closed 26 May-15 Jun, 25 Sep-25 Oct • 4 double rm • Half board €55-65 • Menu €26-38 • Parking, garden, no dogs

Signor Gregorini's friendly management style.

This beautiful classic mountain dwelling has exposed stonework, wood beams and snow white plastered walls. Of 18C origin, it offers panoramic views of the surrounding peaks. The four rooms, deliberately TV free, have an unusual intimacy and warmth which will appeal to those seeking a romantic ambience. The charming an elegant restaurant is renowned throughout the valley for the standards of its cuisine.

Access

From Aosta: SS 27 for 4.5km to Variney, right for 9km, then left for 4km to Rey

Sights nearby: Valley scenery; Aosta: Roman remains, cathedral

3

L'ARC EN CIEL

Sig. Fasolis
Frazione Vert, 1
11010 Sarre (AO)
Tel. 0165 257843 – Fax 0165 257843

45/ 61-66€

Open all year • 5 double rm • Half board €45-47 • Menu €15-22 • Parking, garden, no dogs • Cured meat and cheese tasting

The view of the valley stretching skywards.

The name means rainbow and not without good reason. Guests may well get the feeling that they are up in the sky as they admire the breathtaking views over the Aosta valley and surrounding hillsides with the Ruitor glacier providing an impressive backdrop to the whole scene. Having got over the view, guests can enjoy the restaurant which serves dishes prepared using authentic local produce.

Access
From Aosta: SS 41 for 5km to Vert

Sights nearby: Valley scenery; Aosta: Roman remains, cathedral

4

L'HOSTELLERIE DU PARADIS

Sig. Alberto e Sig.ra Dayne
Località Eau Rousse, 21
11010 Valsavarenche (AO)
Tel. 0165 905972 – Fax 0165 905971
info@hostellerieduparadis.it – www.hostellerieduparadis.it

52-55/ 80€

Closed Nov • 5 single rm, 25 double rm • Breakfast €8; half board €70-75 • Menu €24-35 • Parking, swimming pool

The snowbound alpine refuge.

A classic mountain refuge in appearance, this building of stone and wood with its slate roof seems to invite heavy snowfall in order to provide it with a fairytale setting. Winter is not the only season in which to visit, however, since summer guests can enjoy walking in the woods, some light climbing, or merely strolling in the peaceful surroundings of this national park. Although recently built, the accommodation is largely in wood, very much in keeping with local tradition.

Access
From Aosta: SS 26 for 10km, then left for 16km to Eau Rousse

Sights nearby: Gran Paradiso National Park

5

LA VRILLE

Sig. Deguillame
Hameau du Grandzon, 1
11020 Verrayes (AO)
Tel. 0166 543018
lavrille@tiscali.it – www.lavrille-agriturisme.com

65-80€

Open all year • 6 double rm • No restaurant • Parking, garden, bowls, no dogs • Jam and wine tasting

The generous breakfast served against a backdrop of stone and woodwork.

La Vrille is a typical mountain building in wood and stone, situated among vineyards within sight of Mounts Avic and Emilius. Its location is peaceful, yet convenient for the ski slopes. The quality of the local produce is evident in the hearty breakfasts, where there is no shortage of choice. The area's gastronomic heritage is celebrated in many local events, a good excuse for visitors to explore the mountains and villages of Val d'Aosta.

Access
From Aosta: SS 26 for 4.6km to join A 5, follow towards Torino for 8.2km to Nus exit, then right onto SS 26 for 3.5km, left for 1.2km to Grangeon

Sights nearby: Valley scenery; Aosta: Roman remains, cathedral

ALPEN
Großglockner
3797
Heiligenblut
Brenner
1374
3774
Ötztaleralpen
Reschen
1507
Vipiteno
Brunico
Lienz
Bressanone
Dobbiaco
Merano
ALTO ADIGE
Cortina
d'Ampezzo
20
21
Bolzano
2239
Pordoi
Dolomiti
Tolmezzo
Ora
261
Madonna
di Campiglio
Trento
3
Belluno
Udine
Feltre
10
Conegliano
Pordenone
Brenta
6
Bassano
del Grappa
17
18
19
Piave
Riva
Rovereto
Lago
di Garda
9
2
4
23
11
Portogruaro
VENETO
Treviso
Vicenza
22
14
Mestre
5
Verona
12
VENEZIA
25
Padova
13
Lido di V.
24
1
8
15
Golfo
di Venezia
7
26
Monselice
Nogara
Chioggia
Adige
16
Rovigo
Po
Ferrara
Reggio
Emillia
Comacchio
Modena
Reno
BOLOGNA
Ravenna
Imola

VENETO

It is impossible to describe the Veneto without mentioning Venice, its unique character, art and history having made it the seat of a commercial and cultural empire and subsequently a place of gilded decay. But there is a great deal more to the region than Venice; the rose coloured cathedrals of Dolomites' Cadore district, the evocative Roman remains of Verona, the houses on Treviso's canals, Giotto's frescoes in Padova, not forgetting the smaller towns such as Conegliano and Montagnana, little artistic jewels untouched by the passage of time. The Veneto's landscape of wheat fields on the plains and vineyards in the hills is dotted with the elegant outlines of Palladian villas, reminders of the age when Venice's nobility would retreat to the rural tranquillity of their country residences.

Land and sea are equally represented in the region's cuisine; the traditional peasant staples of *polenta* and rice feature alongside the famous *baccalà alla vicentina* (salted cod) and *sardelle in saor* (sardines in brine).

Soave, Bardolino and Amarone are some of the Veneto's great wines, all of which are a pleasure to get to know.

26 establishments

1

LOCANDA ARCIMBOLDO

Fam. Guidorizzi

Via Gennari, 5
37041 Albaredo d'Adige (VR)
Tel. 045 7025300 – Fax 045 7025201
info@locandadellarcimboldo.it – www.locandadellarcimboldo.it

80/100€

Closed 1-20 Aug • 4 double rm • Half board €75-90 • Menu €37-52 • Parking, garden

The sumptuous rooms, well presented down to the finest details.

This comprehensively restored 19C house is conveniently situated on the road, yet looks onto its garden and parking area, making for a peaceful ambience. The enterprising and hospitable Guidorizzi family has emphasised quality over quantity; the limited number of rooms are elegantly rustic in style and well equipped. The restaurant is also worthy of note, serving local specialities in warm and welcoming surroundings.

Access
From Verona: SS 434 for 20km, then left for 9km

Sights nearby: Verona: amphitheatre, Roman theatre, cathedral, Castelvecchio, church of San Zeno

AL CASTELLO

Sig.ra Moretto e Sig. Cattapan

Via Bonamigo, 19
36077 Bassano del Grappa (VI)
Tel. 0424 228665 – Fax 0424 228665
info@hotelalcastello.it – www.hotelalcastello.it

40-55/70-90€

Open all year • 1 single rm, 10 double rm • Breakfast €6 • No restaurant • Parking, no dogs

The town's lively, colourful atmosphere.

Bassano is situated at the point where the River Brenta leaves the hills and flows into the valley, making this a perfect base for exploring the surrounding countryside. In the heart of the old town, near the Castello degli Ezelini, Al Castello is the most attractive hotel in the area, housed in an old building constructed in the typical architectural style of the Veneto. The entrance stands alongside the elegant and popular hotel bar (a second, quieter bar can be found to the rear of the building). Dark wood predominates in the public rooms and guestrooms, with the occasional wooden beam embellishing the ceiling.

Access

From Vicenza: SS 11 for 1km, then SS 248 for 32km and 3.5km on the link road

Sights nearby: Museo Civico, covered bridge, Monte Grappa

3

NOGHERAZZA

Sig. Miari Fulcis
Via Gresane 78
32024 Belluno (BL)
Tel. 0437 927461 – Fax 0437 925882
amiarif@tin.it – www.nogherazza.it

80/ 100€

Closed 1-15 Nov • 6 double rm • Menu €20-30 • Parking, garden

We most liked

The woodwork, making for a warm ambience throughout.

This pleasant spot is difficult to pigeonhole; a welcoming ambience combined with convenient location halfway betweeen Venice and the Dolomites giving access to the delights of the Veneto and some of the most impressive alpine scenery. The wood panelled rooms are attractive, and there are also sports facilities including riding, football and volleyball, plus the restaurant offering local specialities as well as Tuscan and Umbrian dishes.

Access
3km south-east from Belluno to Castion

Sights nearby: Belluno: Cathedral, Palazzo dei Rettori, Piazza del Mercato

4

COL DELLE RANE

Sig.ra Stefani
Via Mercato Vecchio, 18
31031 Caerano di San Marco (TV)
Tel. 0423 85585 – Fax 0423 650652
info@coldellerane.it – www.coldellerane.it

38/65€

Open all year • 14 double rm • No restaurant • Parking, garden, no dogs • Bicycles available, jam and wine for sale

Breakfast, composed of healthy natural products, looking out over the surrounding countryside.

Halfway between Asolo and Treviso, this comprehensively restored late 18C farmhouse is the ideal base from which to explore the area's famous Palladian villas. At one end of the house is the large breakfast area, also used for functions, overlooking the surrounding countryside through ample windows. The simple yet comfortable rooms are decorated in rustic style. All around are vineyards and orchards, ensuring a ready supply of home made jams.

Access
From Treviso: SS 348 for 18km, then left onto the SS 248 for 5.5km

Sights nearby: Maser: Palladian villa

5

LA MERIDIANA

Sig. Martinelli

Via Zamboni, 11 Località Sandrà
37014 Castelnuovo del Garda (VR)
Tel. 045 7596306 – Fax 045 7596313

42-50/68€

Closed 27 Dec-9 Jan • 2 single rm, 12 double rm • Half board €46.75 • Menu €20-30 • Parking, garden

The sloping wooden ceilings in some of the rooms.

This attractive farmhouse sits in open countryside to the south of Garda, in an area well known for its wines. In addition to its attractive surroundings, it is also well located for access to Lake Garda and the great artistic centres of Verona, Mantova, Padova and Venice, while several natural and theme parks are also nearby. In the main house, there is the tasteful accommodation, showing great attention to detail and personal touches throughout, while the former hay barn now houses the highly regarded restaurant.

Access

From Verona: SS 11 for 17km to Castelnuovo del Garda, then right for 3.5km to Sandrà

Sights nearby: Lake Garda; Verona: amphitheatre, Roman theatre, Castelvecchio, church of San Zeno

6

LOCANDA ALLA POSTA

Sig. e Sig.ra Visentin
Piazza 13 Martiri, 13
31034 Cavaso del Tomba (TV)
Tel. 0423 543112 – Fax 0423 543112

36/55€

Closed 10-31 Jan • 7 double rm • Menu €24-38 • Garden • Home made chocolates for sale (tasting)

The characteristic sign which beckons the arriving guests.

A veritable institution in the district, this building appears in the earliest photos of Cavaso, taken a century ago. Ever since it has provided hospitality to travellers; the bar is popular with the locals, while the accommodation and restaurant cater for tourists. This is a welcoming spot, its rooms mostly refurbished with a personal touch and decorated in a homely style with antiques.

Access
From Treviso: SS 348 for 33km, then left for 5km

Sights nearby: Feltre: Piazza Maggiore, Via Mezzaterra

7

LA TORRE

La Torre Srl

Via Torcolo, 33
37044 Cologna Veneta (VR)
Tel. 0442 410111 – Fax 0442 419245
info@albergoristorantelatorre.it – www.albergoristorantelatorre.it

45-53/ 75-85€

Open all year • 9 single rm, 9 double rm • Half board €60-70 • Menu €30-50

The privilege of staying in such a historic building.

During the days of the Venetian Republic in the 16C, two towers monitored the river traffic which passed this spot. One was subsequently destroyed, the other survives as a hotel. This historic place has evidence of building going back to Roman times, and the existing structure is redolent of its past, with many beautiful features in evidence. This link with bygone days makes a stay here especially pleasureable. Welcoming rooms with functional furnishings and a charming restaurant with brick vaulted ceiling.

Access

From Verona: 9km to Verona est junction, then onto the A 4 for 12km to Soave, then the SS 11 to San Bonifacio, then right for 16km

Sights nearby: Montagnana: walls, cathedral, church of San Francesco

8

VILLA GOETZEN

Fam. Minchio

Via Matteotti, 6
30031 Dolo (VE)
Tel. 041 5102300 – Fax 041 412600
info@villagoetzen.it – www.villagoetzen.it

55/80€

Open all year • 2 single rm, 10 double rm • Menu €33-46 • Parking, garden, no dogs

We most liked

The pleasant new terrace overlooking the river.

Although not the work of Palladio, this hotel is an attractive 18C villa on the river, albeit a little close to the road. It has a charming genteel ambience, is run by family management and offers well laid out, if somewhat compact, accommodation. In the main house are ten rooms, with another two in the former stable block. All are welcoming, with Venetian-style furnishings and every modern convenience. The elegant restaurant specialises in fish dishes.

Access

From Padova: SS 11 for 15km towards Mestre

Sights nearby: Padova: basilica del Santo, Scrovegni chapel, Gattamelata monument, Oratorio di San Giorgio, Scuola di Sant'Antonio

9

LE COLLINE DELL'UVA

Sig.ra Barausse
Via Alteo, 15
36030 Fara Vicentino (VI)
Tel. 0445 897651 – Fax 0445 897092
lecollinedelluva@hotmail.com – www.lecollinedelluva.com

55/90€

Open all year • 3 single rm, 3 double rm • No restaurant • Parking, garden • Bicycle hire, tasting and sale of local produce

The healthy and generous home made breakfast.

Opened in October 2001, this restored farmhouse is out of town and up in the hills and is ideal for visitors, be they tourists or business travellers, in search of elegance and simplicity. The creative management has successfully mixed family pieces with modern objects to create a harmonious minimalist look. In addition to the fine rooms, there is a pleasant breakfast room, a small bar and an attractive garden.

Access
From Vicenza: SS 258 for 13km, then right for 5.5km to Breganze, from where 4km to Via Alteo

Sights nearby: Marostica: Piazza Castello

VILLA GUARDA

Sig. Traina

Via San Nicolò, 47
31050 Follina (TV)
Tel. 0438 980834 – Fax 0438 980854
info@villaguarda.it – www.villaguarda.it

50/ 75€

Open all year • 4 single rm, 16 double rm • Breakfast €6 • No restaurant • Parking, garden

The gushing fountain at the centre of the charming garden.

This large white house is of long and irregular layout. Rising four storeys, it features covered terraces, a wooden gallery, a number of verandas and colonnades. In essence, an unusual and dynamic structure with asymmetrical dimensions and its garden blends well into the hilly Trevisan landscape. Access to the rooms is by external staircases, which might leave visitors unsure as to the efficiency of the service here, but they need not worry. The management's high standards should satisfy even the most exacting guest. Parking for about twenty cars.

Access

From Treviso: SS 13 towards Conegliano for 17km, then left for 18km to Pedeguarda

Sights nearby: Conegliano: cathedral, castle, Scoula dei Battuti

11

VILLA REVEDIN

Sig. Berto

Via Palazzi, 4
31040 Gorgo al Monticano (TV)
Tel. 0422 800033 – Fax 0422 800272
info@villarevedin.it – www.villarevedin.it

66/98€

Open all year • 13 single rm, 15 double rm • Breakfast €7; half board €78 • Menu €22-50 • Parking, no dogs • Organised trips, bicycles available

The splendid park planted with ancient trees.

Situated in the countryside near Treviso, this fine villa was built in the 16C by the Morisini, a noble Venetian family. Towards the end of the 17C it was acquired by the Foscarini Cornaro family, who used it as their summer residence; during this phase of its history it became a port of call for many European aristocrats on their way to Venice. After the fall of the Venetian Republic, the villa and its vast estates became the property of the Revedin family who made it a pioneering farming operation. More recently, it has been transformed into a hotel and restaurant after a lengthy restoration programme which revitalised much of its original splendour.

Access

From Treviso: SS 53 for 30km

Sights nearby: Oderzo: Museo Civico; Treviso: Piazza dei Signori, cathedral, churches of San Nicolò and San Francesco

LE VESCOVANE

Sig.ra Savoia
Via San Rocco, 19
36040 Longare (VI)
Tel. 0444 273570 – Fax 0444273265
info@levescovane.com – www.levescovane.com

55-60/ 78-88€

Open all year • 8 double rm • Half board €62 • Menu €20-28 • Parking, small dogs welcome • Tasting and sale of jams, cured meat and wine

The wood and stone porch leading to the restaurant.

The road to this typical farmstead is located a few kilometres the other side of Vicenza – guests are advised to consult the website or call for directions before leaving the town. Originally built as a hunting lodge in the 16C, the attractive stone farmhouse is now surrounded by a well-tended garden and the peace and quiet of the Monti Berici. Although the style of the house is not as grand as that of a Palladian villa, there is still an elegant, country-house feel to the property. The agriturismo also boasts a busy restaurant which serves a selection of regional cuisine, some of which is produced on the farm.

Access
From Vicenza: SS 11 for 1km, then right on the SS 427 for 8km, then left for 4km

Sights nearby: Vicenza: Teatro Olimpico, Piazza dei Signori, Basilica

13

CA' MARCELLO

Sig. Manfrini

Riviera Bosco Piccolo, 110
30030 Malcontenta (VE)
Tel. 041 420339 – Fax 041 698355
info@camarcello.com – www.camarcello.com

38-55/60-80€

Open all year • 3 double rm • No restaurant • Parking, garden • Bicycle and water scooter hire, vegetables and home grown produce for sale

The wide range of sports and leisure facilities.

Not far from Venice, at the beginning of the Brenta route which winds past the famous villas of the Veneto, this late 19C house has remained in the ownership of the Manfrin family since its original construction. Previously a trattoria, it became an agriturismo in 1995 and has six rooms, four apartments plus camping facilities. Guests can choose from a wide range of activities, including archery, acquascooter on the river, cycling and barbecue facilities.

Access
From Mestre: SS 309 for 4km then right into Via Fusinato

Sights nearby: Venice

14

CA' NOVA

Sig. Zanon
Campalto - Via Bagaron, 1
30030 Mestre (VE)
Tel. 041 900033 – Fax 041 5420420
ca-nova@tiscali.it

40-50/ 80-100€

Closed Jan • 4 single rm, 2 double rm • Breakfast €5 • No restaurant • Parking

The convenient location close to Venice.

Well situated for access not only to Venice itself, but also to the airport and motorway. This 18C villa has been completely restored boasting a genteel cream facade with contrasting blue shutters and surmounted by a classical style cornice. Its small rooms are tastefully furnished and welcoming. Managed in friendly fashion by the Zanon family, who also run the trattoria next door.

Access
From Mestre: SS 14 for 2km to Campalto

Sights nearby: Venice

15

RIVIERA DEI DOGI

Riviera dei Dogi Srl

Via Don Minzoni, 33
30030 Mira Porte (VE)

Tel. 041 424466 – Fax 041 424428

info@rivieradeido.com – www.rivieradeidogi.com

49-57/62-89€

Open all year • 3 single rm, 28 double rm • No restaurant • Parking, no dogs • Bicycle hire

The wooden beams supporting the ceilings throughout.

For four hundred years, this house has watched the waters of the Brenta flow by, and seen generations of visitors come and go. Originally the counts Contarini used it as a weekend retreat, then it became an inn and by the end of the 19C it was the foremost hotel on the Brenta. It subsequently fell into disuse before being brought back to life about ten years ago; the rooms are large and welcoming (although the bathrooms are a little cramped), there is an attractive garden and the public areas have wooden ceilings and floors.

Access

From Padova: SS 11 for 18km

Sights nearby: Padova: basilica del Santo, Scrovegni chapel, Gattamelata monument, Oratorio di San Giorgio, Scuola di Sant'Antonio

ALDO MORO

Sig. Moro

Via Marconi, 27
35044 Montagnana (PD)
Tel. 0429 81351 – Fax 0429 82842
info@hotelaldomoro.com – www.hotelaldomoro.com

66/ 96€

Closed 3-12 Jan, 1-18 Aug • 24 double rm • Breakfast €8; half board €78 • Menu €28-45 • No dogs

The harmonious manner in which the house blends into the local scenery.

Montagnana is often described as a place which has not changed in appearance since the 13C, and this is quite true. Even to the untrained eye, its squares, palaces and churches enclosed by its medieval ramparts have a special charm. Against this backdrop, this establishment fits in well; occupying a historic patrician residence, it is elegantly furnished with carefully selected period pieces. The rooms are comfortable and the restaurant is worth a visit.

Access

From Padova: A 13 for 15km to Monselice exit, then 3.5km to join the SS 10 for 25km to Montagnana

Sights nearby: Walls, cathedral, church of San Francesco

17

CÀ DE PIZZOL

Sigg. De Pizzol
Via Vittoria, 92
31047 Ponte di Piave (TV)
Tel. 0422 853230 – Fax 0422 853462
info@cadepizzol.com – www.cadepizzol.com

30/45€

Open all year • 1 single rm, 4 double rm • Menu €20-30 • Gym, no dogs • Tasting and sale of cured meats and wine

The authenticity of the cuisine and the hospitality alike.

In the finest rural guesthouse traditions, this typical farmhouse is located right next to the home of its owners. It is surrounded by greenery and colourful flowers, beyond which are the vineyards responsible for stocking the cellars with Pinot Bianco, Pinot Grigio, Prosecco and Refosco, to name but a few. The five rustic style rooms are warm and welcoming, while the dining room, which takes up the entire ground floor, serves cuisine largely composed of home grown produce.

Access
From Treviso: SS 53 for 20km to Levada

Sights nearby: Oderzo: Museo Civico

18

RECHSTEINER

Sig. Stepski Doliwa

Via Montegrappa, 3 - Località San Nicolò
31047 Ponte di Piave (TV)

Tel. 0422 807128 – Fax 0422 752155

rechsteiner@rechsteiner.it – www.rechsteiner.it

39-45/ 59-68€

Open all year • 1 single rm, 10 double rm • Half board €44.50-49 • Menu €15-30 • Parking • Bicycle hire, tasting and sale of wine, cheese, cured meat and grappa

The clean and tidy presentation of the establishment.

In keeping with the local style, this large and austere farmhouse has been restored to provide accommodation in the shape of ten rooms. Public areas are composed of the garden, and inside a lounge-cum-dining room with imposing open fireplace. The rooms are given a warm feel by their wooden floors and ceilings, and rustic style furnishings. The estate-produced wines are worth tasting.

Access

From Treviso: SS 53 for 17km to Ponte di Piave, right for 3km, then left for 3km to San Nicolò

Sights nearby: Oderzo: Museo Civico; Treviso: Piazza dei Signori, cathedral, churches of San Nicolò and San Francesco

19

LA LOCANDA GAMBRINUS

Fam. Zanotto

Via Roma, 20
31020 San Polo di Piave (TV)
Tel. 0422 855043 – Fax 0422 855044
lalocanda@gambrinus.it – www.gambrinus.it

55/90€

Closed 9-19 Aug • 2 single rm, 4 double rm • Half board €70-85 • Menu €36-46 • Parking, no dogs • Horse riding, bicycles available, cakes, liqueurs and wine for sale

The villa's pink tower partially obscured by trees.

On sunny days, the contrast between the verdant lawn and the pink exterior of this house viewed through the foliage of its surrounding trees is particularly striking. Elegantly simple, its period feel has not been impaired by restoration. Named after flowers, the six rooms are well presented and each has its individual style, allowing guests to choose between the yellow tones of Sunflower and the gauzy drapery of Violet. Whatever the selection, atmosphere is guaranteed across the board.

Access

From Treviso: SS 13 for 3km, then right for 20km

Sights nearby: Conegliano: cathedral, castle, Scuola dei Battuti

CRISTINA

Sig. e Sig.ra Galler

Borgata Hoffe, 19
32047 Sappada (BL)
Tel. 0435 469430 – Fax 0435 469711
info@albergocristina.it – www.albergocristina.it

55-60/85-98€

Closed May, Nov • 10 double rm • Breakfast €8.50; half board €70-80 • Menu €23-38 • Parking, no dogs

The woodwork of the upper floor, blending equally with winter snow and summer pasture.

This hotel's ten rooms occupy a former hay barn with a striking facade of plastered stone and wood, which in summer is further enhanced by the flowers bedecking its balconies. Inside there is a warm and welcoming alpine feel entirely in keeping with the exterior. Situated in a sunny and peaceful spot which will make any visitor's stay all the more memorable.

Access

From Belluno: SS 50, then left onto the SS 51, right onto the SS 51b, then 13km to Santo Stefano di Cadore, right for 12km

Sights nearby: Sorgenti del Piave, Orrido (gorge) dell'Acquatona

21

HAUS MICHAELA

Sig. Piller

Borgata Fontana, 40
32047 Sappada (BL)

Tel. 0435 469377 – Fax 0435 66131

info@hotelmichaela.com – www.hotelmichaela.com

65/100€

Closed 1 Apr- 19 May, Oct-Nov • 18 double rm • Breakfast €9; half board €60-90 • Menu €32-43 • Parking, garden, swimming pool, gym, no dogs • Bicycle hire

The vast choice of facilities available.

One of the most comprehensive and appealing hotels in the area, this establishment remains very popular despite its location some distance away from the centre. Its strength lies in the wide variety of amenities it offers guests. In addition to the swimming pool, there is a solarium, fitness centre offering a sauna, spa bath and massage facilities, plus a well equipped gym where trained staff can help guests get back into shape. All this against a delightful backdrop of fir trees which cling to the rocky slopes of the mountains.

Access

From Belluno: SS 50, then left onto SS 51, right onto the SS 51b, then 13km to Santo Stefano di Cadore, right for 12km

Sights nearby: Sorgenti del Piave, Orrido (gorge) dell'Acquatona

LOCANDA LE GUIZZE

Sig. Rigon
Via Guizze, 1
36040 Torri di Quartesolo (VI)
Tel. 0444 381977 – Fax 0444 381992
info@leguizze.it – www.leguizze.it

50-80/ 60-100€

Open all year • 6 double rm • Half board €50-75 • Menu €25-39 • Parking, garden, no dogs

Rustic simplicity in the heart of the Veneto countryside.

Set in the midst of the Veneto plain, this brightly coloured farm is typical of rural buildings in this area with an asymmetrical sloping roof covering the central construction. It is not difficult to imagine it as it used to be, with livestock in the stables and peasants returning from tilling the fields. Although modern and functional, the interior is redolent of the rural setting and its attendant tranquillity. The same care lavished on restoring this establishment is evident in the kitchen, where the excellent local cuisine is prepared for guests to enjoy outside under the pavilion.

Access
From Vicenza: SS 11 for 7km, then left for 4km to Larino

Sights nearby: Vicenza: basilica, Piazza dei Signori, Loggia del Capitano, Museo Civico, Teatro Olimpico

23

IL CASCINALE

Sigg. Dotto
Via Torre d'Orlando, 6/b
31100 Treviso (TV)
Tel. 0422 402203 – Fax 0422 346418
info@agriturismoilcascinale.it – www.agriturismoilcascinale.it

35/48-50€

Closed 7-18 Jan, 16 Aug-3 Sep • 2 single rm, 12 double rm • Breakfast €8 • Menu €15-25 • Parking, no dogs • Bicycles available, vegetables for sale

The farmhouse garden with views of Treviso.

Not far from the banks of the river Sile, this establishment is composed of two recently restored buildings, their white facades contrasting with the verdant backdrop of the surrounding landscape. The spacious and modern rooms make for very comfortable accommodation, while parents of young children will be pleased to know that there is a play area. The hotel's pleasant pavilion is the ideal spot to while away the evenings, cooled by a gentle breeze blowing across the garden.

Sights nearby: Piazza dei Signori, cathedral, churches of San Nicolo and San Francesco, Museo Civico Bailo

24

FACCIOLI

Sig. Faccioli

Località Borghetto - Via Tiepolo, 8
37067 Valeggio sul Mincio (VR)
Tel. 045 6370605 – Fax 045 6370571
www.valeggio.com/faccioli

55-60/85-90€

Closed 6-16 Jan • 2 single rm, 17 double rm • No restaurant • Parking

The sloping wooden ceilings in some of the rooms.

Situated in the fertile countryside around Verona, on the border between the provinces of Mantova and Brescia, this village is also conveniently located for exploring the Lake Garda region. Its picturesque setting on the banks of the River Mincio gives the village a film-set appearance. The Albergo Faccioli is a typical country house, with its old stables and hay barn still standing. The rooms here are warm and comfortable, with rustic furniture, wooden ceilings and modern bathrooms. The reception rooms are not particularly large, but are attractively furnished with wicker furniture.

Access

From Verona: SS 11 for 22km to Peschiera, then left on the SS 249 for 11km to Valeggio sul Mincio, 1km to Borghetto

Sights nearby: Segurtà park and gardens

25

LOCANDA CA' FOSCARI

Sig. Scarpa

Calle della Frescada - Dorsoduro 3887/B
30123 Venezia (VE)
Tel. 041 710401 – Fax 041 710817
info@locandacafoscari.com – www.locandacafoscari.com

58-62/75-95€

Closed 25 Jul-8 Aug, 20 Nov-20 Jan • 3 single rm, 8 double rm • No restaurant • No dogs

The central location in the heart of Venice.

This establishment's accommodation is clean and presentable, but the furnishings, view and ambience are unremarkable. Compensation for this is forthcoming thanks to its excellent situation close to the Grand Canal right in the middle of the city, the warm and friendly family management, and the great value for money which this hotel represents.

Sights nearby: Scuola Grande di San Rocco, Scuola Grande dei Carmini, basilica of Santa Maria Gloriosa dei Frari

26

LUCE DEL VENDA

Sig. Menegatti
Via Monte Venda, 1194
35030 Vò (PD)
Tel. 049 9941243
info@lucedelvenda.it – www.lucedelvenda.it

30-40/ 60-80€

Open all year • 3 double rm • Menu €15-20 • Parking, garden

The old stonework of the farmhouse against the backdrop of the Colli Euganei parkland.

In the heart of the protected parkland of the Colli Euganei, this brick and stone building has been converted into a B&B by Signora Cristina. The rooms have an ambience of bygone days, with period style furniture, wooden ceilings and oriental tiles. After exploring the vast garden, where the odd hare or fox may be seen, guests might want to set off to admire Vicenza's Palladian architecture, Verona's Roman monuments, or Padova's masterpieces by Donatello and Giotto.

Access
From Padova: SP 89 for 25km south-west to Vò, then left 2km to Boccòn

Sights nearby: Colli Euganei National Park; Padova: basilica del Santo, Scrovegni chapel, Gattamelata monument, Oratorio di San Giorgio

Feel like getting away from it all? Ready for a change of scenery? Want to get into the countryside and work off some stress or extra pounds? The hotels and country guesthouses listed below offer at least one sporting activity (swimming, cycling, horse-riding, golf, tennis, gym, rambling, etc.).

The Country Guesthouses listed below offer tasting sessions where you can sample local wines, olive oils, jams, home-made pasta, pesto, sun-dried tomatoes and other delicacies. They also often sell regional produce from the local area.

Sarre

Verrayes

VENETO

Belluno

Caerano Di San Marco

Cavaso Del Tomba

Fara Vicentino

Longare

Ponte Di Piave

Treviso

Manufacture Française des Pneumatiques Michelin
Société en commandite par actions au capital de 304 000 000 EUR
Place des Carmes-Déchaux, 63 Clermont-Ferrand (France) - R.C.S. Clermont-Fd B 855 200 507
Michelin et Cie, Propriétaires-Editeurs - Dépôt légal Février 2006

Printed in Italy 01-2006/2.1

Typesetting: Maury Malesherbes (France)
Printing and Binding: STIGE, San Mauro (Italy)

Layout: Studio Maogani
4, rue du Fer à Moulin, 75005 Paris – Tél.: 01 47 07 00 06

Cover layout: Laurent Muller
Illustration and colour: Christelle Le Déan and Maud Burrus

Photos of country guesthouses, hotels and the regions
Project manager – Production photos Alain LEPRINCE
Agence ACSI – A CHACUN SON IMAGE
2, rue Aristide Maillol, 75015 Paris – Tél. : 01 43 27 90 10
Photo credits: Philippe GUERSAN, Lawrence BANAHAN, Romain AIX, Annick MEGRET
p. 61: G. Settembrini/MICHELIN
p. 151: G. Bludzin/MICHELIN

Cover: N. Pasquel/SCOPE
F. Arrighi/MICHELIN

Published in 2006

YOUR OPINION MATTERS!

To help us constantly improve this guide, please fill in this questionnaire and return to:

Michelin "Hotels & Country Guesthouses in Italy",
Michelin Travel Publications,
Hannay House, 39 Clarendon Road, Watford, WD17 1JA, UK

› 1. You are a:

Man .... ❐ Woman .... ❐

< 25 years old .... ❐ 25-34 years old .... ❐

35-50 years old.............. ❐ > 50 years.............. ❐

Student .... ❐

Farmer, Worker in primary industry .... ❐

Technical/Administrative worker .... ❐

Service worker, Craftsman,
Owner of small business .... ❐

Retired .... ❐

Manual worker .... ❐

Manager/executive, Professional .... ❐

Unemployed .... ❐

› 2. How often do you use the Internet to look for information on hotels and restaurants?

Never .... ❐

Occasionally (once a month) .... ❐

Regularly (once a week) .... ❐

Very frequently (more than once a week) .... ❐

› 3. Have you ever bought other Michelin guides?

Yes .... ❐ No .... ❐

› 4. If yes, which one(s)?

The Michelin Guide Italia .... ❐

Other Michelin Guides (please specify titles) ... ❐

....

The Green Guide (please specify titles) .... ❐

....

Other (please specify titles) .... ❐

....

› 5. If you buy the Michelin Guide Italia, how often do buy it?

Every year .... ❐

Every 2 years .... ❐

Every 3 years .... ❐

Every 4 years or more .... ❐

› 6. How do you rate the different elements of this guide?

1. Very Good 2. Good 3. Average 4. Poor 5. Very Poor

	1	**2**	**3**	**4**	**5**
Selection of establishments	❐	❐	❐	❐	❐
Number of establishments	❐	❐	❐	❐	❐
Hotel/country guesthouse mix	❐	❐	❐	❐	❐
Geographical spread of establishments	❐	❐	❐	❐	❐
Prices of rooms	❐	❐	❐	❐	❐
Practical information (prices, activities)	❐	❐	❐	❐	❐
Photos	❐	❐	❐	❐	❐
Description of the establishlment	❐	❐	❐	❐	❐
General presentation	❐	❐	❐	❐	❐
Distribution of establishments by region	❐	❐	❐	❐	❐
Themed indexes	❐	❐	❐	❐	❐
Cover	❐	❐	❐	❐	❐
Price	❐	❐	❐	❐	❐

› 7. Please rate the guide out of 20 / 20

YOUR OPINION MATTERS!

› 8. Did you buy this guide:

For holidays? .... ❐

For a weekend/short break? .... ❐

For business purposes? .... ❐

As a gift? .... ❐

› 9. Which aspects could we improve?

....

....

....

....

....

› 10. Was there an establishment you particularly liked or a choice you didn't agree with? Perhaps you have a favourite address of your own that you would like to tell us about? Please send us your remarks and suggestions.